HISTORY
OF THE
PEOPLE OF ISRAEL

HISTORY

OF THE

PEOPLE OF ISRAEL

FROM THE EARLIEST TIMES TO THE
DESTRUCTION OF JERUSALEM
BY THE ROMANS

WRITTEN FOR LAY READERS
BY
CARL HEINRICH CORNILL, Ph. D., S.T.D.
PROFESSOR OF THEOLOGY IN THE UNIVERSITY OF KONIGSBERG

*TRANSLATED BY W. H. CARRUTH, PROFESSOR OF GERMAN
IN THE UNIVERSITY OF KANSAS*

SIXTH EDITION

THE OPEN COURT PUBLISHING COMPANY
LA SALLE   ILLINOIS
1943

COPYRIGHT, 1898
By THE OPEN COURT PUBLISHING CO.

Printed in the United States of America
By Paquin Printers, Chicago

CONTENTS.

CHAP.		PAGE.
I.	Introductory Observations.—Land and People.—Race Migrations of the Orient in Ancient Times...	1
II.	Israel prior to the Origin of the National Kingdom...	29
III.	The National Kingdom.—Saul and David.......	56
IV.	Solomon.—The Division of the Kingdom.—The Early Years of the Divided Kingdoms........	86
V.	To the Destruction of Jerusalem by the Chaldeans..	115
VI.	From the return out of the Babylonian Captivity to the Outbreak of the Rebellion of the Maccabees...	145
VII.	The Maccabean Rebellion to the Establishment of the Hereditary High Priesthood and Principality under Simon............................	175
VIII.	From Simon the Maccabean to Herod the Great.	207
IX.	The House of Herod.—Judea as a Roman Province...	238
X.	The War in Judea and the Destruction of Jerusalem..	272

HISTORY OF THE PEOPLE OF ISRAEL.

CHAPTER I.

INTRODUCTORY OBSERVATIONS.—LAND AND PEOPLE.
—RACE MIGRATIONS OF THE ORIENT
IN ANCIENT TIMES.

THE history of the people of Israel is the subject to which I desire to call the reader's attention. But am I justified in calling attention to the subject at all? What do we care for the people of Israel? Where is there interest or profit for us in knowing what took place in Palestine in the long period of time from 1500 before Christ to 70 after? Such questions and objections must be anticipated by one who undertakes to present the history of Israel to a general public; and those who make such objections probably regard themselves as upon the very pinnacle of modern impartiality and freedom from bias. But this boasted impartiality is a strange thing: it is too often only a product of ignorance, of entire absence of insight into the situation.

A certain familiarity with the history of Greece and Rome will always be required as a necessary element of general culture. And why? Because our whole civilization has its roots in Hellas and Latium. Our science and our art would simply be incomprehensible without Plato and Aristotle, without Homer, Sophocles, and Phidias. It is true, the Hellenes themselves were heirs of the primitive civilization of the Orient, and their intellectual achievements would have been utterly impossible but for Egypt, Babylonia, India, and Phœnicia. The Phœnicians in their colonizing and commercial activity, which embraced the whole known world, brought to the nations of Europe not only gold and cotton (the Greek word for gold is Phœnician, and our current "cotton" is also a Phœnician word), but also the intellectual possessions of the Orient, and, most important of all, transmitted to the European world perhaps the greatest and most important invention of the Orient, the alphabet, which for the first time rendered possible genuine civilization and real intellectual life.

But the Hellenes acquired this inheritance of the ancient Orient in order to possess it; from the divinely endowed genius of their race they gave it a re-birth as something specifically new and specifically Greek. We, too, know the civilization of the ancient Orient directly only in the form which it received among the Greeks and at their hands. We must know the history of a race to which we owe our whole intellectual life on the secular side. And inasmuch as the inheritance of the Greek mind has reached us through the Romans, whose whole function in the development of civilization consisted in transmitting Greek culture to the nations conquered by them, we must know the history of this race also, the intellectual connecting link between us and Hellas, because only he who knows this can understand his own people and his own present.

Beside Hellas and Rome, third in the group of races to which the arbiter of history assigned an exceptional mission in the world, stands Israel. True, Israel played no important part in universal history in the accepted sense of the word, nor did it ever lead in the march of civilization. In learning and the plastic arts it achieved nothing; it produced no Plato or Aristotle, no Phidias or Praxiteles, no Homer or Sophocles,—but it gave the world Moses and the prophets, and from it alone could be born after the manner of the flesh, Jesus of Nazareth. Just as on the secular side our whole intellectual life is rooted in Hellas and Latium, so on the religious side it is rooted in Israel: Israel gave the world the true God and the true religion.

For all times the truth is established that was uttered by the founder of Christianity himself to the woman of Samaria in the talk by Jacob's Well at Sychar, "Salvation is of the Jews," and which his greatest apostle wrote in an epistle to the Christian community of Rome, that Abraham is the father of us all in the faith. And this applies also to the many millions of Mohammedans, for the prophet of Islam himself wished only to restore in its primitive purity "the faith of Abraham," which Jews and Christians alike had, as he thought, corrupted and disguised under all sorts of strange additions. And can we be indifferent to the history of a race to which we owe our best and noblest possessions? Can we be without interest in such a race?

But, you might reply, we do know it, we have all learned it in school under the title of "Bible History." Very well and good, and that brings me directly to a point which is in urgent need of explanation at the very start. I must simply beg you to forget here all recollections of "Bible History." Not on the ground that everything is untrue that is told in the Bible of the history of Israel; but in the Biblical accounts the material has all gone through the medium of popular tradition, and then again this popular tradition has been treated and presented by later compilers from special points of view. The Holy Scriptures of the Old Testament do not claim to be history, but books of devotion. It is very characteristic that the Jewish canon itself does not know the designation "historical books," but includes the writings which we are accustomed to call the historical books of the Old Testament among the prophetic, with a correct perception that we have not in this case historiography but prophecy. That the historian, who is concerned with these books only as historical materials, looks at them with different eyes from the Bible reader, who is seeking in them only edification, is a matter of course and cannot be otherwise, and accordingly the historian will often be obliged to draw a different picture of the matters reported in them from that made for devotional purposes by the Biblical writers themselves.

There is one misfortune in the limitations of this work : I can only portray and not demonstrate ; if I were to undertake to support my delineation by reference to the sources, I should need at least sixfold the space at my disposal, and I could scarcely hope to awaken interest for such details and investigations, and might not after all convince any one. I must therefore incur the appearance of putting forth in the following work only undemonstrated propositions, and of deviating without evident reason from the current views derived from Bible history. But I earnestly beg my reader to believe that every deviation from the traditional picture is based on careful reflection, and on reasons which my scientific conscience regards as imperative. And I trust it will be felt that everything essential is left, even if certain details disappear.

For I hold the firm and well-grounded conviction that the traditions of the people of Israel itself regarding its earliest history are thoroughly historical in all essential points, and can sustain the keenest and most searching criticism. Poetic legends have, indeed, woven about those ancient traditions a misty magic veil which charms the eye and captivates the heart, and in which lies the spell that those traditions cast over every unbiased mind. Not with rude Vandal hand should we tear away this veil, but with loving care resolve it into its single threads and remove it with considerate hand, so that the original image may stand forth in its unadorned simplicity and naked chastity, and then we shall see that it is really a noble human figure, and not a mere creature of the imagination, that was concealed beneath the protecting cover of this veil. For science there is no veiled image of Sais, and the road to scientific truth does not go through guilt, not even where scientific truth in sacred things is concerned.

If the question is raised : what sources are at our command for the investigation of the scientific truth in connection with the history of Israel, we have first to confirm a fact which for the historian, indeed, is extremely grievous and discouraging, but all the more valuable and significant for the student of race-psychology. Israel is the poorest in history and monuments of all the races that we know. I will not refer to the Egyptians and Mesopotamians, who covered every spot of free space with inscriptions and pictorial representations which recall to us vividly to-day

a life that was lived five thousand years ago.
Even among the nearest relatives and neighbors
of the Israelites the conditions are entirely different. The thousands and thousands of inscriptions which the Phœnicians set up wherever they
went are a familiar fact; from the next kinsmen of the Israelites, the Moabites, we have at
least the triumphal column of their king Mesha,
and from the nature of this monument we may
conclude that it was not the only one. Even the
wandering Bedouins of the Arabian and Syrian
deserts transmitted their memory to future generations by numerous inscriptions. From Israel
we have nothing of the sort, no monument, no
inscription, no tomb. It might be thought that
this was to be explained from outward circumstances. Since the second millennium before
Christ, Palestine has been the battle-field of the
Orient, and all that has visited this land would
make the destruction of its ancient monuments
quite comprehensible. But not even the earth
has brought anything of the sort to light, despite
most careful and painstaking search; and in view
of all that has actually been preserved from ancient times, we have a right to expect that somewhere at least a letter or a written fragment
would appear. One sole exception but confirms
the rule. In the year 1880, the first and thus far
the last ancient Hebrew inscription was found,—
but where? In the tunnel of the conduit of the
Siloam canal, where a human eye could see it

only by accident, as indeed it was discovered by pure chance on the occasion of the cleaning of the canal.

No, the reason lies deeper, and we shall scarcely find anything of importance, even if the search is continued. This is shown by the very character of the literature of Israel that has been preserved. The composer of the Book of Kings had before him the official annals of the ancient kings of Israel and Judah, or at least extracts from them. This work, which if preserved would be for us a historical source of incomparable value, and which we would gladly make great sacrifices to regain, was allowed to perish; it has vanished and left no trace, because it was not appreciated. And yet this work contained everything in the whole matter that would interest us as historians.

We meet an entirely analogous case in the history of David. David was the greatest king and warrior that Israel ever had, and we are more exactly informed about the time of his life and reign than about any other period of ancient Israelitish history; but these very detailed reports speak so incidentally and superficially of David's wars and victories that it is quite impossible for us to obtain a picture of his warlike achievements that shall be clear in all respects. What interested Israel in this its greatest hero, and endeared him to it, was not the warrior and the victor, but the man and the king. It seems as though ancient Israel had no eye for those things, as though it felt itself clearly enough that its function in history and its mission to mankind were not of this world and did not consist in earthly achievements. This undeniable fact has always been to me the strongest proof of a really transcendent spiritual endowment of Israel.

Accordingly, we have no monuments of any sort at hand for the history of the people of Israel, but our only sources are the written traditions of this absolutely unhistorical people itself, which are and profess to be not histories but books of devotion, and after these the direct and indirect reports of alien nations—in fact a scanty and unreliable body of material in dealing with which the greatest caution and self-control are urgently demanded. To present what can be learned from these unpromising materials is the object of these pages.

And first we must endeavor to get a tolerably clear idea of the scene of our history. It will appear that as the people that lived there in historical times was unique in its kind, so is also the land, the features of which could not but exercise a great influence upon the nature and character of its inhabitants.

The land in which the chief part of the history of Israel was played, and which this people regarded as its own, is called by us with a Græco-Roman designation, Palestine, that is, the Land of the Philistines. The Greeks entered the country by way of the coast, and gave to it the name of the tribe that dwelt there, a phenomenon that we shall observe frequently. The inhabitants themselves called it Kenáan. As this name means etymologically "lowland," it must originally have been applied only to the Philisto-Phœnician coast strip. The land occupied by the Israelites, on the contrary, is altogether mountainous and has a considerable lowland only in the plain of Jezreel. This fact is in accord with the report of the Phœnicians that they descended from a tribal progenitor, Chnâ, in which name we recognize immediately the stem of Kenáan. In Israelitish times, however, only the portion of the land situated west of the Jordan is known as Kenáan; the land east of the Jordan has the separate name, Gilead.

What we now call Palestine, the land on both sides of the Jordan, is a comparatively small bit of earth, only about eight thousand five hundred square miles in extent; that is, a little more than the area of Massachusetts, or of Wales and Herefordshire.

Hydrographically, the land is very scantily endowed. Of rivers it has the Jordan alone, with its tributaries, the most important of which, however, are all on the east side: the Yarmuk, the Jabbok, and the Arnon, which latter empties not into the Jordan proper, but into the Dead Sea. The land west of the Jordan can boast really of no rivers save the Kishon in the plain of Jezreel; but in the hottest part of the season this is a slight rivulet and begins to be a considerable river only a few miles above its entrance into the Mediterranean Sea at Haifa.

The fertility of Palestine is dependent exclusively on the rain which falls in winter, and on the dew of summer, wherefore it is more clearly and more perceptibly than in other lands a blessing from above, a gift of heaven, so that the eye of man was here directed upward, toward heaven, by nature herself. The Jordan, the sole river of Palestine, called to-day "esch Scherîat el kebîre," the Great River, has not its like on earth; instead of uniting the adjacent lands and shores, like other rivers, the Jordan separates them as an almost impassable barrier, since its extraordinary fall and its winding and twisting course make navigation on it impossible. Of moderately convenient and always available fords it has only three between the Lake of Gennesaret and the Dead Sea. Thus it comes about that we are obliged to consider the land east of the Jordan and that west of the Jordan as two really distinct lands without connection with each other.

The Jordan plain, called to-day "el Ghôr," is almost entirely uninhabitable, in summer on account of the tropical heat, in winter on account of the floods; it was and is still a notorious resort and hiding-place for all possible beasts. The southern part of the country, too, the region about the Dead Sea and the so-called mountains or wilderness of Judah, is sparsely populated and capable of sustaining only a scant population. In ancient times, as well, it must have been much as it is to-day, since natural conditions have not changed. The country east of the Jordan is but a narrow strip of tillable land wedged in between the valley of the Jordan and the vast Syro-Arabian desert. Only in its middle and northern portions is the land really fertile and adequate for a considerable population, and this especially on the slope toward the Mediterranean coast, the lowlands of Sharon and Sephela, which Israel never succeeded in occupying.

But upon this narrow and limited soil, our astonished eyes meet an infinite variety and diversity of details. Palestine deserves the name of the land of contrasts ; here is found gathered together everything between a sub-tropical climate and the region of eternal snow. The mighty mountain peak of Hermon, which forms the northern boundary of the country, is covered with perpetual snow and rises to an altitude of over nine thousand feet, some three thousand feet more than Mount Washington, or more than twice th height of Ben Nevis. There we have Alpine land scape and Alpine flora. The mountain region o Galilee, the most healthy portion of Palestine, has the most moderate climate ; the southern portions, especially the plain of Jezreel and the seacoast, have a warm climate ; and in the valley of Jordan and about the Dead Sea it is actual! tropical. In Ghôr a temperature of 109 been observed in the shade in the month of May, and along the Dead Sea, even after sunset, when in other southern lands a sudden coolness usually sets in, the thermometer has recorded 95 F.

And accordingly the vegetation here is subtropical: the balsam used to thrive here and the palm still does, wherefore Jericho was formerly called the City of Palms. On account of these great climatic extremes, the flora of Palestine in general is exceedingly rich; some two thousand species of flowers have been noted. It is easy to understand how this natural wealth of the land about him must arouse and inspire the mind and soul of man.

But as a whole, also, Palestine is a land of contrasts, and this in a manner that must be regarded as providential. In the first place, the land is almost entirely shut off from the world outside. On the east and south it is bordered by the desert, like a perfect insulating medium; and on the west by the surging Mediterranean, offering no good harbor on the whole coast of Palestine (to this day a calamity for travelers to the Holy Land), besides being almost unnavigable by the ships of the ancients because of the strong blasts of the trade-winds. Only on the north is the land accessible, though one cannot say open, for here the two great parallel Alpine chains of Lebanon and Anti-Libanus reach across like a natural bar. This same reserve which the land shows outwardly, is manifest within as well. Almost everywhere are mountains with deep, abrupt gorges, which constitute a great obstacle to intercourse, and make travel extremely wearisome and slow.

This is providential: for this isolation guaranteed to the inhabitants the undisturbed development of their individuality; they were exempt from the influences of the great leveler, commerce.

Mountaineers are everywhere men of strongly developed individuality. But there is another side to the matter. It is true that the genuine mountaineer is vigorous and upright, but he is also clumsy and stubborn, revolving complacently about his own axis and distrustful and inhospitable toward all influences from without. From this danger Israel was preserved. For while the land is insulated, at the same time it is a bridge and a highway of world-commerce without a parallel. All the ancient highways of commerce went through Palestine. For instance, that primitive one from the Nile to the Euphrates, which runs through Palestine in its entire length, and after crossing the Jordan touches first at Damascus; and likewise the no less important one from Tyre to the Arabian Gulf, which brought to the Phœnicians the products of Arabia, East Africa, Persia, and India. And so, if I may venture to use the figure, Israel was constantly fanned and refreshed by the wings of world-wide commerce, and thus kept from growing hard and sour, while its individuality ran no risk of being dissolved in a characterless, nebulous cosmopolitanism.

And in still another way this providential tendency to extremes is seen. The land was favored in many ways, but on the other hand it was full of pests. In early times wild beasts, such as the lion and the bear, the wolf and the panther, the jackal and the hyena, must have lived there in great numbers; and even to this day, serpents are a great pest, Palestine having more than twenty species, among them five very dangerous and poisonous ones.

Furthermore, the land is fertile: grain of all varieties, grapes, figs, olives, and pomegranates thrive abundantly, but not without labor and care. Of Palestine especially the old Bible sentence is true: "In the sweat of thy face shalt thou eat bread." These contrasts also are very important. There was no chance for the relaxing and enervating effect that comes when man receives from nature without exertion all that he needs; he was spurred and forced to the full exertion of his powers. But this application was not discouraged by the prospective fruitlessness of his exertions, a condition which makes man as stupid and indifferent as when everything falls into his lap of itself; but prosperity was the reward of toil. He knew that it paid to exert his powers. A land, therefore, which seemed as if made to produce a physically and mentally sound race, that brought thither the capacity to fulfil the mission assigned it by God. The Roman historian, Tacitus, also, in his notoriously unjust description of the Jewish people, dwells especially on the exceptional health, strength, and endurance of this race. And accordingly the Israelite has always clung to his country with sincere gratitude and loving loyalty ; it was to him the paragon of countries, and he recognized the gracious dispensatiyn of his God especially in the fact that this precious land had been assigned and promised to him without any merit and desert of his own.

The limitations of our subject are self-evident. Properly speaking, there is no history of the people of Israel until the exodus from Egypt ; not until this event did Israel become a people, only then does its history begin. It ends with the destruction of Jerusalem by the Romans. Since that time there have been plenty of Jews ; but there has been no Jewish nation since the year 70 after Christ. To be exact, therefore, we should have to begin with the exodus from Egypt. But, as is well known, the recollections of the Israelitish people reach much further back, and we must extend our examination into their history as far back as we can possibly go. This will constitute the primitive or archaic history. A subject of vast importance ! For, as with the individual the child is father of the man, so in the life of a nation the primeval history has a decisive influence on the whole following development. But at this point we must get a clear idea of the character of those earliest recollections of the people of Israel.

We find no history or historical literature in Israel until the period of the kings. Of literary monuments reaching further back than this we have some songs and fragments of poetry, most notably the splendid Song of Deborah. But until the beginning of the monarchy, all the historical recollections of Israel were handed down by word of mouth alone. Now, there are centuries between the oldest authentic reports and the things reported; therefore, the criticism of the sources is especially needed here, and at the same time especially difficult. We must regard this whole body of oldest traditions as popular legends. Popular legend does not invent its subjects, it makes nothing out of nothing; but it handles its subjects very freely and treats them with all the sovereign authority of a divinely inspired poet, to whom the subject is only the raw material which he endows with soul, form, content, and life. Accordingly we must endeavor everywhere to get at the historical germ, the substratum of reality in these legends; it is this that is historically valuable, and may be regarded as an authentic source.

To penetrate into times that antedate history, we have a still more reliable guide: this is language and philology. Let us try to make Israel's language speak, and put it on the stand as a witness regarding the earliest fortunes of the people.

Israel itself calls the language which we know as Hebrew "the language of Canaan"; there is no recollection that the Israelites themselves or their fathers ever spoke any other. Now this designation, "the language of Canaan," is true in a literal sense: it can be proven on philological grounds that this language can have developed in no other country than Canaan.

The Hebrew language calls the west *jam*, "ocean" or "seacoast"; in fact, the Mediterranean Sea constitutes the west boundary, and Canaan is the only race speaking a Semitic tongue which has directly and solely the sea on the west. The south is in Hebrew, *negeb*, literally " the dryland," " the drought-land "; *negeb* is the proper name of the desert into which the mountains of Judah abruptly descend to the south, which is called in the oldest Egyptian records *pa-nagbu* (the very same word, with the Egyptian article prefixed). Here again, this peculiar etymology could have grown up in no other Semitic-speaking land save Canaan. And the creators of the Hebrew language were already tillers of the soil, and no longer nomads. While the Arab, a thorough nomad, uses for all figurative applications of "dwelling" the word *ahl*, "tent" (calling, for instance, a man's family his tent), the Hebrew uses regularly the word *bajith*, "house"; only to a people that had long ceased to be nomadic could it occur to say *scháar*, "gate," for "city" or "dwelling." Most decisive, perhaps, is the word *lechem*, which appears as second element in the name Bethlehem. This word means in Hebrew "bread," while in Arabic the corresponding form of the same stem, *lachm*, means "meat." How is this to be explained? Originally, of course, the word has neither of these meanings, but only the general sense of "nourishment," "food." To the nomad, meat is the absolute equivalent of food; if the Hebrew language understands by it "bread," then those who formed this language as a vehicle for their thoughts and ideas must of necessity have been tillers of the soil.

On these grounds, then, we should conclude that the people of Israel had always dwelt in Canaan and that they had always been agricultural people. But against both assumptions Hebrew tradition raises loud and vigorous protest. No element of this tradition is more permanent than that the ancestors of the people were not born in the land of Canaan, but immigrated thither, and that they were nomads, wandering shepherds, who adopted agriculture and settled abodes only in historical times and in this very land of Canaan. These two points cannot be invention, for the first is very inconvenient for Hebrew tradition, which is thus compelled to make extraordinary efforts to prove or at least to found its claim to the possession of Canaan. Therefore, unless it had had a very distinct recollection of this fact, it would never in the world have invented it. Moreover, traditions have preserved a recollection of the original home; with one accord they report that the patriarchs were Aramæans, and came to Canaan as emigrant Aramæans. In historical times Aram was the hereditary enemy of Israel, which waged a life-and-death struggle against its assaults. Here, too, it is a psychological impossibility that this Aramæan origin should be an invention of legend, particularly when we consider that the Aramæans speak a language wholly different from the Hebrew. The Germans might as easily get the idea that they were descended from the French, or *vice versâ*.

For ancient Israel, Aram is a term of wide extent; but recollection located the primitive home more definitely, though not always in precisely the same place. A tradition, in other respects very good and bearing the marks of antiquity, makes "Laban the Aramæan," the father-in-law of Jacob, dwell not far from Damascus, which the Israelites regarded as a part of Aram. Another and indeed older tradition finds the initial point of the migration of the patriarchs to Canaan in Haran, a place in northwestern Mesopotamia, well known under the Græco-Roman form of the name as Carrhæ, and tells also of a connection with the ancient marvelous city of Ur in the extreme southeast of Babylonia, the modern Mukajjar (Mugheir), whose ruins inform us of a primitive civilization in that region, which we can trace back into the third millennium before Christ, and which is surely much older than that.

How should Israelitish tradition have happened upon these names and localities, which it is not probable that any Israelite ever set eyes on in historical times?

These are no airy creations of the imagination, but even the keenest criticism must recognize here a foundation of reliable tradition. All accounts agree that the ancestors of the people of Israel were conducted from Haran to Canaan by Abraham. The recollection of an occurrence of such importance could not fail to be preserved, and even the name of the person who was the motive power and manager of the whole could not be lost to posterity. I consider Abraham a historical personage in just as strict a sense as Opheltas and Peripoltas who, according to the tradition of the Bœotians, led this people from Arne in the valley of the Peneus in Thessaly to Chæronea in the land afterwards occupied by them. Such particulars and such names are not invented by tradition out of nothing. Let us see whether it is possible to fit these facts into the course of the history of the Orient as known to us from other sources.

In Mesopotamia, where the oldest tradition places the primitive home of Israel, our historical knowledge reaches back almost to the year 4000 before Christ. According to the reports of the Babylonians themselves, the two earliest kings of whom they have any recollection, Sargon of Agade and his son Naram-Sin, ruled about the year 3800 before Christ; of Sargon it is already reported that he made expeditions as far as the Mediterranean Sea. These two rulers are absolutely historical personages, since we possess to-day authentic monuments of them with full identification of their names.

And even then the land had already a long and eventful history behind it. Sargon of Agade already bears a genuinely Semitic name. But there can be no doubt that the primitive Babylonian civilization, which has given even to the present day the names of the seven planets, and of the corresponding days of the week, the division of the circle into 360 degrees, the division of the year into 12 months, the week into 7 days, the day into 24 hours, and the hour into 60 minutes, is older than the year 4000 B. C. and derived from a non-Semitic people. This people called themselves Sumerians, and by their language belonged to the Finnish-Turkish-Tartar race, the so-called Turanians.

This highly civilized but unwarlike people was overwhelmed by a great Semitic migration, and with the Semitizing of the Sumerians our knowledge of the history of Mesopotamia begins. We can follow this process step by step. The more energetic and powerful Semitic race succeeded in the course of centuries in completely absorbing the Sumerians, and adopted, without adding anything of their own, their primitive civilization, especially the cuneiform writing invented by the

Sumerians and long in use among them. They organized city principalities and district kingdoms whose rulers we can name and identify in great numbers from their own inscriptions and the accounts of the Babylonians. Especially interesting for us among these is Gudea of Sirgurla, about 2800 B. C., from whom we have a considerable number of sculptures and inscriptions. These sculptures show already a high degree of skill; in the inscriptions he mentions expressly cedars from the Amanus mountains and from Lebanon, so that the connection with the Mediterranean was still maintained. Furthermore, it is as good as certain that there existed already a lively and uninterrupted intercourse with Egypt; in these very sculptures of Gudea, Egyptian influences are said to be manifest. We must assume about the year 3000 B. C., a high degree of civilization and some international commerce in southwestern Asia. We see, therefore, at the beginning how the course which Israelitish tradition assigns to the patriarchs had been traveled for a thousand years or more.

About the year 2300 B. C., these Mesopotamian Semites are assailed by a new enemy who seems about to deal out to them the same fate which they had before dealt to the Sumerians. The Elamites, the non-Semitic inhabitants of the mountain region east of the lower course of the Tigris, invade Babylonia and conquer the land. Their king, Kudur-Mabuk, must have ruled over a mighty realm reaching even to the Mediterranean, and of this Elamite kingdom we have left a trace in the king Chedorlaomer of Elam, who, according to the account in Genesis, chapter 14, ruled over Palestine and waged wars there. But their dominion was to be of short duration. About 2250 B. C., the great city-king, Hammurabi of Babel, led a victorious attack of the Semites against the Elamites, destroyed their power and became the founder of a greater Babylonian empire, combining under his scepter all that was later known as Babylon.

This greater Babylonian Empire founded by Hammurabi seems to have continued over five hundred years peaceful and unassailed. In the eighteenth century before Christ, it is true, the Assyrian power began to develop to the north of it, but for some time this did not threaten Babylonia. It was a more serious matter when in 1550 B. C. a new conquest came upon the country. The Cossæans, or Kassites, a mountain people related to the Elamites and dwelling northeast of Mesopotamia, invaded the country under the lead of their king, Agu-kak-rimi, whose very name shows that he was no Semite. They succeeded in completely subduing the north part of it and in establishing a Cossæic dynasty which ruled for several hundred years, the members of which called themselves, after the name of Middle and North Babylonia, "Kings of Kar-Duniash." The Semitic part of the people and their rulers were forced southward, where they continued to live an inactive life, and suffered severely from the attacks of the Bedouins of the Arabian Desert.

By this time another enemy had appeared on the scene. About the year 2000 B. C., Egypt had been invaded by foreign conquerors—Hyksos, the Egyptian historian Manetho calls them—who settled permanently in Lower Egypt, which they subdued to their sway. The origin of these Hyksos is disputed; according to the report of the Egyptians themselves, we can see in them only hordes of Asiatic Bedouins, who, however, soon became acclimated and adopted Egyptian civilization to a certain degree. After the reign of the Hyksos had lasted a considerable time, Pharaoh Ahmes, the vigorous founder of the Eighteenth Dynasty, succeeded in breaking their power and taking from them their last support in Egypt, the border fortress of Abaris.

The Hyksos went back to Asia, but the Egyptians followed their track, and now themselves advanced into Asia as conquerors. Thotmes II., the great-grandson of Ahmes, overran all southwest Asia, even to the further side of the Euphrates, which he descended with his army in ships, and hunted lions and the still numerous elephants in Mesopotamia. Even the king of the rising Assyrian Empire sought the favor of the powerful Egyptian and several times sent him valuable presents. Even though this Egyptian rule was only nominal in the lands along the Euphrates, it established itself firmly in Palestine and on the Mediterranean coast. At this period Palestine was a regular Egyptian province, ruled by subject kings and Egyptian governors. And so the Cossæic kings of Kar-Duniash sought the friendship of the Egyptian Pharaohs, and maintained with them the relations of friend and neighbor.

Here again I must mention one of the most remarkable and valuable discoveries given to the world in recent years. The last Pharaoh of the powerful and mighty Eighteenth Dynasty was King Amenhotep IV., the so-called Heretic King. This remarkable man wished to reform the Egyptian religion and put in place of the old and confused polytheism a solar monotheism in which the sun was to be worshiped as the sole god, under the name of Aten. The king especially disapproved of the ancient imperial god, Amon, whose name he ordered erased everywhere, and changed his own name from Amenhotep to Chu-en-aten, "Glory of the Sun." And so too, the old metropolis of Thebes, the very city of Amon, had become distasteful to him, and he moved his capital to Middle Egypt to the modern Tell-el-Amarna. It is no wonder that the reformation was a failure, and that the king, who was besides so unfortunate as to leave no son but only daughters, died amidst the curses of his subjects, and pursued by the fanatical hatred of later generations. Hence the place where he had dwelt was regarded as plague-ridden and haunted by evil demons.

And as a result of this belief it happened that the complete royal archives, his own and his father's diplomatic correspondence, were preserved at Tell-el-Amarna; they were found in the fall of 1887. This highly interesting correspondence covers the whole of Palestine and the Phœnician coast; Mesopotamia and Babylonia, and even the Cossæic kings are represented. And this correspondence is in the Assyrio-Babylonian language and written in Babylonian cuneiform characters. If even the proud Egyptians, who so thoroughly despised everything foreign, condescended to this and had their subjects and vassals write to the king in a foreign language which the Egyptians themselves had first to learn with much pains, this is the clearest evidence of the great power and dominant influence exercised by Babylonian culture on southwest Asia; it explains also very naturally how precisely the oldest Hebrew tradition shows the most remarkable kinship with the Babylonian.

This, then, is the historical picture shown us by southwest Asia at the time of the migration of the ancestors of the people of Israel; Babylonia shaken to its foundations by the Cossæic conquest, Egypt in uncontested possession of southwest Asia and recognized even by the rulers of Mesopotamia as chief power of the age. Let us try to fix the time a little more closely. The exodus of Israel from Egypt must have occurred, according to Egyptian chronology, about 1300 before Christ;

the residence of Israel in Egypt lasted, according to the oldest tradition, three generations, or in round numbers a hundred years. This would place the migration to Egypt about 1400 B. C. If we estimate the events between the immigration of Abraham to Canaan and the further migration to Egypt at about one hundred years also, or perhaps somewhat more, we would arrive at the time for the immigration of Abraham to Canaan as between 1550 and 1500 B. C.

Now if the unquestionably Semitic inhabitants of Mesopotamia whom Abraham led leave Mesopotamia at exactly the same time when the Cossæic conquest was suppressing and expelling the Semitic element from Mesopotamia; if these Semitic emigrants follow a long familiar highway of international commerce into a land where they will be under the potent protection of Egypt; if later they go from the recognized Egyptian province to Egypt itself,—not a migration from one country to another, but only a migration from one part of a land to another—well, am I saying too much when I declare that the substance and the historical pith of the oldest traditions of Israel fit most perfectly into the picture of the general history of the time and are completely confirmed by it? What in fact the primitive history of Israel was, we shall examine in the next article.

CHAPTER II.

ISRAEL PRIOR TO THE ORIGIN OF THE NATIONAL KINGDOM.

HAVING satisfied ourselves that Israel's oldest traditions fit very easily into the course of the ancient history of the Orient as known to us from other sources, our task will now be to translate these oldest traditions out of the language of legend into that of history, or in other words, to ascertain their historical content. To this end we must first of all have a clear idea of the point of view that is to be our guide in the process.

With most earnest conviction I have already recognized Abraham as a strictly historical personage, and it might be thought that what is true of the father should hold for the son and grandchildren. But this conclusion would be premature. Greek tradition ascribes to Lycurgus, the lawgiver of Sparta, two sons: Eunomos and Eucosmos, i. e., Law and Order. No reasonable person will doubt that Lycurgus was a historical personage, but that he actually had two sons named "Law" and "Order" will scarcely be believed. The tradition will be understood to mean that by his whole public activity he became the father of law and order for Sparta.

I have purposely chosen the example of Lycurgus because here the names themselves speak plainly. It is the same with Hebrew tradition. The names which it gives us in connection with Abraham are all names of races and tribes, and accordingly we are beyond question in the realm of personification; for races never adopt the names of individuals, but the patronymic tribal ancestor is first and ever a composite, a personification of the people. When the Hellenes derive themselves from a patriarch Hellen, who has two sons, Æolus and Dorus, and two grandsons, Achæus and Ion, no one will dream of looking for historical individuals here, but will immediately recognize in them the entire race of the Hellenes and the tribes into which it was divided. Or when, in the well-known list of races in Genesis, Shem has the five sons, Elam, Asshur, Arpachshad, Lud, and Aram, every one will see in this directly a very evident way of representing that those five peoples were regarded as branches of the great Semitic race and language group to which Israel itself belonged.

And thus also must the primitive history of Israel be regarded. However plastic and distinct the individualities of Ishmael and Edom, Israel and Joseph may seem to us, they are all only personifications and representations of the races or tribes whose names they bear. A glimmer of this truth is seen quite clearly in Hebrew tradition itself. When Rebekah, before the birth of the twins whose mother she is to become, receives the divine annunciation:

"Two nations are in thy womb,
And two peoples shall be separated even from thy bowels:
And the one people shall be stronger than the other people;
And the elder shall serve the younger,"

it is said with all directness that we are dealing here not with single individuals, but with races. And when Jacob and Laban together set up a boundary-stone upon Mount Gilead and make a solemn and sworn covenant that neither of them henceforth will pass this boundary with evil intent, it is perfectly plain that this is not a private agreement between father-in-law and son-in-law, but a legal regulation of tribal boundary rights between Israel and Aram, which according to the Hebrew manner of speaking reaches unto southward of Damascus and to the mountain of Gilead.

What is historically significant in this tradition is the purely genealogical element, the relations of age and kinship between the various personages. To return once more to the Greek illustration cited, just as we must conclude when Æolus and Dorus appear as sons, and Achæus and Ion as grandsons of the patriarch Hellen, that the Æolians and Dorians are older tribal organizations and entered history earlier than the Achaians and Ionians, so it is in the case of Hebrew tradition: those tribes which were consolidated earlier in a political and national way are regarded as older, and the genealogical kinship corresponds to the ethnographic relationship. When Moab and Ammon appear as sons of the nephew of the patriarch, and Edom and Israel on the contrary as his twin grandsons, this means: Moab and Ammon are closely related to each other, and Israel too recognizes its kinship with them, but only as cousins, not as close kin, while with Edom it feels very closely related, in a kinship as of brothers, even of twin brothers. And when of these twin brothers Edom is the elder, this signifies: Edom was earlier consolidated into a political body, a nation, became a people, in the historical sense, earlier than Israel. And when Ishmael is represented as the son of the patriarch by a concubine, this means: Israel recognizes a race relationship even with the Bedouins of the Syro-Arabian desert, which borders on Palestine, but regards this relationship as a very remote one. Having thus established the correct point of view for an historical understanding of the oldest traditions of Israel, let us now proceed to loose their tongue and hear their testimony as historical witnesses.

As we have seen, about 1500 B. C. a party of emigrants from Mesopotamia set out for Palestine under the lead of Abraham, and among them must have been, along with the ancestors of Israel, those of Moab, Ammon, and Edom as well. That these races so closely related to Israel are also not natives of the lands occupied by them in historical times, but are immigrants, is declared quite expressly, and certainly not without reason, by Hebrew tradition. The new arrivals were nomads, wandering shepherds, going about the country peacefully and seeking pasture for their flocks. It is therefore only natural that they turned to the portions of the land best suited to grazing. One branch soon crossed over the Jordan and settled in the luxuriant pastures of the country east of the Jordan; and here where the Egyptian dominion did not reach they succeeded in a comparatively short time in forming a political and national organization as Moab and Ammon. Separated from the others by the Jordan these tribes thenceforth went their own way.

West of the Jordan the march went mainly towards the south. The more thinly populated south with the abundant growth of grass in the mountains of Judah seemed made for such nomadic shepherds, and it is therefore not accidental, but rests on sound historical tradition, when the legend locates Abraham as well as Isaac in the south. In Canaan they adopt the language of Canaan: this important process, too, must have taken place in the pre-Egyptian time, and at the same time and in the same way among all related tribes; for the Moabites, too, speak a language differing from the Hebrew only in unimportant dialectic respects.

But we have to examine another important element of the tradition. It represents Abraham as a religious leader and hero, and I find myself compelled to regard this feature also as historical. The appearance and achievements of Moses would be entirely inexplicable unless the people already had a distinctly marked religious character: for it is "the God of the Fathers" whom Moses proposes to bring and proclaim to Israel. The details of this matter are of course beyond inquiry and recognition, but we must maintain the fact unqualifiedly.

The next occurrence of historical importance is a further division within the portion of the Abrahamitic expedition that remained in Palestine. Not too soon after the settlement in Canaan,— Edom and Israel are late-born grandsons of Abraham,—the chief part turned further toward the south, where on Mount Seir dwelt the evidently uncivilized tribe of the Horites, and where the very nature of the land was a guarantee that the dominion of Egypt was but nominal. They succeeded in overcoming the Horites and in forming a political and national unity as Edom. More than a thousand years they remained in undisputed possession of this territory. About the time when these events must have taken place, the Egyptian prefect in Jerusalem, Abdichiba, writes to the Pharaoh Amenhotep, in the before-mentioned correspondence of Tell-el-Amarna, of Chabiri tribes that were making him much trouble and against whom he urgently begs the Pharaoh for support. There has been an attempt to find the Hebrews in these Chabiri, and the identification is possible from a linguistic point of view; but it is too much out of harmony with the whole character of Israelitish tradition itself for us to adopt it. Yet we may learn from these letters that southern Palestine was at that time in ferment and turmoil, and thus we have even here the appropriate historical background.

Of course, the Abrahamitic expedition was much reduced by the separation of Moab, Ammon, and Edom, and perhaps it would have been unable to maintain its identity if help had not come from the original home in Mesopotamia. This is Jacob, whose name means "reinforcement," "straggler." Jacob appears as father of twelve sons: these are the tribes into which Israel was divided in historical times. Legend has these sons, with the exception of Benjamin, born in Haran and the patriarch brought thence by them to Palestine: this is significant and shows that we are dealing here with fresh additions from without. Among these twelve sons the genealogical relationship is especially important. They fall into four groups, personified by the legend in four mothers: two wives and two concubines of the patriarch. We have four groups: a Leah group, a Rachel group, a Bilhah group, and a Zilpah group. The oldest and most important of these groups is the Leah group, and next to it the Zilpah group; but not less in power and nobility was the Rachel group, with which the Bilhah group was more closely connected.

In the origin and formation of the tribes we have one of the obscurest points in the primitive history of Israel; but weighty reasons confirm us in thinking that we must place the beginnings of tribal formation in the pre-Egyptian period. In order to avoid false conceptions, we must endeavor to get a clear idea of what a tribe is, according to oriental views. We are inclined to conceive of a tribe as something great and important; but that would be a great mistake. The Turkish Bureau of Statistics publishes a list of the Bedouin tribes that wander in Dscholan, the region east of the Sea of Galilee; there are 29 enumerated and their number given by tents, the tents being estimated at an average of five persons; of these 29 "tribes" two consist of 4 tents, two of 6, five of 8, and the most numerous of 300. This, then, would make for the largest in round numbers 1500 souls, while groups of only 20 souls are reckoned as separate tribes. On an average each of these 29 tribes has 40 tents, or in round numbers 200 souls. Such are the ideas of size with which we have to deal in treating the earliest tribal history of Israel. Even in historical times the tribe of Dan is estimated at 600 fighting men, and all Israel at 40,000.

It is not to be assumed that the Abrahamitic expedition had no connection with the formation of the tribes, and there has been a disposition to see in the Leah group, which is generally regarded as the oldest and comprising the firstborn sons, the portions of the Abrahamitic expedition that remained in Canaan, and in the Rachel group the reinforcements from Haran, so that Jacob and Joseph would at bottom be terms of the same size historically. At any rate we must distinguish two expeditions; the second we shall call the Jacobitic. This one united with the portions of the Abrahamitic expedition that remained in Canaan—the legend has Jacob also settle in the southern part of the land—and now becomes the representative of the historical development. And the two expeditions were united not outwardly alone, but spiritually as well: the faith of Abraham was transmitted to Jacob and was perpetuated in him as the noblest inheritance from his ancestors.

The next feature reported by tradition is the internal strifes among the tribes. Presuming upon his power and upon being the representative of the national history, Joseph, from whom Benjamin had probably not yet separated, laid claim to the hegemony, but had to give up in the face of a coalition of the other tribes, and went to Egypt, whose fertile and grassy borderlands on the side of Asia, on the isthmus of Suez, had been from early times the scene of strife among Semitic nomads.

With Joseph the Bilhah group had lost its chief

support. Now the Leah group attempted to gain control of it, and the first-born of the Leah group, Reuben, seemed to have planned to achieve this by violence; but the tough and doughty tribes of Dan and Naphtali maintained their independence, and Reuben retired from the contest so reduced that he lost forever his birthright, i. e., his former power and standing. The only case in which the tribe of Reuben, or members of it, play a historical part, is in the insurrection of the Reubenites, Dathan and Abiram, against the Levite Moses, to whom they deny the leadership, —another contest for the hegemony. Legend has personified these occurrences in a crime on the part of Reuben with Bilhah, his father's wife, on account of which he is cursed and deprived of his birthright.

But soon conditions must have arisen which forced all the tribes to migrate. They followed the path of Joseph, and the latter now took noble revenge; forgetting the cause of offense and mindful only of the old kinship, he hospitably opened to his distressed brethren the territory occupied by himself.

Thus all the sons of Jacob had come to Egypt. At first the Egyptian government, to which such settlements of Semitic nomads in the borderlands was a very common affair, seems to have met the strangers with kindly neutrality; but soon there was a very keen change in their situation, and the reason for this is to be found in a change of the historical and political conditions. Even in the Tell-el-Amarna correspondence, Ribaddi, the Egyptian prefect of Gebal (the Greek Byblos), complains of the Chatti (spelled also Cheta, and Khita) who are advancing threateningly against northern Palestine. This people, the Hittites of the Old Testament, did in fact at this time, during a temporary decline of the Egyptian power, set up a great kingdom between the Euphrates and Lebanon. Judging by the names of their rulers and the numerous monuments left by them, they were not Semites, and the attempt has been made to identify them with the Armenians, and even to designate their language as ancient Armenian.

When under Seti I. the Egyptian power began to revive, it undertook immediately the recovery of the former dominion in Asia; but Seti was diverted toward the West and had to devote his chief attention to the Libyans. His son, Rameses II., however, equipped a great expedition against the kingdom of the Cheta and claims to have subdued them completely. But the end of the long contest was a treaty which proves the very opposite: the two opponents, who had apparently recognized themselves as well matched, concluded a perpetual peace, the letter of which is preserved to us as the oldest political treaty in history. When this treaty, — the Egyptian version, it should be added, in which alone it is preserved, — begins with the words: "Chetasar, the great king of Cheta, enters into treaty from this day on with Ramessu, the great prince of Egypt," one sees directly that this is not the style in which the vanquished deals with the victor. Evidently the kingdom of the Cheta remained unreduced and embraced all northern Palestine, while only southern Palestine returned into the former subjection to Egypt.

That this perpetual peace was not a finality was probably clear to both the contracting parties, and at least it was a heavily armed peace. Therefore we can understand why Rameses regarded distrustfully the alien elements on his eastern border facing Asia; besides, for his great architectural undertakings,—he was unquestionably the greatest builder of ancient Egypt,—he needed laborers, and so he resorted to the measure of impressing as public slaves the Semitic settlers on the isthmus of Suez and forced them to do heavy labor under strong military guard. It is claimed that there is a direct reference to the Israelites in a papyrus of the time of Rameses II. which speaks of "Apuriu," who drag stone for the constructions of King Rameses. These Apuriu, who are also mentioned elsewhere, are not, indeed, the Hebrews, but the papyrus is incontestable evidence that under Rameses II. alien settlers were really treated as the Israelites were treated by him according to their traditions. In the very Land of Goshen there have been discovered numerous structures of bricks made of Nile mud and chopped straw, and bearing the arms of Rameses II.

And so from free nomads the Israelites had become Egyptian serfs. It will be easily understood that of all people Bedouins, in whom the proud spirit of independence is most characteristic, could not endure such treatment; among them especially it was inevitable that nature should rebel against the outrageous constraint which struck and wounded mortally the very heart of their being. As long as Rameses ruled, indeed, all resistance and all attempts at escape seemed vain. But under his son and successor, Merenptah, an entire change in affairs took place. In the fifth year of Merenptah there poured over Egypt an invasion of several distinct foreign races, which brought the government to the verge of ruin. Merenptah claims, indeed, to have beaten and completely overcome the enemy, but it remains true that the Egyptian power received in these occurrences a blow from which it was long in recovering.

These enemies from without seem to have come simultaneously with all sorts of domestic troubles and distresses, and thus the hour of freedom for Israel had struck. Moses, a Hebrew of the tribe of Levi, had by favorable providence had access to the learning and civilization of Egypt,—even his name, Mesu, is genuinely and specifically Egyptian. But his heart inclined him to his people; he preferred to be a brother of these despised slaves rather than to live in the enjoyment of Egyptian glory and Egyptian splendor. One single thought dominated him; how to become the rescuer and liberator of his people. With keen insight he perceived that the only possibility of rescuing them from the iron clutch of the Egyptian border fortresses and garrisons was a desperate course : through the sea to the desert. He gathers more detailed information about places and conditions, enters into connections with the related Bedouins of the Arabian Desert, and when he thinks the proper moment come they start with wife and child, with flocks and belongings. By skilful zigzag marches he succeeds in eluding the Egyptian border-guards, and already the strait of Suez lies before them when they are overtaken by a troop of Egyptian scouts. Before them the breakers, behind them the pursuers thirsting for vengeance,—a moment of extreme distress ! But where need is greatest there God is nearest. A mighty northeast wind lays dry the shallow strait and they go through on the bottom of the sea, into the desert, into freedom. The pursuing Egyptians are surprised by the returning waters ; Israel is saved. Then, as Exodus says briefly, but with magnificent effect, " then the people feared the Lord and they believed in God and in his servant Moses." This overwhelming moment created the people of Israel ; they never forgot it ; here they recognized the God of their fathers, who with strong hand and outstretched arm had saved his people and brought them out of the house of bondage, out of Egypt.

Under Merenptah, as we know from documentary evidence, southern Palestine and the seacoast was still in uncontested Egyptian possession, and the neighboring kingdom of the Cheta was obliged, according to the treaty referred to, to deliver Egyptian deserters and fugitives; therefore Moses led the liberated people into the gorges of Sinai, whither a troop of wandering nomads could indeed make its way, but never an army of any size. Israel remained for some time in Sinai, and here in this mighty highland scenery tradition locates the capital achievement of Moses, his religious reorganization of the people. It is one of the most remarkable moments in the history of mankind, the birth-hour of the religion of the spirit. In the thunderstorms of Sinai the God of revelation himself comes down upon the earth: here we have the dawn of the day which was to break upon the whole human race, and among the greatest mortals who ever walked this earth Moses will always remain one of the greatest.

But Sinai was only a station, not the goal of the expedition. Soon the people, strengthened by the rest and compacted by discipline, wandered on as far as Kadesh-barnea in the desert south of Canaan, very probably the modern Ain Kudês on the southwest slope of the plateau of Azâzimeh. This place, sufficient as a settlement for simple shepherds, was out of reach of the Egyptian arms, and yet at the gate of the land of the fathers. Here for a time they could quietly await the development of affairs, and from all we can judge the stay in Kadesh must have been a tolerably long one. Probably here too occurred the death of Moses. That he personally did not enter the Promised Land, nor any one else of those who left Egypt, is an important feature of the tradition, the more essential when one remembers that the distance involved is one that can be covered easily under normal conditions in two weeks.

After the death of Merenptah Egypt fell into a condition of wild anarchy, which made any interference in the affairs of Palestine impossible. His grandson, Setnecht, finally succeeded in restoring order; but then there came a new danger. In the eighth year of his successor, Rameses III., a general race-migration swept in upon northern Syria and Palestine. We are told of a whole series of races who came bringing with them their wives and children to seek new dwellings. Rameses was obliged to take measures against the impending danger. With a great army and a strong fleet he set out for Palestine, and the experienced military art of Egypt was successful in defeating the undisciplined hordes. The danger to Egypt was removed, and the glory of the Egyptian name in Palestine was revived—but it was a final flickering before extinction. After this we hear no more of the deeds of the Egyptians in Canaan; indeed when the first great Assyrian conqueror, Tiglath-Pileser, advanced to the Mediterranean, the Pharaoh hastened to send him presents.

This race-migration in the time of Rameses III. had two great results. It evidently destroyed the kingdom of the Cheta, of whom no more is heard, and it brought the Philistines to Palestine. In the army of these hordes Rameses repeatedly makes prominent mention of the "Pursta." As the Egyptian script regularly represents the "l" in foreign words by "r" and makes no distinction in the sounds, we may also read the name "Pulsta," and have probably to recognize in them the Philistines, who were of course also immigrants, and whose alien race character was especially felt. In nature and customs they were entirely different from all the other races of Palestine, and are therefore justly to be regarded as the remnant of that migration which remained in Palestine.

But we have almost lost sight of Israel, and shall now return to it. It was in all probability the consequence of the just-mentioned disturbances which brought Israel to the end of its wanderings. Driven in turn, perhaps, by the Philistines who were settling in their country, the Canaanites, led by their king, Sihon, made an advance into the country east of the Jordan, expelling the Moabites and the Ammonites from the most fertile parts of their territory and founding a new kingdom with Heshbon for its capital. At this point the conquered bethought themselves of their kinsmen in the desert of Kadesh. Perhaps called to aid by Moab and Ammon themselves, in any case they were welcome allies, and the fresh and unexhausted vigor of Israel accomplished the work. King Sihon was defeated at Jahaz and his kingdom destroyed, but Israel took up its dwelling in the bountiful land and kept for itself the reward of the contest and victory. Soon, however, the fertile valleys and fields ceased to suffice for the constantly increasing men and flocks : it was necessary to seek homes west of the Jordan. Judah led the advance. He crossed the Jordan and turned southward toward the mountains and fertile lowlands which afterwards bore his name. Here Judah succeeded, indeed, in establishing himself, but only after heavy losses. Many mixtures with alien races took place, but after long and persistent struggles the intruder finally overcame the native; at the time of David, when Judah enters the clear light of history, the Israelitish part of the population is in unquestioned control of the land and it is recognized as distinctly Israelitish.

A second and entirely unsuccessful attempt was made by Simeon and Levi. Through treachery they got possession of the Canaanite city of Shechem which is the key to the mountain region of Ephraim ; but Israel recoiled in horror from the disgraceful deed, and the transgressing tribes fell victims to the vengeance of the Canaanites.

Levi was obliterated as a tribe, to reappear by a most remarkable metamorphosis as a sacerdotal tribe; the remnants of Simeon took refuge with their nearest kinsmen, the tribe of Judah, and were absorbed by it.

The third and most successful invasion was conducted by the house of Joseph. Only Reuben and Gad remained behind in the country east of the Jordan; the other seven tribes united under the lead of the Ephraimite Joshua for a combined expedition against middle Palestine. They took advantage of unusually low water in the Jordan to make a sudden assault upon Jericho, which they captured and destroyed; they also succeeded in taking Ai and Bethel.

Only now did the Canaanites, who were evidently enervated by luxury, and no match in respect of bravery for the impetuous sons of the desert, rouse themselves to united resistance; but Joshua defeated them at Gibeon, and so Israel was firmly established in middle Palestine. But this does not mean that Israel was in full possession of the land: by far the best and most fertile portions of it, and especially the majority of the cities, whose strong fortifications made them impregnable to the primitive military skill of the Israelites, remained in possession of the Canaanites; it was chiefly the woody mountain-chains of northern and middle Palestine that had come into the power of Israel, and the Canaanites had partly to be subdued by force and partly to be peacefully absorbed—a long and difficult task.

That Israel had the ability to carry on this struggle of centuries deliberately and with final success is due entirely to Moses and his work. Moses had given the people a nationality and in this an inalienable palladium which, purified and strengthened by the power of religion, could not be destroyed, but of itself led on to victory. Thus it came about that Israel in Canaan did not become Canaanitish; but, on the contrary, the Canaanites became Israelitish.

But this outcome of the contest of the nationalities was by no means certain to human foresight. In Canaan, Israel adopted from the Canaanites agriculture and all the arts of domiciliated life. How easily this might have led to a change in national character, a loss of national individuality, so that Israel would have been conquered and subdued spiritually by the Canaanites!

Besides, quite apart from the superior numbers and civilization of the Canaanites, Israel had within itself the worst of enemies and a germ of destruction. This was the proud sense of independence and the strongly-developed family feeling of the nomad, which did not immediately vanish from the national character with the surrender of the nomadic fashion of life. After the united effort under Joshua had but barely laid the foundation, the people again broke up into tribes and clans, which now aimlessly sought new places of settlement, each on its own account and unmindful of its neighbors.

Judah had been entirely lost sight of by the other tribes. Zebulun and Naphtali went into the extreme north, where under the leadership of a certain Barak of Kedesh-naphtali, they succeeded in defeating King Jabin of Hazor and thus secured their tribal territory in the North. A part of the tribe of Manasseh, the families of Jair and Machir, crossed the Jordan and conquered the land east of the Sea of Galilee—an event of much importance, since thus was established the permanent connection between the country east of the Jordan and that west of it. The tribe of Dan tried first to establish permanent homes in the fertile plain sloping toward the Mediterranean; but in spite of all its bravery it did not succeed in conquering territory from the powerful and warlike Philistines : the poetic, one might almost say romantic, expression of this fruitless struggle between the tribe and the Philistines is preserved in the story of Samson. They finally left this region and in the utmost north conquered the city of Laish on the slope of Mount Hermon, giving it their own name of Dan. The division of Benjamin from Joseph, and its continuance as a separate tribe must also be dated from this time. Shamir in the mountains of Ephraim was occupied by the family of Tolah of the tribe of Issachar ; Pirathon in the same region, by the family of Abdon ; Aijalon, by the family of

Elon from the tribe of Zebulun. Only an extreme danger could bring about union among these, and not even this a complete or permanent union.

After the time of Joshua, the Canaanites seem to have made only one more effort, by gathering and exerting all their forces, to overcome the intruders. Under the leadership of a certain Sisera of Harosheth-haggojim a powerful coalition of Canaanitish kings was formed, which undertook a war of extermination against Israel. And it seemed about to succeed: the Israelites were already withdrawing into the hiding-places of their woods and mountains when aid came from heaven. Deborah, a divinely inspired woman, rekindled the spirits of the discouraged troops. Under the lead of Barak of the tribe of Issachar the fighting-men of seven tribes assembled upon the venerable and sacred Mount Tabor, and the Canaanites gave way before the impetuous attack of these troops fighting for God and their existence. At Taanach by the river Kishon they were beaten and scattered; Sisera himself was slain on his flight by a woman. After this battle we hear no more of any resistance on the part of the Canaanites: it settled the destiny of Palestine for good in favor of Israel.

While Israel had thus obtained relief from the Canaanites, it was now threatened by another enemy. The races related to Israel looked enviously upon its success, and now wanted a share of the Canaanite booty. Moab advanced across the Jordan, and its king, Eglon, received at Jericho homage and tribute from the tribe of Benjamin, but the Benjaminite Ehud stabbed him and freed his people from the foreign yoke. Ammon, too, advanced to the Jordan, and the hard-pressed tribe of Gad was saved only by the bravery of Jephthah, whose victory was made especially memorable by the tragic circumstances connected with it,—the hero was forced by a too hasty vow to sacrifice upon the altar his only child, a beloved daughter. Jephthah had also to wage domestic war. The tribes of Ephraim and Manasseh regarded with jealous and anxious eyes the rising power of the tribe of Gad, which lay between them, and tried to extend their own territory by an act of aggression against Gad; but they were repulsed by the Gaddites, under Jephthah, and suffered a fearful defeat.

If Israel was so lacking in inner harmony, it is no wonder that its enemies had free play. Even the marauding Bedouins of the desert made plundering incursions into the land which was exposed to them as a defenceless prey. Such a band of Midianites advanced even to Mount Tabor in the extreme north of the country, not far from the Sea of Galilee. But this very expedition was to bear far-reaching consequences. In pure wantonness the Midianites had slaughtered on Tabor some captured members of the noble family of Abiezer, of the tribe of Manasseh. Thereupon,

Gideon, or Jerubbaal, the head of the family, took up the sword to avenge the blood of his murdered brethren. He summoned the members and dependents of his family, three hundred men all told, and with these pursued the retreating Midianites. Far beyond the Jordan, on the very border of the desert, he overtook them; he succeeded in dispersing the enemy and in taking captive their two kings, Zebah and Zalmunna, whom he himself struck down in expiation for his murdered brethren, after his eldest son, Jether, had refused to do it. On his return he chastised the inhabitants of Succoth and Penuel, who had scornfully refused to aid him in his pursuit of vengeance. After this victory Gideon must have established a regular tribal kingdom; in his ancestral city of Ophrah he erected a great ephod, or idol, from the gold of the Midianitish booty, and maintained there a regular court and numerous wives.

Thus, the first attempt at political concentration, the establishment of a tribal kingdom, had originated with the house of Joseph, and from this tribal kingdom might have grown a national kingdom, but the time for it had not yet come. During his life Gideon was in undisputed possession of the sway over Joseph; but after his death harem politics, the curse of all oriental royal houses, overthrew his family. Abimelech, his son by a woman from the still purely Canaanitish city of Shechem, with the aid of kinsmen in this city, appropriated the inheritance of his father. He attacked Ophrah and slew there upon one stone all of his brothers, seventy in number, according to the legend; only the youngest escaped. Of course this was not the way to establish the kingdom in the hearts of the Israelitish people. Abimelech enjoyed the usurped throne only three years. At the end of this period he fell into a quarrel with the Shechemites. Toward them, too, he acted the Israelitish king, and the proud Canaanitish nobles would not endure this of their creature. An open insurrection against him took place, in consequence of which he sacked and utterly destroyed Shechem. But before the Canaanitish city of Thebez, which he was threatening with the same fate, destiny overtook him. As he was on the point of setting fire to the tower in which the inhabitants of Thebez had taken refuge, a woman threw a millstone down upon him from the battlements of the tower and killed him.

Thus the first attempt at an Israelitish kingdom ended in blood and murder. But it failed not on its own account, but because of the manner of its execution. Conditions called for a repetition of the attempt; only it must be no tribal kingdom, but a national one. It was an absolute necessity. Only through the union, in one strong hand, of all the divided, and therefore impotent forces, could the way be paved for order, and race and nationality be maintained. True, it required first a great danger to overcome all the centrifugal forces in Israel, and a gigantic danger really came; but in the fire of this extreme distress Israel was welded together into a united and strong nation.

The truculent people of the Philistines, well trained in war, took advantage of the weakness of Israel and advanced toward the mountain region of Ephraim into the fertile plain of Jezreel. The first clash at Ebenezer resulted unfortunately for Israel. Thereupon they fetched from the temple at Shiloh, the old military shrine of the house of Joseph, the ark of the covenant, in order to make sure of the help of God. But as though God had wished to give his people an impressive lesson on the folly of such reliance upon outward things, this second battle ended with a more terrible and complete defeat; thirty thousand Israelites covered the field of battle; the sacred ark itself was captured by the heathen victor. With this, the power of Joseph was broken. The Philistines burned and destroyed the temple at Shiloh, carried the captured sacred ark to the temple of their chief god, Dagon, and subjected the land, even to the Jordan; the people were disarmed and held in check by Philistine prefects and strongholds. And from all evidence this Philistine domination must have lasted a considerable time. Israel seemed paralyzed, and submitted, though with gnashing of teeth. After all, it was no disgrace to have succumbed to the lion. But when, in addition, the ass came to give a kick to the powerless people, the measure was full. The Ammonites renewed the attempt which Jephthah had checked, and spread out as conquerors on the east bank of the Jordan. They laid siege to the city of Jabesh-gilead; the inhabitants, recognizing the impossibility of resistance offered to capitulate. But the Ammonite king, Nahash, answered them: "On this condition will I accept a capitulation from you, that I may thrust out all your right eyes, and lay it for a reproach upon all Israel." The inhabitants of Jabesh beg for seven days' time, during which they propose to call on all Israel for help. Scornfully the Ammonite grants them the respite, and calmly permits the messengers to leave the beleaguered city. But he was destined to have erred in his reckoning. The God of Sinai had not forgotten his people; he who had freed it from the bondage of the Egyptians delivered it now from the Philistine subjection. Already his spirit had touched the heart of the hero whom he had chosen as the liberator of his people; this liberator is still following the plow in the field inherited from his fathers, but humbly, yet confidently, he bides his time. Then, when the call for help from Jabesh reaches his ear, there is no delay; the districts of Israel are stirred as by a spring tempest; the liberator, the king, has come.

CHAPTER III.

THE NATIONAL KINGDOM.—SAUL AND DAVID.

WE have seen the messengers of the hard-pressed city of Jabesh go out through all Israel; will they bring help? King Nahash thinks not, otherwise he would not have let them go, and very likely they themselves have little hope of it; but only a few weeks before, in an obscure and quiet corner of the mountain region of Ephraim, had occurred an event which was to give a wholly new turn to the destinies of Israel.

At Ramah in the hill country of Ephraim, in the district of Zuph—not to be confused with the better-known Ramah of the tribe of Benjamin near Jerusalem—dwells a seer already high in years, Samuel by name, highly esteemed among his own people, but otherwise little known in Israel. He feels Israel's degradation more bitterly and more keenly than the rest of the people, who had already submitted with dumb indifference to what seemed inevitable. To his illumined eye the causes of the national misfortune are evident: the lamentable division alone, in spite of all the personal bravery of individuals, has made the people the almost defenseless prey of its neigh-

HISTORY OF THE PEOPLE OF ISRAEL. 57

bors. If the nation is not to succumb utterly and be absorbed gradually by its oppressors the only remedy is the union of the divided and undisciplined forces in one strong hand,—in other words, the national kingdom. Among the enemies of Israel it is precisely and solely this organization and centralization due to the kingdom which guarantees to them their superiority in the field. But whence shall come the king who with strong hand will shake off the yoke of foreign rule and lead the people to victory and freedom? Full of pious trust, Samuel lays the question before the faithful God who has always hitherto sent the right man at the right time.

In this crisis there appears before him one day a distinguished Benjaminite seeking Samuel's prophetic gift for an event of daily life: Saul the son of Kish, from Gibeah of the tribe of Benjamin. In this Gibeah a Philistine prefect held his court. This is significant. With this visible evidence of the bondage of his people constantly before his eyes, Saul could not but feel with especial keenness the humiliation of his people. Doubtless he bore the yoke of the uncircumcised with gnashing of teeth, and probably looked often in silent grief for a rescuer out of this distress. But with the childlike guilelessness of a generous and unspoiled heart he seems to have no presentiment of the powers that slumber within him. That he himself might be destined to become this ardently-longed-for rescuer from distress is a thought that does not enter his head. Thus unconscious of his own worth, in the noble adornment of modesty, he appears before Samuel. The seer is struck with the chivalrous bearing and the majestic appearance of this Benjaminite who towers above the rest of the people by a head; when he catches sight of him an inner voice calls to him: This is the man for whom thou waitest; God himself sends him to thee. By mysterious remarks he cunningly rouses in Saul's heart thoughts and feelings that till now had slumbered within him. A sacrifice, combined with a festal meal, to which Samuel takes the Benjaminite, serves to give to the developing thoughts of Saul a religious consecration, and the honorable distinction with which Samuel treats him, a stranger, at this solemn ceremony, arouses within him the presentiment of great things that await him.

When after this Samuel takes the stranger to his own house as a guest, where a familiar conversation loosens his tongue and reveals the innermost thoughts of his heart, Samuel grows ever more certain that he has found the one whom God has chosen for the liberation of his people. When Saul takes leave of his host the following morning the seer anoints his head with oil, reveals to him for what high things he is destined, and bids him bide his time and then do what his hand may find to do, for God will be with him.

Saul returns to his home, and his people notice that a change has come over him—as our account says briefly and significantly, God had changed him into another man; but quietly as before he tills his field, awaiting the moment when the spirit of God shall come upon him. Now the messengers from Jabesh make their appearance also in Gibeah. Everywhere they have found tearful sympathy, but no hand is lifted to help. And in Gibeah also it seemed to be the same. When Saul drives home his yoke of oxen from the field he finds the whole city in tears. In reply to his question he learns of the insolent mockery of the Ammonite. He flames out in sacred wrath, cuts his oxen in pieces and sends the bloody portions all about with the message: "Whosoever cometh not forth after Saul, so shall it be done unto his oxen." His enthusiasm has its effect; a considerable troop gathers around the brave leader, the enemy are surprised in the gray of morn and utterly routed; the hard-pressed city of Jabesh is saved.

Now the scales seem to fall from their eyes: they have found the right man and they propose to keep him. Rejoicing in the first victory after long subjugation and humiliation the people bring to Gilgal in triumph the one to whom they owe the fresh victory, to deck him in this ancient sacred city with the royal diadem. Now Israel too has a king, like all the nations round about. Will the new king accomplish what they expect of him and what he needs must accomplish ? Or was the ceremony at Gilgal perhaps too hasty, a mocking air-phantom of the overflowing enthusiasm of the moment ?

The defeat of that troop of Ammonite skirmishers was after all no great affair. The real test of power for the new kingdom was rather whether it would succeed in breaking the domination of the Philistines. It had been possible, indeed, to attempt a peaceful settlement with the national enemy. Perhaps the Philistines would have recognized Saul as a feudal king or Philistine vassal if he had submitted to their authority as had been done before. But this was an impossibility for the popular king who had just been raised to the throne. Only the sword could arbitrate now. Therefore Saul keeps about him three thousand men selected from the exultant concourse at Gilgal, waiting to see what attitude the Philistines would assume in view of the new turn of affairs. But the whole situation demanded a settlement ; both sides needed a decided clearing away of uncertainties. In order to bring Israel face to face with an accomplished fact which should shut out all retreat, Jonathan, Saul's first-born son, the most ideal and purely heroic figure of the Old Testament, does a bold deed and slays the Philistine prefect at Gibeah, and Saul has the trumpet sounded throughout all Israel and the fighting men summoned to join him at Gibeah.

To meet this open outbreak the Philistines march
into the rebellious district with a strong force,
and so great is Israel's fear of her long-standing
oppressors, so great the dread of this victory-
wonted enemy that the people about Saul flee, all
save six hundred men, at the approach of the
Philistine army. Again it is Jonathan who takes
the lead in manful action. By a movement executed with unparalleled audacity he carries disorder into the Philistine camp: Saul takes advantage of this disorder to make an attack, and
after a hot struggle the victory is his. But in
the ardor of pursuit of the fleeing enemy he issues
an imprudent order which makes it impossible to
secure the full benefit of the victory. His glorious son Jonathan, the real hero of this memorable
day, came near falling a victim to his father's in-
discretion,—and thus in this very first deed of
liberation there is a faint shadow which settles
upon the new kingdom as an omen portentous of
misfortune.

We do not know much more of Saul's reign.
Saul's first measure was to put the military forces
of the people upon a war footing; for he had
enemies all about, first of all, the Philistines.
That first victory at Michmash was only a tran-
sient achievement which had scarcely destroyed
the Philistine tyranny; the struggle with this
ancestral enemy, conducted with fluctuating fortunes, constitutes the chief part of Saul's reign
and his life. He owed the crown to his sword

and had to maintain it by the sword; his whole reign was an incessant warfare. In such a condition of affairs the need of a standing army became evident; it would not do to be forced in every separate case to summon the militia of Israel. And so Saul kept those three thousand men about his person and strove to increase the number and their efficiency: wherever he saw a brave and capable man, he attached him to himself, he himself and his son Jonathan at their head, a genuine leader of his men and supported by the enthusiastic love of his people. So much the more puzzling and incomprehensible seems the tragic turn of events which soon ensued. The oldest account gives no explanation for it but simply says: "An evil spirit from the Lord troubled him." Plainly we have to do here with severe derangements of mind and soul, an incurable melancholy which at times gave way to fits of madness. And if we examine more closely, we shall easily find the psychological reasons for this.

It had really been a hasty proceeding when they put the crown upon Saul's head in Gilgal. Saul was not equal to the inner difficulties of the situation. If he had been introduced into settled conditions, reared upon the throne in possession of an inherited and established power he would have been, with his noble and chivalrous nature, one of the best kings of Israel: but here everything had first to be created, and Saul was not equal to this task : he was a nobleman and cavalier, but here was needed a ruler and king. His whole character has a cast which I would almost call commonplace; the original and sunny, the winning and all-compelling personality that sways men by moral conquest, this he lacked. And this is just what he needed; for the office did not carry the man, but the man had first to create the office.

It was no easy thing for the Israelites who were accustomed to perfect freedom and local independence to renounce these congenial and familiar conditions and subordinate themselves to a single will. When there was combat with the national enemy involving the struggle for existence, they followed him willingly and gladly; but to feel themselves members of a commonwealth even in times of peace and to abandon perhaps well-founded personal claims in the interest of the state and public order, was more than could be expected of them, and the people had to be accustomed to it slowly and gradually. In fact, it was achieved only when they had a sense of doing, as a personal favor to the king, whatever came hard to them, somewhat as a child on first going to school can be accustomed and reared to the discipline of the school only when he does all that is asked of him with the joyous feeling of showing the teacher a personal kindness. And to awaken this feeling in Israel Saul was not the man. Of decidedly choleric temperament, bold and energetic, but at the same time abrupt and inconsiderate, it was not natural for him to sue for love; indeed, he had no compunctions about offending Israel in its most sacred feelings when state policy, as we would express it to-day, seemed to call for it.

Israel had a solemn league and covenant with the Gibeonites, a Canaanitish alliance of four cities. We can understand that Saul felt it as a severe restraint to have an enclave of alien people dwelling a few miles from the gates of his capital. In his zeal for Israel, as the report says, he attacked the Gibeonites and undertook to defeat them. Furthermore, it became a necessity to reduce the predatory and dangerous people of the desert, the Amalekites. The solemn curse was pronounced against them, and Saul marched against them and conquered them, but considered it more expedient not to execute the curse, and spared the captive king and the best part of the booty. This could not but seem a great sin to the religious consciousness of that time, being a breach of promise and perjury toward God himself, and robbery or at least embezzlement of God's property. So even Samuel lost faith in the man of his choice, and in deep grief abandoned him to whom, as king, law and right ought to have been inviolable and sacred.

When we realize further that even in the war with the Philistines there were no great and decisive victories, and that the enthusiastic uprising finally ended in a spiritless and wearisome guerrilla warfare, we can understand the change in public sentiment and understand, too, how Saul himself was forced to recognize that he was not equal to his position and was not accomplishing what was expected of him and what he ought to accomplish. Now, for a noble man striving only for the best with honest purpose and consecrated zeal, there is no more terrible spiritual torment than the consciousness of his own insufficiency; Saul's strong and yet sensitive nature succumbed to this infernal assault, and darkness settled upon his great soul.

When I contemplate this picture that so moves the depths of the heart, I am always impressed with the parallel in the figure of that most unfortunate of rulers on the Prussian throne, personally perhaps the most gifted of all, the son and counterfeit of an incomparable mother, and richly endowed with all advantages of mind and soul, who was welcomed at the beginning of his reign with rejoicings and enthusiasm beyond what any Hohenzoller had ever received, and yet ended at last alone and forsaken in the night of insanity, because a pitiless destiny had placed him in a position and before tasks to which his empyreal nature was not equal.[1]

It is a touching proof of the genuine and grateful love bestowed upon Saul that Israel remained

[1] Frederick William IV., son of Queen Louise, and brother of Emperor William I.

faithful to him in his misfortunes, and that no one undertook to remove him from the throne, not even after he had actually become a danger to his people. On the contrary, they did everything possible to subdue the evil spirit. The magic power of music was invoked to dispel the melancholy of the unhappy king. Some one in Saul's retinue knows a man especially talented in singing, and at the same time of tried valor, knight and troubadour in one, the Judean David of Bethlehem. David is summoned to court and obeys the summons. Thus enters upon the scene the man, who after Moses, is the greatest personage of ancient Israel, and for whom it was reserved to complete the work of Moses.

David is one of those divinely favored, sunny natures whom all hearts acknowledge, the born ruler whom all willingly and gladly acknowledge and serve. Distinguished by all the advantages of mind and body, radiant with youth, beauty and power, compelling all hearts to love by his fascinating amiability, thus he appears before the king. At first all went well. Even Saul could not withstand the charm of this personality; he made the young man, who soon became indispensable to him, his armor-bearer, what we would call his personal adjutant. The chivalrous Jonathan recognizes in the chivalrous Judean an affinity, and the two hearts are united in a most devoted, fraternal league of pure and generous friendship, while the king's daughter Michal also is inflamed with ardent love for her brother's bosom friend and her father's favorite, and Saul, for whom it was a matter of great concern to keep such a hero near him, gives him his daughter to wife.

But soon the evil spirit began its fiendish work even here. It is not clear what aroused the wrath of the suspicious king. According to one account it was jealousy of David's warlike deeds and success. True, it was necessary in those days that the king should be at the same time the chief in bravery, but there was his glorious son Jonathan, who at least equaled David in military fame. According to another account he sees in David a pretendant to the crown, a possible rival in the dominion over Israel. This account owes its origin wholly to the fact that David actually did become his successor; but it is wholly improbable that at that time anybody, even David himself, should have thought of such a thing; when Saul resigned the crown it would simply descend to Jonathan, and the most that David could have expected would be to become perhaps grand-vizier of his friend and brother-in-law. On the other hand the oldest account offers us what seems to be the first credible and plausible clue: here Saul suspects that David had entered with Jonathan into a conspiracy against him, a plan to depose him and put Jonathan in his place.

David cannot have failed to see that such a change of rulers would be a real blessing for Israel in the condition of the people at that time, and many a good patriot may have thought the same. Whether David some time uttered an incautious expression to this effect, or whether the suspicious king imagined this thought in the heart of his son-in-law,—at all events, in an attack of his malady he threw a spear at him, and David fled. The priests at Nob, who had innocently aided the fugitive, were overtaken by a fearful judgment: they were summoned before the king's tribunal and executed as traitors, and their city and sanctuary destroyed; only one, Ebiathar by name, escaped and fled to David.

Meanwhile David had fled to his home in Judah, and had there gathered about him a band of desperate men, four hundred rash and reckless fellows, whose leader he became. He is often represented as a regular robber chief, before whom no man was sure of his life, no woman of her honor; and there is some support for such a view in the familiar story of David's relations with the rich Nabal and his prudent wife, the fair Abigail. But such stories must be judged from the oriental point of view. To this day any Arab would shoot down on the spot like a mad dog a man refusing his hospitality in such an insolent and offensive way as Nabal does David's. No, we have rather to picture him to ourselves like the knights-errant who go out seeking adventures and are always ready to draw their swords where there is need. For instance, David is informed that the city of Keilah is hard beset by the Philistines; his people remonstrate with him, saying : " We are scarcely sure of our lives in Judah, and shall we now begin a feud with the Philistines?" But David undertakes the foray and rescues the city. On this occasion, however, and in general we see that the members of his tribe are rather in sympathy with Saul and regard David and his band with evident distrust.

Despite the critical condition of his kingdom, Saul did not shrink from civil war, but led his standing army against David and his men. David succeeded, indeed, in evading him, but finally the soil of Judah became too warm for him and there remained nothing for him but to take refuge with the enemy : he became the vassal of the Philistine king, Achish of Gath, who received him with open arms and gave him the city of Ziklag as residence. Even here he was helpful to his people and fought their enemies while pretending to Achish that he was fighting with Judah and Israel, and in order to keep the matter secret he took no prisoners. Achish, too, was completely fascinated by him and trusted him blindly.

When David had dwelt a year and four months in Ziklag, destiny overtook Saul. The Philistines prepared for a decisive campaign against Israel, and David was expected to join the army of Achish. How David would have acted if the Philistines had insisted on the fulfilment of his feudal obligations we cannot say, but the other

Philistine kings did not trust David and protested against such an ally. David probably never thanked his God more ardently than when he was thus sent home. Saul with his troops was stationed on Mount Gilboa, and the battle ended in his total defeat. When he saw all lost and his three sons fallen, in despair he fell upon his own sword. The Philistines cut off the head of the corpse and sent it, together with the armor of the fallen king, to the temple of Astarte; the headless body and the corpses of his three sons they hung upon the walls of Beth-shan, the nearest considerable city. But now the men of Jabesh, which Saul had once rescued from utmost need, remembered their debt; they took down the bodies from the walls by night and carried them across the Jordan to Jabesh, where they gave them honorable burial and mourned them for seven days.

Saul is one of the most tragic figures in history. A great and nobly endowed nature, heroic and chivalrous, inspired with fiery zeal, he finally accomplished nothing; the dream of Gilgal proved a cruel illusion; the man of the people, whose very name signifies "the desired" and in whom the longing of Israel seemed embodied, had been a will-o'-the-wisp. At his death the situation was again just what it had been at his coronation: Israel prostrate, the power of the Philistines greater and firmer than ever before. He had not shown himself equal to the task which destiny and circumstances had set for him.

And I would call attention to one more point: he lacked appreciation of the true character of Israel; in this regard tradition has given a wholly correct picture of him. He was exclusively a soldier, and was in a fair way to change Israel into a secular military state and thus divert it from its religious function in universal history. Saul may claim our deepest compassion and our heartiest sympathy, but the fall of his power was a blessing for Israel. We have no direct information as to the length of his reign; from such sources as we can command it did not last long. Five years is the least that we are obliged to estimate, but ten is the utmost possible. According to the most probable estimate of dates, based on the very accurate Assyrian chronology, Saul's death would fall in the year 1017; this will not deviate more than a few years at the utmost from the actual date.

But Saul's blood was not to flow on Mount Gilboa unavenged; an avenger and the real finisher of his life-work arose in the Judean whom he had fought and persecuted. For a while, it is true, David had to remain inactive. It would have been madness to begin the contest against the Philistines with his six hundred men; he took care first to save what he could, and was annointed tribal king of Judah under Philistine suzerainty, and took up his residence as such at Hebron. It seems that Saul had left a single, minor son, named Ish-bosheth (or Eshbaal);

Abner, Saul's cousin and commander-in-chief, took up his cause and established for him out of the ruins of Saul's dominion a kingdom at Mahanaim in the country east of the Jordan, in all probably under Philistine suzerainty also, while the whole territory west of the Jordan reverted to the Philistines. We know scarcely anything about the period immediately following: it is evident that they did not like to recall it in later times. When Abner had in some measure established himself, he attempted to subject David and Judah also to the dominion of Ish-bosheth: a battle was fought at Gibeon, but the Judeans under the lead of David's nephew and general, Joab, won a complete victory, and Abner fled with the remnants of his army across the Jordan.

Soon, however, dissension arose between Abner and Ish-bosheth. Saul had left a concubine named Rizpah, and Abner took her. Ish-bosheth could see in this nothing but a design against his dominion, and called Abner passionately to account, whereupon the latter renounced allegiance to his ward and went over to David. He had probably recognized for some time that there was no prospect under existing circumstances that Ish-bosheth's reign could last long. David then demanded back Saul's daughter, Michal, whom after David's flight Saul had given in marriage to a noble of the tribe of Benjamin. Abner himself brought her to Hebron and was splendidly entertained by David. He went away with a promise to win all Israel over to David. Thereupon Joab hastens after him and stabs him on the pretext of revenge for blood.

Joab is the most remarkable figure among David's followers,—the man to whom he owes most. He has something terrible but at the same time grand about him, and reminds me vividly of one of the most characteristic personages of our German legends, the fierce Hagen of Tronje. Like Hagen, Joab is dominated and impelled by one single feeling, that of absolute fidelity to his master. Whatever is for the interest of his master he does, even if it should be a crime; for the crime he himself takes the responsibility in order that his master may reap the benefit. Abner was in fact, a questionable friend who was liable to become inconvenient and even dangerous, and his death was a desirable thing for David, although the latter denied, and very justly, all responsibility for the deed; that he knew about it, or instigated it, is wholly out of the question, for that would have been, to use the familiar and shocking *mot* of Talleyrand, more than a crime, it would have been a blunder.

Soon after, Ish-bosheth, too, fell a victim to blood vengeance: he was assassinated by two Gibeonites. The murderers cut off his head and brought it to David thinking to win a reward; but David had them cut down by his guards and the head of Ish-bosheth deposited in Abner's tomb. Thus ended the son of Saul after a reign of seven and a half years.

There were still left two sons of Saul by the concubine Rizpah, but no one thought of them. The situation was such that experiments could not be risked, and David was the only one who could be regarded as equal to it. And so the voice of the people called him to the throne: the elders of the districts hitherto ruled by Ish-bosheth came to Hebron to offer the crown to David, and the terms of his regency were accepted by him with a solemn oath. Now the Philistines began to suspect their late vassal, and they attempted to destroy the kingdom of David in the bud. But the undertaking on which Saul had made shipwreck was accomplished by David and accomplished to last. In what were evidently long continued and bitter contests, from which tradition gives us a number of exciting episodes and individual deeds of heroism, he succeeded in breaking forever the Philistine dominion. He destroyed all their relish for returning to the attack in his realm, but disturbed them no more in their own. He did not take from them a single foot of their land or a stone of their fortresses, and thus by his wise moderation paved the way for a peaceable footing of arbitration between the two countries, which fortunately for Judah remained permanent.

While David thus had his hands full with the Philistine wars, the Moabites appear to have fallen upon his rear; they, too, are beaten and severely chastised, and joined to the kingdom of Israel as a tributary province. During the Philistine wars, perhaps, or in any event directly after the close of them, David took a step which gives shining evidence of his statesmanship. As king of all Israel he could not continue to reside at Hebron in the extreme south of the country. Only about six miles north of his native place, Bethlehem, lies Jerusalem, at that time still in possession of the Canaanite tribe of the Jebusites. The almost impregnable location of this city could not fail to strike a man of David's military insight; he selected it for the capital of his new kingdom; he conquered it but did the Jebusites no harm, and thus made sure from the start of an element of grateful and devoted citizens. Jerusalem is situated pretty near the central point of the entire country, and belonging to none of the tribes it stood on neutral ground above them and their rivalries. When it is called the City of David this is no mere phrase, for Jerusalem is altogether the creation of David; and when we consider what Jerusalem was to the people of Israel, and through the people of Israel to all mankind, we shall recognize in the foundation of this City of David an event of world-wide importance.

In characteristic contrast to this, Saul, even when he was king, continued to reside quietly in his native village. And another characteristic contrast between the two kings forces itself here upon our attention. David immediately set about securing in the political center of his kingdom an ideal center of interest. The ancient popular shrine, the ark of the covenant, had once been captured by the Philistines and then given back; Saul had let it run down without concerning himself about it. David made it one of his first concerns to bring it from the out-of-the-way country town to which it had been taken, to his new national capital. In a great popular celebration in which the king himself officiated as a leading performer, the shrine was brought to Jerusalem, and thus the God of Israel himself made his entrance. If anything in the Psalms was really composed by David, it is the words of the twenty-fourth Psalm, which may very well have been sung on the occasion of that great celebration:

> "Lift up your heads, O ye gates;
> And be ye lift up, ye everlasting doors;
> And the King of glory shall come in.
> Who is this King of glory?
> The Lord strong and mighty,
> The Lord mighty in battle."

That the Lord was mighty in battle David was soon to experience. Nahash, the king of the Ammonites, Saul's old opponent, died, and David sent an embassy of condolence to his son and successor Hanun. But Hanun took the messengers for spies and sent them back to their master covered with insults. Hereupon the Ammonites united with the Aramæans, Israel's neighbors on the north border, who probably were also somewhat uneasy at the sight of Israel's ambitious growth. At the Ammonite capital a battle was fought : while Abishai, Joab's brother, held the Ammonites in check, Joab beat the Aramæans in a decisive combat and the campaign was won. But now the Aramæans called other allies into the field. David took the command himself, and there was a decisive battle fought at a place called Helam, the location of which we do not know ; the Aramæans received a still more crushing defeat, and the hostile leader was among the slain. David captured rich booty, and the region about Damascus was added to his realm as a tributary province. And thus, too, the northern border was made secure.

But while David was thus occupied in the extreme north, the Edomites invaded the land from the south. Joab proceeded against them in forced marches, and beside the Dead Sea they were beaten and fearfully punished ; their land too became a tributary province. After a long siege the capital of the Ammonites fell also ; but in this case David exercised leniency and only required certain public labors of them, indeed he even seems to have permitted the native dynasty to continue, of course as vassals of Israel.

Thus under the lead of David, Israel had become in a few years the dominant race, the most important nation between the Euphrates and the Nile, and it deserves to be once more emphatically pointed out in closing this part of the subject that it cannot be proved or even claimed with plausibility that David began a single one of these wars : only to ward off unwarranted attacks and for the defense of the most vital interests of his people did David draw the sword, but when he did, it was with might and as in a war of God. The close of his life might have been full of light and of peaceful enjoyment of the power he had acquired, but at the height of his renown and his career David incurred a heavy guilt, and this guilt went on bearing evil deeds; thus a series of trials was prepared for him which plunged him into the depths of woe.

While his troops were in the field against the Ammonites he was smitten with a sinful passion for Bath-sheba, the wife of one of his officers; he had the officer put out of the way and took the woman. If we look into the whole wretched affair without prejudice, we must come to the conclusion that the blame was just as great on the woman's part, if not greater. Few kings, indeed, would have made such frank confession of the sin as David did, and we get the impression that of all his numerous wives this demoniac woman was the only one whom he really and deeply loved.

Thus David had sinned against the sanctity of the family, and the heaviest retribution was to come upon him from his own family. His eldest son, Amnon, is enamored of his fair step-sister, Thamar, and accomplishes his shameful purpose by cunning and force. Very likely he thought :

If my father has done such things, I need not restrain myself. In fact David does not venture, probably in view of his own guilt, to punish his wicked son; but two years after, Amnon is murdered by Absalom, the full brother of the ravished Thamar. Now Absalom has to flee, but the king longs for this son, who after the death of Amnon was the successor to the throne, and who had slain in Amnon rather the crown prince than the violator of his sister. Joab sees through the situation and manages to procure for Absalom permission to return; but he is still banished from his father's presence and is not allowed to come to court. This was extremely unwise, and could not but embitter the son. Two years passed thus, and again Joab acted as intercessor and Absalom was restored to favor and now appeared as officially recognized crown-prince.

But Absalom's ambition was not satisfied with this. It is easy to imagine that many elements, and these not the worst, were dissatisfied with the new conditions and saw with deep regret the former simplicity and informality giving way before the pomp and splendor of the new monarchy. Absalom took advantage of this sentiment and even cultivated it. The description of the malcontent crown-prince and the way in which he wins popularity and steals the hearts of his father's people is nothing less than classic. When he thought the time had come he procured leave of absence to go to Hebron, and there the insurrection broke out ; Absalom was proclaimed king and marched with his Judean supporters directly upon Jerusalem.

That the insurrection broke out in David's first capital, Hebron, and in his own tribe of Judah, is significant and highly complimentary to David : the Judeans evidently felt offended and slighted because David did not favor them, and because as king of all Israel he no longer would or could be tribal king of Judah. David was taken so completely by surprise that he barely managed to escape; he fled across the Jordan, but did not neglect to provide for representation of his interests in Jerusalem. And the cunning Hushai actually succeeded in detaining Absalom from an immediate pursuit of his father and in persuading him to a fatal delay. The militia of all Israel was first summoned and then Absalom crossed the Jordan.

Meanwhile David had found time to gather about him his old and tried guards ; under the leadership of Joab these easily scattered Absalom's rabble hosts and Absalom himself, contrary to David's express command, was slain by Joab's own hand. The scene that follows, David breaking out into bitter lamentations over the death of his still loved son and taking no pleasure in his victory, is familiar to all ; Joab is obliged to remind him by a frank admonition of his duty as king, but the king takes the death of his son so to heart that he dismisses Joab and puts in his place Absalom's general, Amasa. Now there was nothing to interfere with his return to Jerusalem, but in the spiritual anguish of these days and weeks he had lost his old discretion and wisdom. It may well have cut him deeply that his Judeans had been the first to desert him, and accordingly he persuaded them now to come alone and fetch him back to Jerusalem. This was done. But when the forces of the northern tribes came to the Jordan and saw how things stood, dissension and strife arose, which finally became so bitter that a Benjaminite named Sheba blew the trumpet and cried: "We have no portion in David, neither have we inheritance in the son of Jesse. To thy tents, Israel!" And all Israel actually followed Sheba, and David was left alone with his Judeans. He immediately gave orders to his newly-appointed general, Amasa, to get the army ready to march; but when Amasa proved unable to execute the order he turned again to the tried and trusty Joab, and as though nothing had happened meanwhile, Joab did his duty with inflexible fidelity. He cut down his incapable successor, and the old and invincible warriors gathered enthusiastically about his standard. The rebels were promptly dispersed and driven into the extreme north of the country; Sheba took refuge in the city of Abel-Bethmaacah, and as Joab was preparing to besiege the city the inhabitants threw out over the wall to him the head of the rebel.

With this achievement David's kingdom was

saved, and the evening of his life seems to have been passed in undisturbed repose. He reigned forty years in all; seven and a half years as tribal king of Judah at Hebron, and thirty-three years as national king of Israel in Jerusalem. When he reached the age of seventy the infirmities of age made themselves felt; he seems to have become quite torpid, a plaything without will in the hands of his followers, particularly of Bath-sheba, who entirely controlled him. Adonijah, the eldest son after the death of Absalom, was generally regarded as the successor to the throne, and David's old companions, Joab and Abiathar, were on his side, while Bath-sheba, supported by certain ambitious men who hoped thus to open a future for themselves, tried to divert the succession to her son Solomon, the youngest of David's sons.

Be it that Adonijah could not wait for the death of his father, or that he merely incurred the appearance of so doing,—under pressure of the report that Adonijah had caused himself to be proclaimed king and homage to be paid him, Bath-sheba managed to have Solomon formally recognized by the dying king and introduced to the people as his successor. As Benaiah, the captain of the guard, who wished to succeed Joab as general and actually did succeed him, was for Solomon and Bath-sheba and they thus had the whole military force at their disposal, all resistance was in vain and the outwitted opponents were constrained to make their peace with the newly appointed youthful king. Adonijah and Joab did not long survive the defeat of their hopes and died by the hand of the executioner; the priest Abiathar was merely deposed and banished.

David must have died soon after this settlement of the succession. He is the most luminous figure and the most gifted personage in Israelitish history, surpassed in ethical greatness and general historical importance only by Moses, the man of God. It is not possible to overestimate what David did for Israel: Israel as a people, as a representative of political life, as a concrete quantity in the development of universal history, as a nation in the fullest sense of the word, is exclusively his work. With this he completed what Moses had begun in quiet and inconspicuous labors on Sinai and at Kadesh. And all of this David created as it were out of nothing, under the most difficult conditions conceivable, with no other means than his own all-inspiring and all-compelling personality.

However far I let my gaze wander among the ranks of the great figures of history, I find no parallel among them for so completely a "self-made man." He is one of those phenomenal men such as Providence gives but once to a people, in whom a whole nation and its history reaches once for all its climax. David created Israel and at the same time raised it to its highest eminence;

what Israel was under and through David it never again became. And so we can easily understand how the eyes of Israel rested in grateful reverence upon this figure, and how a second David became the dream of Israel's future.

True, the picture of David does not lack the traits of human frailty, which Israelitish tradition, with a truly admirable sincerity has neither suppressed nor palliated; but the charm which this personality exercised over all contemporaries without exception has not yet faded for us of later day; whoever devotes himself without prejudice to the contemplation of David's history and character cannot fail to like him. A saint and psalm-singer, as later tradition has represented him, he certainly was not; but we find in him a truly noble human figure, which, in spite of all, preserved the tenderest and most fragrant bloom of its nature, perfect directness and simplicity; nowhere any posing, nothing theatrical, such as is always found in sham greatness; he always acts out what he is, but his unspoiled nature, noble at heart, generally comes very near to the right and good. At the same time the whole personality is touched with a breath of genuine piety and childlike trust in God, so that we can wholly comprehend how he appears to tradition as the ideal ruler, the king after God's own heart.

This king, who did more for the worldly greatness and earthly power of Israel than any one else, was a genuine Israelite in that he appreciated also

Israel's religious destiny : he was no soldier-king, no conqueror and warrior of common stamp, no ruler like any one of a hundred others, but he is the truest incorporation of the unique character of Israel, a unique personality in the history of the world, and we understand how he could become the impersonation of an idea,—how the highest and holiest that Israel hoped for and longed for appears as the Son of David.

CHAPTER IV.

SOLOMON.—THE DIVISION OF THE KINGDOM.—THE EARLY YEARS OF THE DIVIDED KINGDOMS.

TO be the successor of David was a great inheritance, but a much greater responsibility. Will Solomon, upon whose youthful shoulders the dying father laid the heavy burden, be equal to it? There is perhaps no other personage of Israelitish history of whose true character and its historical significance it is so difficult to get a clear conception and give a correct picture, as Solomon; for what we know of him is scant and self-contradictory. It is possible to represent him as an oriental despot of the most common stamp and support every trait of the picture thus drawn with Bible references, and to take credit into the bargain for one's objectivity and freedom from prejudice. But such a judgment would be absolutely unhistorical: Solomon cannot have been an ordinary and insignificant man,—on this point history speaks loud and clear.

He was the acknowledged favorite of his father. This may have been due solely to the fact that he was a late offspring, considerably younger than David's other sons, and born in his father's old age. Now it is deeply rooted in the nature of a man that his desire for children and his fondness for them grows with advancing age. A grandson is usually loved more fondly than a son, and Solomon might have been David's grandson as far as years were concerned. But this is not the whole explanation of their relation. Solomon was plainly made of different clay from his brothers. The elder sons of David, so far as we know them, were mere caricatures of their father, rude, wild fellows, who had inherited their father's strength and beauty indeed, but not his lofty mind and noble spirit.

Moreover, in estimating Solomon, his mother is a factor to be considered. Bathsheba, this demoniac creature, must have been a quite unusual and extraordinary woman ; for to attach to herself such a man as David, not merely in the fleeting intoxication of a criminal passion but permanently, and to be indispensable to his heart for twenty years, required more than simply a beautiful face, especially when one considers how quickly physical charms decay in oriental women. From this extraordinary mother also Solomon had received a rich endowment for his career. Thus we can easily comprehend how the aged king took into his heart of hearts this highly gifted, clever and animated boy who played about him, growing under his very eyes into the image of his fondly-cherished mother, and how he came to the honest conviction that this son was the fittest and worthiest to sit upon the throne after himself. And in diverting the succession to him he committed no wrong according to Israelitish ideas. In ancient times custom seems really to have conceded to the father unrestricted disposal of the right of primogeniture: the Hebrew language devised a regular formal expression for the transference of the right of primogeniture to a son who was not the first-born, and this right was expressly taken from the father only with the giving of the Second Law (Deuteronomy). Solomon was eighteen years old when he ascended the throne, at least no older than this. The fact that in spite of this he maintained his dominion for forty years under the most trying conditions is of itself sufficient evidence of his great qualities, and that his father had not been deceived in him.

The new king's tasks were given in his conditions. David himself had really not been a conqueror. To extend the realm further would have been folly; rather could the loss of provinces be endured if only domestic conditions were strengthened and consolidated. The kingdom of David was the creation of enthusiasm, an achievement of a mighty national tendency which his masterful personality had released and guided : if this creation was to be permanent it was necessary that institutions should take the place of persons.

David had in the main left domestic conditions unaltered. He was satisfied if Israel always responded to his summons, and the tribute of conquered peoples sufficed to meet the expenses of the still comparatively simple court. True, David does seem to have contemplated some measures of taxation—the great census of which we are told can have had no other end in view—but when a severe pestilence broke out he saw in it a divine warning and gave the matter up. What united the Israelites under David was free obedience and voluntary subjection; it was not forgotten, and he himself did not deny, that his rule was the outcome of popular choice. In comparison with the neighboring peoples, having long-established monarchical forms of government, conditions in Israel were still thoroughly patriarchal and primitive, and David was only a sheikh on a large scale. Now it was Solomon's accomplishment and merit to have rid the Israelites of the last trace of their Bedouin character, and to have trained them in a severe and even harsh school into national citizenship. Tradition sees in him preeminently the judge and the ruler who establishes everywhere solid order and strictest discipline. And in this respect his activity was unquestionably beneficent and laid the foundation for all after time. If David created an Israelitish nation, Solomon created an Israelitish state.

But,—and now we come to the reverse of the medallion—Solomon was thoroughly imbued with the sentiment : *L'état c'est moi*. His government has a decidedly personal character, and all that he did was done not for the benefit of his people, but for his own glorification. Love of splendor and desire for display are the most prominent traits of his picture. He looked for the essence of dominion in outward show : extensive buildings, an extravagant court with innumerable servants and concubines,—that was his taste. But for this he needed most of all money, and so his whole reign has a marked financial character. This necessity grew more imperative in so much as the tributes from foreign peoples soon ceased.

Right at the beginning of his reign Edom secured its independence. Hadad, a descendant of the Edomite royal family, had escaped the catastrophe that came upon Edom at the hands of Joab and David, by fleeing to Egypt and had there formed an alliance of marriage with the Pharaoh. When he heard that David and Joab were dead Hadad returned to his country. He despised Israel and became king in Edom, as the Book of Kings briefly and dryly reports. The commercial highway by way of the Arabah valley to the Red Sea must, indeed, have remained in Solomon's possession, otherwise he would not have been able to make his famous trips to Ophir ; but Hadad evidently ruled without molestation in the Edomite mountain-land proper.

Moab, too, seems to have shaken off the Israelitish yoke. At any rate, it was necessary soon after to subdue it anew. But it was a matter of much more moment that Solomon did not, or could not, prevent the secession from Israel of the Aramæans whom David had conquered. They established a new kingdom with Damascus as center, which was destined to become the mortal enemy of Israel.

Thus the conquests of David were quickly lost, and Solomon was left dependent on the resources of his own land and people alone. He divided the land into twelve districts for fiscal purposes, each of which had to meet the expenses of the court for one month. In conjunction with the Phœnicians he undertook from his seaport of Eziongeber expeditions to South Arabia and East Africa, which brought him abundant profit. From the caravans which crossed his territory he collected high tolls, and monopolized the Egyptian horse trade with Asia. And when these resources failed he borrowed of his friend and neighbor, Hiram of Tyre. The Tyrian loan had finally reached the amount of 12,000 pounds of gold; that is, according to current value of the metal, about $2,880,000, but taking into consideration the purchasing power of money at that time it would in fact correspond to $48,000,000 ; and as Solomon could not pay back this immense sum he had to cede to Hiram a border district with twenty towns.

But Solomon's chief need was workers. To supply it he robbed of all their rights and liberties the Canaanites who still dwelt among the Israelites, making them state slaves, just as Pharaoh Rameses II. had done to the Israelites in

Goshen in his day. This was not exactly commendable, but it was an enormous advance in the centralization of the state. Saul had planned something of the sort, but had not been able to carry it out. But this was still insufficient, and accordingly Solomon had levies made of 30,000 Israelite citizens, who were compelled to work in sections of 10,000 every fourth month.

Among the buildings of Solomon none became of such importance to succeeding generations as the temple. Yet the temple was originally planned merely as a chapel—only a part, and by no means the largest and most important, of Solomon's palace. The royal residence of David had long ceased to satisfy the increased requirements. Solomon worked for thirteen years on his palace at Jerusalem.

Solomon's activity in building and his development in splendor were doubtless increased by the fact that he had won for a wife the daughter of his powerful neighbor, Pharaoh Pashebchanen II., and had to supply her in some measure with what she was used to at home, as indeed he did build her a palace for herself with quite exceptional splendor. The Pharaoh had furnished Egyptian troops to conquer the ancient Canaanite city of Gezer which was evidently indisposed to submit to forced annexation by Solomon, and surrendered it to Solomon as dowry for his daughter.

This is a symptom of great military weakness or at least of indolence, and it is in keeping with the fact that Solomon's buildings were chiefly of the nature of fortifications. He endeavored to protect by fortresses all the strategic or otherwise important points of his country, and especially to make his capital of Jerusalem impregnable. We see that Solomon places himself wholly on the defensive and desires only to put his country into condition to maintain and defend itself within his own borders. Here the difference from David becomes most conspicuous, but here also the question may be asked whether Solomon's policy was not the more correct and suited to the situation. If he succeeded in securing his own country against attack and strengthening it within, that was enough.

That these new conditions seemed very strange to the Israelites, who were accustomed to the most unrestricted freedom, and were very distasteful to them, we can easily imagine. So much the more significant is the fact that there was only one revolt against Solomon's authority, and that easily suppressed. A young Ephraimite named Jeroboam had attracted Solomon's attention and Solomon had made him overseer of the laborers of the house of Joseph, who were working on the fortifications of Jerusalem. Jeroboam induced those who were under him to rebel, though they probably followed unwillingly, but was obliged to flee to Egypt. There the throne was no longer occupied by Solomon's father-in-law, but a new dynasty had arisen, the founder of which, Sheshenk I. (Shishak), of course received with open arms the enemy of his neighbor who was allied to the previous dynasty.

Otherwise Solomon's reign seems to have passed off altogether peacefully and without disturbance within the country itself. And in one respect it bore the most important results for Israel. Solomon was what one might almost call a cosmopolitan nature : he extended immensely the intellectual horizon of Israel, and opened his country in all directions to intercourse with the world. He placed Israel in the ranks of the great nations. Not only gold and ivory, sandalwood and peacocks came to Jerusalem ; but also the art of the Phœnicians and Egyptians, the wisdom and the fairylore of the East found their way into Israel, giving everywhere the most powerful impulses, and rousing to new life.

Solomon was just as striking and winning a person as his father David, only in a different way : what is told of his wisdom and his wit, his artistic and scientific tastes and interests is certainly to be regarded as historical. The epigram has come down to us which he uttered on the occasion of the dedication of the temple, and it is among the most profound and original in all Israelite literature. It runs :

"God hath set the sun in the tent of heaven,
But He Himself hath chosen to dwell in the thick darkness.
And yet I have dared to build Thee an house
As habitation and a dwelling-place for ever."

It is quite conceivable that about the person of just such a ruler a whole circle of legends and anecdotes was woven, and his portrait was especially ornamented by poetry. Judah never had occasion to regret that it remained faithful to his son and preserved the solid structure of the state founded by Solomon.

After a reign of forty years Solomon died and thereupon a serious crisis came upon his realm. The imposing personality of Solomon had restrained opposing forces; now they were determined to bear the heavy burdens no longer. In Jerusalem, it is true, Rehoboam, the oldest son of the deceased king, was promptly recognized; but in northern Israel they had not forgotten that David was not a member of their tribes, but that the house of Joseph had submitted to him as an electoral king and on the terms of a solemn electoral compact.

And so all Israel gathered at Shechem to set terms for the new king: "Make thou the heavy yoke which thy father put upon us lighter, and we will serve thee," so ran their demand. Rehoboam was clearly disposed to consent, but his advisers succeeded in changing his purpose. Legally considered, the men assembled at Shechem were rebels; he was urged to make no concessions to the revolution, but to suppress it by an appearance of energetic firmness. When on the third day the people came to get the royal response Rehoboam answered: "My father did lade you with a heavy yoke, but I will add to your yoke; my father hath chastised you with whips, but I will chastise you with scorpions."

After these fateful words the rebellion was openly declared. The terrified king sent Solomon's overseer, Adoniram, to negotiate, but he could not have chosen a less acceptable negotiator; the people stoned the odious officer to death before the eyes of the king, and the latter hastily sought his chariot and barely escaped to Jerusalem. But those who were at Shechem proclaimed Jeroboam, who meanwhile had returned from Egypt, king over Israel.

And thus the work of David was destroyed; what he had united through the pains and labors of a beneficent life was divided forever by the imprudence of his grandson. Of course the might of the nation was broken by this division, and it is a real wonder and an astonishing evidence of its toughness and vitality that it maintained itself, divided as it was, for centuries.

We have very scanty information regarding the next two centuries. The Hebrew sources themselves run low, and we receive nothing worth speaking of from without. Even the kings of this period are known to us by little more than their names. Only a few, here and there, are for us concrete figures with individual features.

In the beginning the two hostile brothers made war upon each other for life and death. At first the advantage seems to have been upon the side of Judah, where Rehoboam had at his disposal the well-filled arsenals and garnered treasures of his father, and lived amid established conditions, while Jeroboam had to create everything from the beginning. Thus Jeroboam considered it advisable to transfer his residence from Shechem, where he had at first dwelt, to Penuel on the east bank of the Jordan.

But at this point a severe storm broke over Rehoboam. The Egyptian Pharaoh, Shishak (Sheshenk), marched against his country and plundered Jerusalem, carrying off all the treasures accumulated by Solomon. As Shishak is the former host and protector of Jeroboam one might be led by the account of the Old Testament to suspect that Jeroboam had called him in to relieve him of his neighbor and enemy; but from the report of his victory made by Shishak himself in the great temple of Amon at Karnak we learn that he conquered and plundered north Israelitish cities also, and accordingly that his expedition was directed against both kingdoms alike. So we see that it was just an ordinary marauding expedition on which Shishak expected to secure easy booty and cheap laurels, and succeeded.

This is all that is told us of the seventeen years' reign of Rehoboam,—this and the fact that there was constant war between him and Jeroboam. It is the same with Rehoboam's son and successor Abijah, though it appears that he entered into alliance with the kingdom of Damascus, in order, of course, to make with it common cause against Israel. Abijah reigned but three years; he was followed by his son Asa, of whom we learn that he was obliged to take measures against his own mother, because she had devoted herself to the worship of an unclean idol.

Meanwhile Jeroboam had died after a reign of twenty-two years, having transferred his residence back to the west side of the Jordan at Tirzah. He was followed by his son Nadab. But the latter was murdered in the second year of his reign. While engaged in the siege of the Philistine border fortress of Gibbethon—for we learn thus that war had again broken out between the people of northern Israel and the Philistines—he was slain by a certain Baasha and the whole house of Jeroboam destroyed.

This performance is typical of the whole history of the northern kingdom. Israel had rebelled against the heavy yoke of Solomon, and now it was never rid of revolutions and anarchy; the throne was regarded as derelict, and every bold robber took possession of it, only to be dispossessed by the next more lucky comer. Baasha who was perhaps Nadab's general (the usurpers are generally officers and the revolutions military revolutions), and who must have been an efficient soldier, turned his whole force against Asa of Judah. At Ramah, about six miles north of Jerusalem, on the border of his country, he established a close blockade, and as the Book of Kings says, "suffered no one to go out or come in to Asa, king of Judah." Asa was thus brought into such straits that he gave all his remaining gold and silver to purchase the aid of the king of Damascus. The latter immediately invaded and devastated the whole north of Israel, whereupon Baasha was obliged to hasten to the aid of his hard-pressed north-border. Now Asa summoned all Judah to arms, had the fortifications at Ramah taken down and the material transported across the border where with Baasha's stone and timber he strongly fortified Geba and Mizpah on his own territory. The Book of Kings also attributes to him the fortification of other cities.

Baasha ruled for twenty-four years. But fate overtook his son Elah. Once more the Israelites were in the field against the Philistines and besieging Gibbethon; but the king, as it is said, lay drunken at Tirzah in the house of his minister, Arza. Here a cavalry officer named Zimri murdered him and exterminated the whole house of Baasha and all his relatives and friends. But the glory of Zimri was to last but seven days. Scarcely had the army which lay encamped before Gibbethon, learned of the palace-revolution when it proclaimed its tried leader Omri as king. In forced marches Omri moved against Tirzah; Zimri realized that all resistance was in vain, but was resolved at least to die like a king: he set fire to the palace and perished in the flames. Omri, however, was not destined to receive general recognition; a certain Tibni was set up as opposition king. But after several years of civil war Omri succeeded in overcoming his rival; Tibni fell, and now Omri was the undisputed monarch.

Omri's very first deed after attaining the sole rule bears testimony to his statesmanship. Zimri had burned the palace at Tirzah, and there was need of building another. Omri may himself have learned with dismay what an easy game the capture of the capital had been; therefore he moved the royal residence to another place and founded Samaria. The very name, which we may translate with watchtower (*Wartburg*), is significant enough. Proud and free the hill of Samaria rises from the surrounding valley, sloping gently only to the east, but falling off steeply on the other sides. A gigantic circle of higher mountains surrounds it with a protecting sweep. Moreover this particular region is extraordinarily fertile and comparatively well watered. From a strategic point of view especially the choice of the site is a strikingly fortunate one; that the kingdom of Israel survived for a century and a half the lamentable times that soon came upon it is due first of all to its almost impregnable capital, which resisted even the Assyrians for three years. Through the foundation of Samaria Omri became the real founder of the kingdom of Israel, and it is not without reason that the Assyrians always designated the kingdom of Israel as Omriland.

Further than this we know only a few facts regarding Omri's reign, and these only indirectly. He made successful war against Moab, colonized the northern parts of Moab with Israelites, and made the king Kemosgad pay tribute. On the other hand, he was not successful against Damascus : he had to cede several border districts and acknowledge a sort of feudal overlordship. Therefore he sought the support of his powerful neighbor on the west, and married his son Ahab to Jezebel, the daughter of the Tyrian king Ethbaal. With Judah, where king Asa still reigned, he seems to have maintained peace and to have taken steps toward closer relations with the brother kingdom. On the other hand, the first conflict with Assyria occurs in his reign.

Under Asurnazirpal, who ascended the Assyrian throne in 884 B. C., the power of Assur experienced a mighty revival after a long period of decrepitude ; Asurnazirpal is the first of the great conquerors who lived wholly in war and by war and carried the terror of the Assyrian arms everywhere. In the year 876 he marched as far as the Mediterranean and Mount Lebanon, and Omri among others hastened to lay his offering at the feet of the mighty monarch ; but Asurnazirpal never came again.

Omri was succeeded by his son Ahab. We know relatively the most of him, because the great prophet Elijah was his contemporary, and his career throws also important light on the king. True, this light is not favorable for Ahab, and his conflict with Elijah was fateful for him. He is one of the most ill reputed personages in Israelitish history. But if we examine carefully and with the searching eye of criticism the reports preserved regarding him, the result is a materially different picture. His religious conflict with Elijah, as reported in the Book of Kings, is pure legend; the historical residue turns out to be quite innocent, leaving no occasion for any just reproach to Ahab, and the only actual crime that is laid to his door, the judicial murder of the Jezreelite Naboth, was the work of Jezebel, which he simply did not interfere with; when Elijah openly and frankly reproached him with the wretched deed, he bitterly repented it and did heavy public penance for it.

What remains of the reports concerning Ahab shows him to have been a worthy son of Omri and one of the best kings and most powerful rulers that Israel ever had. The situation of his kingdom was very critical, and to this were added exterior misfortune, crop-failure and shortage, famine and drouth, so as to shake the state to its foundations. But Ahab was equal to the situation, and managed to win the respect and admiration of friend and foe. First of all, he took steps for a peaceful and friendly relation with Judah. Under him we find again for the first time Israel and Judah fighting shoulder to shoulder; the old feud is forgotten, and to seal their friendship the two reigning houses ally themselves by marriage: Jehoshaphat of Judah, who meanwhile had succeeded his father Asa, married his heir, Jehoram, to Athaliah, the daughter of Ahab.

It is notable, although Jehoshaphat reigned twenty-five years, and is praised by the Book of Kings as one of the best kings of Judah, that we really know nothing about him save his relations to the ruling family of Israel. When we find express mention that under him there was no king in Edom, but that a governor from Judah ruled the land, we may indeed infer that Jehoshaphat again subdued the land and deposed the dynasty of Hadad, but the conclusion is not inevitable. He attempted to resume the Ophir expeditions of Solomon from Eziongeber, but characteristically refused to let his Israelitish friend and neighbor take part in them. However, he did not in the end carry out his purpose, for the ships, though constructed with much pains, were wrecked, probably because they were not managed by the skilled seafarers of Phœnicia, who in Solomon's undertakings had been the leaders.

The most important matter in the reign of Ahab is his wars with the kingdom of Damascus. Omri had been obliged to recognize its overlordship in a certain fashion, and evidently Ahab did the same for some time; but he could not suffer this state of things to continue. After he had increased the power of resistance of his country by fortifying the most important cities, he made an attempt to secure his independence. At first fortune did not favor him, and Ahab found himself shut up in Samaria. King Ben-hadad sends word to him: "Thy gold and thy silver are mine." And with truly royal mind Ahab does not hesitate to take upon himself the misfortune of his people, and consents.

Now Ben-hadad who had evidently not expected such prompt yielding, demands further that his people shall also plunder Samaria. But Ahab cannot consent to this; he says: "All that thou didst send for of thy servant at the first I will do; but this thing I may not do." Then Ben-hadad answers: "The dust of Samaria will not suffice for handfuls for all the people that follow me;" and to this brutal boast Ahab replies with dignity and decision: "Let not him that girdeth on his armor boast himself as he that putteth it off." While Ben-hadad and his officers lie in their drunken midday sleep Ahab makes a desperate sortie with the seven thousand two hundred and twenty-three men whom he had in Samaria; the Syrians are taken wholly by surprise and defeated, and hasten back to Damascus in confusion with additional heavy losses on the way.

The following day they again measure strength in open battle at Aphek, and again, despite greatly inferior numbers, Ahab wins a complete victory; the army of Damascus is destroyed, and Ben-hadad himself, with the remnants of his forces, shut up in Aphek. But Ahab nobly and magnanimously spares his defenseless opponent, and makes peace and friendship with him on condition of the surrender of all the territories that had been taken from Israel.

This performance on the part of Ahab is only explained by a very surprising piece of information which we receive from the Assyrians. Shalmaneser II., son and successor of Asurnazirpal, takes up his father's plans, and in 854 B. C. leads all the forces of his empire against Cœlesyria. At Karkar on the river Orontes there is a battle. Here Shalmaneser meets a coalition of many kings and tribes, at the head of which Ben-hadad of Syria and Ahab of Israel are fighting shoulder to shoulder. True, the Assyrian king claims a complete victory, but this victory results in his beginning a very hasty retreat, and it is five years before he attempts to come again.

If Ahab had been a king of common mold he would certainly have used the opportunity to fall upon the rear of this his mortal foe of many years' standing and the natural enemy of his people; but he looked further and recognized the greater danger; and as he had put an end to the fraternal dissension with Judah, it was plainly his intention here by conciliation and magnanimity to put an end to the quarrel with Damascus and conquer his opponent by moral force; and he steadily and faithfully carried out this noble and magnificent policy.

But Ahab had made the mistake of judging others by himself, and in his nobility and large-heartedness overlooked a factor with which the practical statesman unfortunately must deal, and that is human meanness. When the danger was past Ben-hadad never dreamed of keeping his plighted word, and Ahab is compelled to demand the rightful possessions of his people at the point of the sword.

One year after the battle at Karkar the allies of that occasion are facing each other in open battle. Ahab was supported by Jehoshaphat of Judah; for the first time since the days of David we see all Israel united against a foreign foe. The campaign is to secure the important border fortress of Ramoth in Gilead. How high Ben-hadad rated his opponent may be learned from the order he gave his captains: "Fight neither with small nor great, save only with the king of Israel."

Ahab may have known or suspected this; he does not wear his usual armor in the battle, but his fate was sealed. By chance a man shot into a joint of his breastplate an arrow which was to put a premature end to his precious life. But Ahab proposed to die as he had lived, a king and a hero. Although he immediately recognized the wound as mortal he held himself, by superhuman efforts, upright in his chariot until evening, in order not to discourage his troops; then his strength gives way and he falls down dead. At this dreadful tidings a wild panic seizes the Israelite ranks ; they think only of saving the king's body ; battle and campaign are lost. This is the historical Ahab of Israel.

The consequences of the death of Ahab are seen forthwith. Now that his strong hand was cold, the Moabites again became aggressive. Their king, Mesha, reconquered the parts of his country that had been taken by Omri, and massacred the Israelites that had settled there without respect to age or sex, "as a delight for the eyes in Kemosh and Moab," as he himself says. There was no opposition, for Ahab's eldest son and successor, Ahaziah, seems to have been an incapable and insignificant man. Fortunately for Israel, one is inclined to say, he died in the second year of his reign in consequence of a fall from the window of his palace, and as he had no children he was succeeded by his much abler brother Jehoram. The latter immediately undertook a compaign of revenge against Moab. In conjunction with Jehoshaphat of Judah they advanced from the south by way of Edom into that country and wasted it terribly ; but Mesha succeeded in holding his own in the fortress of Kir-haresheth, and the allied kings were obliged to depart finally with their purpose unaccomplished.

Soon after this Jehoshaphat died and was succeeded by his son Jehoram, husband of Athaliah. The Book of Kings reports from his eight years' reign nothing but these two misfortunes : the

Edomites freed themselves from their subjection to Judah, while an attempt on the part of Jehoram to subject them again failed utterly, and the king himself barely escaped; furthermore, the city of Libnah revolted from Judah and allied itself with the Philistines. Jehoram was followed by his son Ahaziah who reigned but one year, for then a terrible catastrophe broke upon the royal houses of both kingdoms.

In the years 849, 848, and 845 B.C., Shalmaneser was again in Cœlesyria, and thus we can understand how Jehoram of Israel succeeded in recovering from the power of Damascus the city of Ramoth, before the walls of which his father Ahab had fallen. Besides there had been a violent change of dynasty in Damascus, Benhadad having been murdered by one of his courtiers, Hazael, who himself mounted the throne. Jehoram was wounded and withdrew to Jezreel to be healed of his wound. And then the calamity which had long been creeping in the darkness suddenly burst forth.

The great prophet Elijah had died; his pure and sacred work was carried on in a very impure and unholy spirit. The impression grew up that the whole house of Ahab must be exterminated root and branch for the honor of God. And now the favorable moment seemed to have come. Elisha sent into the camp at Ramoth a disciple of the prophets to anoint as king the man whom he had selected to execute the judgment against the house of Ahab. This was Jehu, a dashing cavalry officer, as we would describe him: no match for him in madness rode horse in Israel.

Jehu had been an eye-witness of the memorable scene when Elijah, after the judicial murder executed against Naboth, had denounced upon Ahab the divine judgment which would demand of him and his children the blood of Naboth and his children. Ambitious and full of restless energy, he seemed to be the most suitable instrument. The anointing takes place, and his comrades do homage to him. Jehu immediately forbids any one to leave the camp, and himself with a troop of cavalry takes the road for Jezreel where lay the wounded king, and where meanwhile Ahaziah of Judah had arrived to visit his sick uncle. The guard sees a troop of cavalry approaching; after two messengers sent out to meet them fail to return, the two kings themselves mount their chariots and ride out to meet this mysterious troop. Jehoram recognizes Jehu and calls out to him: "Is it peace, Jehu?" and Jehu answered: "What peace, so long as the whoredoms of thy mother Jezebel are so many?" Then Jehoram turned his chariot and cried: "There is treachery, Ahaziah!" But with fatal accuracy Jehu shoots an arrow into his back, piercing his heart; the body of the king he orders thrown into Naboth's vineyard. Ahaziah had fled, but is pursued by Jehu's command and likewise fatally wounded; he dies in Megiddo, not far away, and his servants bring the corpse to Jerusalem.

Meanwhile the red-handed murderer has reached the royal palace in Jezreel. The aged Jezebel is minded at least to die like a queen: in full royal attire she looks from the window and receives the ruthless Jehu with the haughty greeting: "Goes all well, Zimri, thou murderer of thy master?" Jehu has her thrown out of the window, her blood spattering his horse. Then he coolly rides over the quivering corpse, leaving it lying on the street, and enters the palace to proceed to a royal meal; when he is through he says: "See now to this cursed woman and bury her; for she is a king's daughter."

But there were still many royal princes in the capital Samaria. Therefore Jehu writes to the chief officials there: "Ye have arsenals and fenced cities; look ye out the best and meetest of your master's sons, and set him on his father's throne and fight for him!" For reply the intimidated people ask his orders. Thereupon he wrote: "If ye be on my side, take ye the heads of your master's sons and bring them to me to Jezreel." The horrible order is executed, seventy royal princes are murdered, and their severed heads packed in baskets and sent to Jezreel. There Jehu has them piled in two pyramids beside the city gate and feasts his eyes on the terrible sight, casting to the people that stood about a cynical witticism.

Now he starts for the capital of the kingdom, having first caused all the friends, supporters, and officials of the overthrown dynasty remaining in Jezreel to be slain. On the way there is more bloody work. At Beth-ekeb he meets a party of forty-two persons of distinction. They profess themselves royal princes from Jerusalem, coming to visit Ahaziah and Jehoram in Jezreel. Jehu has them seized, and the forty-two princes of the house of David follow the seventy of the house of Omri. Thus he enters Samaria.

A supposedly religious movement had brought him to the throne; he now paid in his own fashion those who had elevated him. He makes proclamation: "Ahab served Baal a little; but Jehu shall serve him much." He makes pretense as though he would offer his coronation-sacrifice in the temple of Baal erected by Ahab, and summons thither on pain of death all worshipers of Baal. When they were all in the trap, he had them cut down by the guards and desecrated the temple in the most brutal manner. Of course, the boards were now swept clean in Samaria also, and all the relatives, friends, supporters, and officials of the exterminated royal house were slaughtered. The peace of the grave dwelt in Samaria.

The fanatical prophets could not have chosen for the execution of their purpose a more unholy instrument than this bloodhound; even a century later, almost, Israel still stands aghast at the memory of this horror, and the prophet Hosea sees in the bloody deeds of Jehu an unatoned guilt which rests upon the kingdom and its royal house, and can be atoned for only by the destruction of both. And if ever in history God himself has clearly spoken and pronounced condemnation upon human delusions, it was here: by the fall of the house of Omri Israel itself was brought to the brink of destruction, and the reign of Jehu and of his son, Jehoahaz, is the most miserable period that Israel ever experienced.

It is one of the most remarkable ironies of fate that these murders which were alleged to have been done to the honor of God, and which actually did completely root out the worship of Baal in Samaria, led in Jerusalem to exactly the opposite result. King Ahaziah and forty-two princes of the royal house had succumbed to the murderous steel of Jehu; how will the future of Judah fare? A wholly unexpected turn of affairs ensues. When the queen-mother, Athaliah, learns that her son is dead, she proceeds to finish Jehu's work, and has the whole royal family put to death. Only one little grandson, Ahaziah's one-year-old son, Joash, escaped her frenzy; a sister of Ahaziah, Jehosheba, who was married to the priest Jehoiada, saved her little nephew and concealed him in the temple from his grandmother.

Athaliah now assumes the reins of government as sovereign queen. She seems to have met no opposition; Judah submitted with just as much resignation to Athaliah and her wickedness as had Israel to Jehu and his monstrous deeds. Athaliah now erected at Jerusalem a temple of Baal, and, if we may credit the report which even gives us the name of the priest appointed by her, celebrated the worship of Baal officially. It is asked, What can have moved Athaliah to turn thus madly against her own flesh and blood? How is it possible that a grandmother would have her own grandchildren exterminated? On this very point an explanation is not far to seek. Conditions in the Orient are such that the first lady of the land is not the wife but the mother of the king; she is the only person to whom the king himself, the sovereign lord of all, shows reverence and even submission—whom he recognizes as superior to himself; he goes to meet her, does obeisance to her, seats her at his right hand. So we see that the position of the queen-mother was actually a court office, and the highest of all; King Asa formally deposed his wicked mother from this dignity. The moment her grandson ascended the throne Athaliah would have been compelled to vacate this first position in the kingdom in favor of her daughter-in-law, and her proud heart could not bear this. Lust of power, and the gift for ruling,—generally, alas! combined,—must have impelled her and made a fury of her; it is possible also that the thought arose that the ruling house in the little land of Judah should not fare better than that in her own mighty Israel,—if she could have had her way the house of David would have perished from the earth. But God held his hand over it; he cared too much for it to let the family be destroyed by an inhuman woman.

The destruction of the house of Omri and the catastrophe in the house of David constitute a milestone in the history of the people of Israel at which we may tarry and turn away overcome. Unspeakable horrors at Samaria, unspeakable horrors at Jerusalem, and the curtain falls on blood and corpses. Is this terrible picture an omen for the future? Yes, and no. In the next chapter we shall see both kingdoms fall, but their fall is not a blood-curdling melodrama, rather a genuine tragedy; they fall like heroes, after a manful struggle with destiny, and there is a mitigating feature: they fall, indeed, but they do not perish; new life will spring from the ruins.

CHAPTER V.

TO THE DESTRUCTION OF JERUSALEM BY THE CHALDEANS.

OUR minds still bear the fresh impression of the terrible events in Samaria and Jerusalem. What will be the fate of the blood-stained usurper of the throne?

It was but six years until righteous retribution overtook Athaliah. Jehoiada the priest, who had taken his nephew, the crown-prince Joash, into the temple for safety and there kept him hidden, established relations with the captains of the royal body-guard and managed to win them for his plan. We learn in this connection that the whole royal body-guard did duty in the temple on the Sabbath, and that only one-third of them returned to the palace for service there, while two-thirds remained in the temple as a sort of guard of honor. One Sabbath when there was a numerous concourse in the temple Jehoiada detained the whole body-guard in the temple, so that the royal palace was without any military protection whatever and Athaliah had no troops of any kind at her command. Now Jehoiada brings the seven-year-old crown-prince to what we would call the royal box in the temple, and there anoints and crowns him, whereupon a thundering "Hurrah" from the guards and the whole people greets the legitimate ruler. At the sound Athaliah goes to the temple to learn the cause of it; at the command of Jehoiada she is seized and taken out and slain at the entrance to the temple; the temple she had erected to Baal is destroyed and the priest appointed by her likewise slain.

From the forty years' reign of Joash only one occurrence is reported in detail, which, however, throws a peculiar and glaring light upon the conditions of the time. As a matter of course the priest Jehoiada at first conducted the government as guardian for his nephew, and the authority and influence of the priesthood was greatly increased by this relationship; but unfortunately the priesthood made a very material use of this. In the twenty-third year of Joash there was a sharp accounting between him and his uncle the priest. The priests were in the habit of receiving from the people voluntary offerings for the service and the temple, but were evidently allowing these gifts to find their way to their private coffers; therefore the king deprived them of this office of trust, and a contribution-box was placed in the temple, into which thereafter all offerings were to be put. When this "chest with a hole in the lid," as the Bible account briefly but clearly describes it, was full, royal officials came and emptied it, and carried the money away; and this arrangement became permanent, being expressly mentioned as late as the time of King Josiah.

Jehu died without having been molested, and bequeathed the usurped throne to his descendants even to the fourth generation; but then an even more fearful fate than in the case of Athaliah overtook the ruler.

From this point on, Assyria is the determining factor, and the whole history of Israel is intelligible only when we know the history of Assyria. This may also be maintained in a certain sense for earlier times. The pan-Israelitish kingdom of David would not have been possible save for the fact that Assyria, which had already prepared under Tiglath-Pileser I., 1110 B. C., to establish itself in Cœlesyria, was in David's time in such a condition of weakness and impotence that we do not even know the names of its kings for a century and a half.

From the time of Shalmaneser II. on, Assyrian and Hebrew history are, as it were, two connected vessels, where the height of the water in the one is always governed by that in the other; if Assyria was powerful, Israel was prosperous; but if the power of Assyria was declining, Israel suffered accordingly.

In the year 842 B. C., probably the date of the two violent usurpations in Samaria and Jerusalem, Shalmaneser marched for the fifth time against Damascus. This time he succeeded in inflicting upon King Hazael a decisive defeat. He besieged him in his capital, but could not take Damascus. Under the cirumstances it was a correct and reasonable policy, humanly considered, for Jehu to throw himself into the arms of the Assyrians, the mighty enemies of his hostile neighbor : he sent a considerable tribute to Shalmaneser, which the latter caused to be depicted, among other things, upon his famous black obelisk.

And yet Jehu had reckoned without his host, as the saying goes. Shalmaneser came again, indeed, in 839 B. C.; but then there followed a period of thirty-eight years in which no Assyrian made his appearance in that region. Now the people of Damascus threw themselves with all the force of hatred and revenge upon Israel,—with what result we will let the Book of Kings tell : "In the days of Jehu the Lord began to cut Israel short, and Hazael smote them in all the coasts of Israel." He seems to have taken from Israel the whole of the territory east of the Jordan, and he carried his warlike and victorious incursions even to the country of the Philistines : he took and destroyed Gath, and Joash of Judah was enabled to ransom Jerusalem from siege only by the delivery of all the treasures in the temple and palace.

While the situation under Jehu was sad, it became absolutely hopeless under his son and successor, Jehoahaz. "At that time," says the Book of Kings, "the anger of the Lord was kindled against Israel, and He delivered them into the hand of Hazael king of Aram (Syria) and into the hand of Ben-hadad, the son of Hazael, continually. He left to Jehoahaz but ten chariots and fifty horsemen and ten thousand foot soldiers, for the king of Aram (Syria) had destroyed them and ground them to dust."

By the most probable assumption, Jehoahaz is the unnamed king in whose reign occurred the siege of Samaria reported in the story of the prophet Elisha, when famine raged so frightfully that mothers slew and devoured their own children, and when one of these wretched women appealed to the king because she had shared her son the day before with another woman and the latter now refused to reciprocate in kind. But this siege was suddenly raised because Ben-hadad received tidings that his own land was threatened by an invading foe. This foe must have been the Assyrians.

In fact the Assyrians are again found in Cœlesyria in the years 805, 804, and 803 B. C., and strange to say it is a woman who begins the mighty advance of the Assyrian arms. The nominal ruler in Nineveh was King Ramman-Nirari III., but being yet a boy, his mother, the Babylonian princess Sammuramat, wielded the scepter for him, and with a strong hand : she resumed the policy of her father-in-law, Shalmaneser, and sent out her generals and troops into all quarters of the world to announce to astonished humanity that a woman was preparing to renew the glory of Assur.

There can be no doubt that we must recognize in this vigorous and energetic Babylonian princess and Assyrian queen-mother the Semiramis of the Greeks. And among other places she sent her troops three years in succession into Cœlesyria, and thus Israel had a breathing spell ; Joash, the brave and vigorous successor of Jehoahaz, succeeded in defeating Ben-hadad three times decisively, and in giving Israel relief from this tormentor. But Joash must needs turn his victorious arms against Judah also. There King Joash, after a reign of forty years, had been murdered by two high officials and succeeded by his son Amaziah, who avenged the death of his father upon the murderers, but had only the murderers executed and not their families. He also succeeded in defeating the Edomites and in again subjecting this old province.

What follows must be told in the very language of the Bible account : " Then Amaziah sent messengers to Jehoash (Joash) king of Israel, saying : ' Come let us look one another in the face ! ' And Jehoash answered Amaziah, saying : ' The thistle that was in Lebanon sent to the cedar that was in Lebanon, saying : " Give thy daughter to my son to wife." And there passed by a wild beast that was in Lebanon, and trode down the thistle. Thou hast indeed smitten Edom, and thy heart hath lifted thee up ; glory thereof, and abide at home ; for why shouldst thou fall to thy hurt and Judah with thee ? ' But Amaziah would not hear.

And so they looked one another in the face at Beth-shemesh. And Judah was put to the worse before Israel; and they fled every man to his tent. And Jehoash took Amaziah prisoner at Beth-shemesh, and brought him to Jerusalem, and brake down the wall of Jerusalem a space of four hundred cubits, and took away all the gold and silver in the temple and in the palace, and hostages also, and returned to Samaria." Indeed the conjecture has been put forth, and the attempt made to support it, that Jehoash put a complete end to the kingdom of Judah for the time being and formally incorporated it with the kingdom of Israel.

Amaziah came to a like end with his father Joash. The people grew weary of the rule of the indiscreet and thoughtless monarch and murdered him. They took his sixteen-year-old son, Azariah or Uzziah—he has both names—and seated him upon his father's throne. Uzziah was evidently not the eldest son and heir-apparent, but this time the popular choice had hit upon the right man. His reign of fifty-two years must have been powerful and prosperous and a period of new progress for Judah, although we know surely from this whole long time only the one fact that Uzziah reconquered the Edomite seaport Elath and fortified it. But the descriptions by the prophet Isaiah, who was consecrated prophet in the year of Uzziah's death, declare loudly and clearly that outward conditions in Judah at that time were prosperous and even flourishing.

But we must now return to Israel. In the year 797 B. C. the Assyrians had finally taken Damascus, though they did not immediately dethrone King Mari, son of Ben-hadad, but allowed the country to continue its existence. But in the following fifty years they returned five times, so that a lasting restoration of the kingdom was impossible. Thus Israel was left free, and the son of Jehoash, Jeroboam II., succeeded not only in regaining the former possessions, but in taking from Damascus a part of its territory and subduing all Moab, and thus in restoring the kingdom of Israel to the same compass as in the time of David. He ruled over the whole country from Edom to Damascus, and seems to have been on friendly terms with Uzziah of Judah; at least we hear of no dissension between them.

Unfortunately we know no details of the forty-one years' reign of Jeroboam II. But the light which Jeroboam caused once more to illumine Israel was only the glow of evening, a last flickering of the dying taper. Under Jeroboam's son, Zechariah, Nemesis overtook the house of Jehu: after a rule of six months he was murdered by a certain Shallum, who in his turn was overthrown after one month by Menahem and slain in a war waged with barbarous cruelty. And now destiny came upon Israel with giant strides.

In the year 745 B.C. a usurper named Pul had

mounted the Assyrian throne, and as a sort of
declaration of his purposes he adopted the name
of the first great Assyrian conqueror, Tiglath-
Pileser. And he carried out his program with
brilliant success. As early as 745 B. C. he had
begun systematically to conquer Cœlesyria. Menahem took pains to purchase his friendship and
protection by means of a tribute of a thousand talents of silver. This tribute was raised by a poll
tax, and Menahem demanded of every man of
means in Israel fifty shekels of silver. This is
an interesting item for the student of national
economy, as it proves that there were at that time
in Israel 60,000 men of means. And Menahem
did manage to die a peaceful death and was able
to bequeath the kingdom to his son Pekahiah,
who, however, was soon slain by an adjutant
named Pekah, who mounted the throne destined
to be the next to the last king of Samaria.

And now begins an almost incredible spectacle.
The doves over which the hawk is already hover-
ing ready for his mortal swoop, begin pecking
and fighting one another. In Jerusalem the
crown had just been assumed by Ahaz, the grandson of Azariah, evidently still very young and of
very youthful character. Israel and Damascus
profit by his weak and unpopular rule. They
combine against Judah in order to drive the house
of David from the throne and make the king a
vassal dependent on them. First they expel the
Judeans from Elath, which they give back to the

Edomites, and invade Judah itself, bringing it into direst distress. The capital, Jerusalem, was besieged and hard beset, and this situation probably brought about that resort to the last remedy of despair, reported of Ahaz by the Book of Kings: he sacrificed his own son, just as King Mesha of Moab in extreme distress made a burnt offering upon the walls of his beleaguered city of the son who was to succeed him as king.

Finally Ahaz knew no other way out of the difficulty but to send a message to Tiglath-Pileser, saying: "I am thy servant and thy son; come up and save me out of the hand of the king of Syria (Aram) and of the king of Israel." That this petition was supported by jingling arguments is a matter of course. Under the circumstances Tiglath-Pileser would perhaps have interfered of his own accord; at any rate he did not wait for a second invitation, but came straightway. Damascus was besieged and a part of the army sent against Israel. Pekah's life was ended by the murderous steel of a certain Hoshea, who was recognized as an Assyrian vassal but was compelled to resign the country east of the Jordan and the entire North to Assyria. After a siege of three years Damascus was taken, King Resin was executed, and his country appropriated as an Assyrian province.

Thus the kingdom of Damascus had vanished and Judah and the decimated remainder of Israel had become dependencies of Assyria. Ahaz understood the situation, and was shrewd enough to keep quiet, but in Israel the old, defiant spirit of independence flashed forth mightily.

In the year 727 B. C. the powerful Tiglath-Pileser had died, and at about the same time Egypt had received an energetic and enterprising ruler in the forceful Ethiopian prince Shabaka (also Sabe, Sebech, Sewe), the Biblical So. For Egypt it was a vital matter that the Assyrians should not establish themselves on her border; self-preservation compelled her to interpose. Therefore Shabaka entered into negotiations with the rulers in Palestine, and Hoshea allowed himself to be deluded by the voice of the siren, and broke his allegiance to the Assyrians. Forthwith the son of Tiglath-Pileser, Shalmaneser IV., marched against him. Hoshea indeed surrendered and was imprisoned; but Samaria itself, even without a king, made desperate resistance; only after three years did the Assyrians succeed in overcoming the creation of Omri. It was taken in the year 722 B. C., while the Egyptians and Ethiopians never lifted a hand for its relief.

This is the end of the Kingdom of Israel. The Assyrians seized the country as a province and put it under the immediate rule of Assyria. But they did not destroy Samaria itself. On the contrary it became the seat of the Assyrian prefect, after 27,280 persons, that is, certainly the whole population which had survived the siege, had been carried away from it into exile.

The opinion is very prevalent that the whole population of Israel was carried away to Assyria, but this is decidedly an error. On the other hand, the Assyrians flooded the land with foreign colonists, thus entirely destroying its nationality; in Judah it soon became the custom to regard the Samarians as half heathen. The fact that the race, surrounded by powerful enemies and in the midst of domestic anarchy and constant revolutions, nevertheless maintained itself with honor for over two hundred years and finally perished honorably, is a shining proof of its inherent worth and of its indestructible vitality. Yet even after its destruction the kingdom of Israel was pursued by misfortune: an undeserved reproach clings to its memory.

Later Judean historiography, which fixed the picture of Israelitish history for all following times, and whose views have entered into our very flesh and blood as Bible history, sees in the House of David the legitimate and divinely appointed dynasty for all Israel, and in the Temple of Solomon the only legitimate sanctuary for all Israel, and accordingly regards the Ten Tribes as rebels and heretics, who have renounced through wicked arrogance and sinful defiance the legitimate dynasty and the true religion. The final consequence of this view appears in the latest historical book of the Bible, the Book of Chronicles, to which only Judah is Israel, and which consequently ignores entirely the

Kingdom of the Ten Tribes and tells after the division in the kingdom only of the Kingdom of Judah. Indeed, some have gone so far as to regard the claim of the Kingdom of the Ten Tribes to the name of the Promise, the name Israel, as boundless presumption and an utterly unjustified pretension. But this whole point of view is unhistorical. The center of gravity of the race, materially as well as intellectually, was in fact with the Kingdom of the Ten Tribes: it was really the People of Israel, beside which Judah can only be regarded as a part which had separated from the whole body. That the Kingdom of Judah was only an appendage to the more powerful neighbor kingdom until after the destruction of Samaria is shown as plainly as possible by the accounts of the Book of Kings itself.

The religious judgment of later times has been influenced by the bull-cult, which was practised officially in the Kingdom of the Ten Tribes. But in this connection the fact is highly noteworthy, and yet is not generally given a clear explanation, that we do not hear a single word of rebuke on this subject from the prophet Elijah. When he denounces Baal in Samaria and Israel, he is simply advocating the "calves of Dan and Bethel," the only customary form of worship in the kingdom of Israel,* which he himself did not attack. The view that this whole species of worship was pure heathenism, and the worship

* Cp. 1 Kings, 12 : 28.

of God in an image folly and absurdity, is first found in the prophet Hosea, and is an outgrowth of literary prophecy.

In the pre-prophetic times according to the express testimony of the Book of Kings itself, religious conditions in Judah were not a whit better than in Israel, indeed we have documentary evidence of the worst distortions and perversions only in Judah. And especially let us not forget that the greatest spiritual power that ever arose in Israel, prophecy, is, if I may use the expression, an exclusive growth of North Israel, which bloomed and developed on the soil of the Kingdom of the Ten Tribes : Joseph, and not Judah, gave this divine blessing to mankind. Samuel, Elijah, and Hosea were North Israelites, and even the native Judean Amos worked exclusively in and for Israel.

With the loss of national and political independence this relation changes immediately : Samaria is thenceforth only an Assyrian province, and Judah receives the inheritance. After 722 B. C. Judah really became Israel, and the spiritual life too is centered in Jerusalem ; the prophet Nahum, for instance, although a native of Galilee, regards himself altogether as a Judean, and does not even connect with the destruction of the universal empire of Assyria the hope of a restoration of the Kingdom of the Ten Tribes.

True, Judah was also an Assyrian dependency, and remained so a whole century ; but if it despatched its annual tribute dutifully and conscientiously to Nineveh, that was all the Assyrian government cared for. In domestic affairs it was still wholly its own master, and could develop unchecked and unhindered; indeed, the question may fairly be raised whether the dependency on Assyria was not actually a blessing for its interior development, inasmuch as it guaranteed a positive security and permanence of conditions and relieved it of the necessity of cultivating international politics, for which the petty state of Judah, about the size of the English county of Kent, or half again as large as Rhode Island, had neither the power nor the means, and in which it would inevitably have worn itself out. Hence we can fully comprehend how a man like the prophet Isaiah, who was certainly a genuine patriot and did not underestimate the destiny of his people, could actually regard it as the object of his life to keep Judah in peaceful subjection to Assyria and preserve it from unwise adventures.

The conquest of Samaria was not achieved under Shalmaneser IV., but belongs to the beginning of the reign of Sargon. This Assyrian ruler, perhaps the mightiest of all, was, as it seems, a descendant of the old Assyrian royal family overthrown by Tiglath-Pileser. He was obliged to continue warfare in Palestine. In the year 720 B. C. there occurred a general revolt of the countries from Hamath to the Egyptian border, which had but shortly before been subjected by Assyria.

And now Shabaka finally prepared for armed intervention. But the whole coalition was dispersed by Sargon, the Egyptians were defeated at Raphia southward from Gaza, and when, five years later, Sargon returned to these regions the Egyptians hastened to lay tribute at his feet,— the decadent empire of the Pharaohs was no match for the rising power of Assyria, and the time was past for Egypt to pursue an international policy. Its only resort was to plot and instigate in order if possible to derive some questionable advantage from the dissensions of others. These conditions were characterized most drastically by Isaiah in the words he applies to Egypt, "blustering and doing nothing,"* that is, making a mighty clanking with the sword and finally when matters become serious refusing to draw.

In the year 715 B. C. King Ahaz died and was followed by his son Hezekiah. Ahaz had persisted steadfastly until the end in his voluntary subordination to Assyria, and thus secured for his country twenty years of unbroken peace. Hezekiah was differently constituted. Even from the descriptions of the tradition, which

* The passage referred to is Is. xxx. 7, which Prof. Cornill translates: *Lärmen und Sitzenbleiben*. This is the literal rendering of the traditional Hebrew text, the meaning of which is precisely that of the English "to bark and not to bite." The *Polychrome Bible* translates on the basis of a conjecture. "Whose help is but vapor and emptiness."

greatly favors and glorifies him we derive the impression that he was an undecided, vacillating character, easily influenced and partial to great plans, but just as easily discouraged and dispirited. Under him the national party again came to the surface, regarding the dependency upon Assyria as a disgrace and disposed to use the first opportunity to regain their former independence. The danger became so great that Isaiah went about for three years in the humiliating garb of a military captive, as a standing warning that such would be the fate of all enemies of Assyria.

In the year 711 B.C. especially the situation became critical. In Ashdod a certain Yaman had expelled the Assyrian vassal king Achimiz, and raised the standard of rebellion; according to the report of Sargon he had entered into the plots with Judah, Edom, and Moab. But the Assyrian army made a swift end of this war of liberation. When he recognized that his cause was lost Yaman fled to Egypt, but was delivered to Sargon in chains by the Pharaoh,—with this disgraceful act Egypt with her own hand effaced her name from the list of first-class powers.

During the life of Sargon we hear no more of disturbances in Palestine. But in 705 B. C. the great king died suddenly a violent death, murdered, it appears, by his son and successor, Sennacherib. This was the signal for revolt and rebellion in the whole extent of the great empire, for it was not to be expected that a second Sargon would follow the murdered king, and fear and submission had been due alone to the person of Sargon. The threads of conspiracy run from Babylon to the Nile. The Book of Kings informs us that there came to Hezekiah an embassy from the Babylonian king, Merodach-baladan, to whom Hezekiah showed all his armories and treasures: this embassy must have come in the first year of the reign of Sennacherib (704 B. C.), in order to win Hezekiah as an ally, for in the very beginning of the year 703 B.C. Sennacherib threw himself with all his might upon Babylon and expelled Merodach-baladan.

Furthermore Isaiah gives us a vivid description of an embassy of tall, bronzed Ethiopians, who also came to Jerusalem with the evident purpose of forming an alliance against Assyria. In the year 704 B. C. the young and vigorous Tirhakah had become king of the Ethiopians and had succeeded in carrying Egypt with him. Now with two such great powers as support, there was no stopping the movement. All the Phœnician and Philistine rulers, Edom, Moab, Ammon and Judah were in outspoken rebellion. King Padi of Ekron, who remained loyal to the Assyrians, was taken prisoner by his own people and brought in chains to Hezekiah at Jerusalem, in order that the latter might hold him in safekeeping. This shows how general was the confidence in the impregnable position of Jerusalem.

In one of his most powerful and most stirring

appeals Isaiah describes half in fierce mockery, half with bleeding heart, the delirium of heroism and warlike enthusiasm that seized upon Judah on this occasion : he sees these holiday troops already dispersed and scattered to the winds, captured without the shooting of an arrow. And all too soon it became manifest how justly Isaiah had judged his people.

In the year 701 B. C. Sennacherib moved with the whole force of his kingdom against the rebels, and the petty kingdoms sank one after the other like barley blades before the sickle. The very beginning of the attack brought the whole coast of Phœnicia and Philistia to terms. Then Hezekiah too lost courage. "And Hezekiah," so the Book of Kings reports, "sent to the king of Assyria to Lachish, saying : 'I have offended! Return from me ; that which thou puttest on me will I bear.' And the king of Assyria appointed unto Hezekiah three hundred talents of silver and thirty talents of gold. And Hezekiah gave him all the silver that was found in the house of the Lord and in the treasures of the king's house. And he even had all the gold stripped from the doors and pillars of the temple, and gave it to the king of Assyria."

Further King Sennacherib informs us that Hezekiah set free King Padi of Ekron, whom he held captive, and delivered over to him his daughters and the women of his household. Gladly we would doubt this statement. But it is

not possible ; we are really obliged to believe that
Hezekiah made a contribution of his own flesh and
blood to the harem of the mighty Assyrian monarch. It was not possible to humble himself more
deeply before Sennacherib. But the situation
soon changed. The combined Ethiopian and
Egyptian forces actually began to advance, and
now it appeared to Sennacherib hazardous to leave
in his rear an unreliable vassal like Hezekiah in
such an important strategic position as Jerusalem. Therefore he now demanded the surrender
of the capital and the acceptance of an Assyrian
garrison.

But now Hezekiah remained firm : he could
not consent to this. According to the account of
the Book of Kings it was chiefly the prophet Isaiah who urged him to hold out, promising him
most positively that the Assyrian would not send
a single arrow into Jerusalem, but would return
again the way he had come. And contrary to
all expectation this bold prophecy was fulfilled.

The immediate results of Hezekiah's refusal
were indeed terrible for the land. The Assyrian
captured forty-six walled cities, and countless fortresses and smaller places, devastated the land
systematically, and took two hundred thousand
one hundred and fifty persons and all the cattle
as booty to Assyria. He himself reports that he
at least undertook the siege of Jerusalem, and
there is no reason to doubt this. But he did not
accomplish his object. The final result of this

undertaking is veiled in obscurity. At El Tekeh, on the border between Judah and Philistia, Sennacherib came upon the combined Egyptian and Ethiopian armies, and defeated them completely.

Several Egyptian princes and a considerable number of the enemy's highest officers were made captives by the Assyrians. Sennacherib pursued the retreating hosts and had doubtless already determined upon an advance into Egypt, but was compelled to turn back on the Egyptian border. Herodotus was told by the Egyptians that an army of mice attacked the Assyrian army in the night, destroying all the leather of their equipment and weapons, thus disabling the army of Sennacherib.

The Bible account also tells of a great catastrophe that befell Sennacherib : "The angel of the Lord went forth in the night and smote in the camp of the Assyrians an hundred four-score and five thousand." At any rate the great expedition came to naught. It is possible that a threatening turn of affairs in Babylon urgently demanded Sennacherib's presence at home and hastened his return. Before going he assigned all the cities of Judah to his loyal Philistine vassals and returned to Nineveh. He never saw Palestine again. Jerusalem was indeed saved, but in what a condition ? The prophet Isaiah shall tell us :

> "Your country is desolate ;
> Your cities are burned with fire ;

> Your land,—strangers devour it in your presence,
> And the daughter of Zion is left as a booth in a vineyard,
> As a lodge in a garden of cucumbers,
> As a besieged city.
> Except the Lord of Hosts had left unto us a very small remnant,
> We should have been as Sodom,
> We should have been like unto Gomorrah."

Of the next hundred years we know almost nothing. For the history of Israelitish religion, it is true, scarcely any other period is so significant and important as this very seventh century: yet concerning the secular history we know but little. The Book of Kings goes on to tell that Hezekiah drove the Philistines beyond Gaza : so he evidently succeeded in regaining those portions of his territory which had been separated from Judah by Sennacherib and promised to the neighboring Philistine kings. But we are obliged to infer that he returned to his former dependence upon Assyria and sent his yearly tribute to Nineveh afterwards as before, for his son and successor, Manasseh, appears always and everywhere in the ranks of the tributary vassals of Assyria.

Of Manasseh we know only that he was twelve years old when he ascended the throne, that he ruled fifty-five years, that he persecuted the prophets with fire and sword, and filled Jerusalem with the blood of the innocent. His son and successor, Amon, was murdered in the second year of his reign by a conspiracy in his own household, but the people slew the conspirators and placed upon the throne Josiah, the eight-year-old son of the murdered king. And here a ray of light falls upon the history of Israel: Josiah, from all that we know of him, must have been a good and noble character, who took his duties as regent seriously, ruled with justice and mildness, and was a father to his subjects. His contemporary, the prophet Jeremiah, bears the best of testimony for him, and the Book of Kings praises him as a second David; but unfortunately we have no details regarding his reign.

The ninety years which we have just hastily covered include the greatest splendor and the greatest power of the Assyrian Empire as well as its sudden end. The wild and barbarous Sennacherib was murdered, 681, B.C., by two of his sons, who thus avenged his act of parricide, but the throne was not their reward. Another son, Esarhaddon, who had evidently been selected by Sennacherib for the succession, marched against his brothers and was generally recognized as king. He was destined to attain the utmost goal of Assyrian ambition and conquer Egypt.

Tirhakah still kept up his interference in Palestine in order to stir up revolts. Therefore Esarhaddon determined to put an end to the matter: he entered Egypt in 670, B.C., defeated Tirhakah completely and subdued the whole country, and Tirhakah withdrew into his native Ethiopia. Thus Egypt also became an Assyrian province, and remained so a considerable length of time. Under

Asurbanipal who ascended the Assyrian throne, 668, B. C., came the turning-point. Outwardly, indeed, the empire is more brilliant and more powerful than before, but within are seen already unequivocal signs of dissolution. Asurbanipal continued, indeed, to wage wars, more cruel and bloody than any of his predecessors ; but he himself no longer appears in the field. On the contrary he has the captive enemies and rebels brought to Nineveh, there to feast his eyes upon their torture and death, pursuing in the intervals the pleasures of the chase and the harem—he is the Sardanapalus of the Greeks—and incidentally showing an active interest in art and science. In his palace he establishes an immense library, into which he gathers all that could be found of Babylonian and Assyrian literature.

It deserves attention, and is the evidence of a very unusual personality, that no one throughout his reign of forty-two years ventured to contest the throne with this unwarlike monarch. Nevertheless the beginning of the end was at hand. Egypt seems to have freed itself soon from Assyrian domination, and enters upon a new period of political and national progress in the long and prosperous reign of Psammetichus I. In the Aryan mountaineers, the Medes, a dangerous enemy, arise in the rear of Nineveh, and at the same time another fearful storm sweeps over all Asia. From the north, the countries about the Black Sea, hordes of predatory horsemen, similar in nature to the later Huns and Mongolians, invade the civilized countries of Asia, marching through and plundering them for about thirty years: Herodotus calls them Cimmerians. As a matter of course all political ties were loosened by this, and the Assyrian Empire was shaken to its foundation.

Now Phraortes, king of the Medes, considered the time come to venture an attack upon Nineveh; but he was utterly defeated and met his own death in the undertaking. His son, Cyaxares, proposed to avenge his father, and already had assailed and besieged Nineveh when an invasion of the Cimmerians into his own country recalled him and relieved Nineveh. But this was only a stay of execution. About fifteen years later Cyaxares united with Nabopolassar, king of Babylon, for a final blow at the Assyrian Empire, of whose last two kings we do not even know the exact names. After a siege of three years Nineveh was taken and razed to the ground, and the whole nation obliterated. This took place in the year 606 B.C., just twenty years after the death of the mighty Asurbanipal.

The whole history of the world shows no catastrophe equal to the destruction of the Assyrian Empire; no nation was ever so completely destroyed as the Assyrian,—a just retribution for the abominations which it had perpetrated for centuries. The two victors divided the spoil, the lion's share falling to Media.

But meanwhile a third rival had arisen. In Egypt Necho, son of Psammetichus, had ascended the throne of the Pharaohs in 610. This enterprising and restless monarch also wanted to secure his share of the Assyrian spoil, and set out for the Euphrates with a mighty army in 608 B. C. King Josiah of Judah tried to arrest him but was utterly defeated at Megiddo and himself mortally wounded. The people, who knew well what they had to expect of the crown-prince Jehoiakim, made Jehoahaz, the younger son of the deceased, king in his father's stead. But only three months had passed when Necho summoned the young man before his tribunal at Riblah and sent him in bonds to Egypt. He punished the people for their arbitrary action by a heavy tax, and put Jehoiakim upon the throne at Jerusalem as an Egyptian vassal.

But the Egyptian glory was not to last long; a year after the destruction of Nineveh the Babylonian crown prince, Nebuchadnezzar, met the Egyptians at Carchemish on the Euphrates, and Necho was so completely defeated that he sought safety in wild flight. Nebuchadnezzar followed closely after him, but was overtaken by the news of the death of his father, Nabopolassar, so that his presence at home became absolutely necessary. Accordingly he made peace with Necho, who ceded to Babylon all his conquests in Asia as far as the Egyptian border in consideration of being allowed to return to his country unmolested.

Thus Jehoiakim of Judah had been transformed from an Egyptian vassal into a Babylonian. His policy was prescribed by his cirumstances : unconditioned submission to Babylon. But he would none of this, and rebelled against his feudal lord. At first Nebuchadnezzar did not consider it worth the while to go himself, but stirred up the neighboring peoples against the unhappy land. In the midst of this situation Jehoiakim died. His eighteen-year-old son, Jehoiachin, entered upon an evil inheritance, and had to atone for his father's sins. After a reign of three months he was forced to capitulate and surrender to the Chaldeans without conditions. Nebuchadnezzar took the treasures of the temple and the palace with him and led the young king and ten thousand of the best inhabitants, the whole aristocracy of birth and intellect, into exile in Babylon, where Jehoiachin himself was kept in close confinement. But Nebuchadnezzar made one more attempt with a native ruler and placed Zedekiah, the full brother of Jehoahaz, who had formerly been chosen by the people, and an uncle of the captive Jehoiachin, upon the throne in Jerusalem as a Babylonian vassal prince. This took place in 597 B. C. Before four years of Zedekiah's reign had passed Jerusalem was again filled with discontent, and there were plots which however finally came to nothing. Of course the matter could not remain concealed from the Babylonian government and the seriously compromised Zedekiah went in person to Babylon, but came off cheap and conducted himself discreetly for the next five years. The misfortune brought it about that the restless and aggressive Uahabra (Apries, the Hophra of the Bible) ascended the throne of the Pharaohs and immediately resumed the policy of his grandfather, Necho. So all eyes were turned longingly toward the Nile, whence the liberator from Babylonian subjection was expected. Uahabra promised assistance, and Zedekiah could no longer resist the pressure: he actually rebelled, and thus the fate of Judah and Jerusalem was sealed.

On the 10th of January, 587, B.C., the Chaldeans began to besiege Jerusalem; but Uahabra kept his word: a mighty Egyptian army started for Palestine, and the Chaldeans withdrew. The rejoicing in Jerusalem knew no bounds. But the prophets of evil were justified: the Chaldeans returned, and after a resistance conducted with the heroism of despair, when the most terrible famine was already raging in Jerusalem, such that women were devouring their own children, the city fell into the hands of the Chaldeans, on the 9th of July, 586, B.C. In the first confusion Zedekiah escaped with a few attendants, but was overtaken and brought before the tribunal of Nebuchadnezzar at Riblah. But now Nebuchadnezzar knew no such word as mercy. All the captive nobles were executed and Zedekiah's children were all butchered before the eyes of the wretched father. That was the last thing he was ever to see, for he himself was blinded and taken to Babylon in chains, where he declined and perished miserably in prison. Thus ended the last descendant of David that had ruled in Jerusalem.

The city itself was looted and then given over to the flames; the whole people that had escaped hunger and the sword was led into exile at Babylon. "Only of the poorest of the land did they leave some in Judah as vinedressers and husbandmen." Over this miserable remnant was set a certain Gedaliah as Babylonian prefect; but when Gedaliah perished soon after by the hand of a murderer, those who had remained in Judah fled to Egypt from fear of the vengeance of the Chaldeans, and there they vanished and left no trace. Edomites and other neighbors spread over the unclaimed land—Judah had ceased to be.

If Israel had been merely a race like others it would never have survived this fearful catastrophe and would have disappeared in the Babylonian exile. But Israel was the bearer of an idea; this was not to be annihilated with the state, and its eternal destiny was not closed with its political life. On the contrary. It seems as though only now, when the body was dashed to pieces, was the spirit really able to develop unhampered. The death that Judah died was a death suffused with dawn. While its sun seemed set in eternal night, already in the east new day was breaking, destined in the fulness of time to illumine the whole world with its light. Israel went down to the grave with the hope of early resurrection, and this hope was not disappointed. Forty-nine years after Nebuzaradan, the Babylonian captain of the guard, set fire to city and temple, a burnt offering from those who had returned to the fatherland was again smoking to the God of Israel on the spot where the brazen altar of Solomon had stood. The flame that had consumed Jerusalem was for Judah a purifying fire; from the seed-field of the exile sown in tears was to spring up a precious and immortal harvest.

CHAPTER VI.

FROM THE RETURN OUT OF THE BABYLONIAN CAPTIVITY TO THE OUTBREAK OF THE REBELLION OF THE MACCABEES.

THE history of the people of Israel begins with the migration of Abraham from the Euphrates to the Jordan ; it closes, one may say in a certain sense, with the compulsory migration of the exiles from the Jordan back to the Euphrates. The Babylonian exile constitutes the crisis in the history of the people of Israel from both the political and the religious standpoint. Politically and nationally the Babylonian captivity put an end for ever to the people of Israel. Even when, three hundred and fifty years later, there was once more a Jewish state, those who formed it were not the people of Israel, not even the Jewish nation, but that portion which remained in the mother country of a great religious organization scattered over all Asia and Egypt. It would on this account be technically correct to entitle the second part of our theme, which is to occupy us in the last five chapters, simply Jewish history, or history of the Jewish people. Yet still more tremendous is the change which the Babylonian exile produced in the religious life of Israel, though indeed the two are most intimately and inherently connected. The very overthrow of the Judean state and the destruction of the national life had the effect of entirely reconstructing the religion of Israel. Even in the last periods of Judean independence there had been evolving a movement which had for its aim to spiritualize religion as much as possible. In order to guard it against growing worldly and to avoid with all care the danger of sullying its purity, the leaders in this movement had aimed at separating religion from its foundation in nature and basing it absolutely upon itself and the spirit.

This was a dispensation of Providence; for thus it became possible for the religion of Israel to survive the fall of the state and the destruction of the nation, and yet to preserve them both by reconstructing them. If the destruction of the body had freed the spirit and given it an unhampered career, this spirit must needs shape for itself a new body. And Israel could constitute this new body only if it developed in accordance with the demands of this spirit. No one felt this more clearly and no one expressed it more distinctly than the Great Unknown of the last years of the Babylonian exile, whom we are accustomed to call Deutero-Isaiah, because his writings are transmitted to us as the second portion of the book of Isaiah. This Deutero-Isaiah announced the universal mission of the religion of Israel more grandly than any one else : Israel is set for a light of the heathen ; it is called to carry the revelation of God to the whole world even to the ultimate islands, the house of the God of Israel shall become a house of prayer for all nations ; but in order to be able to fulfil this mission God must first make of Israel itself a covenant. Israel must become a covenant nation ; that is, after Israel had broken the covenant and therefore perished as a nation, it must become a new people which will identify itself with the covenant, or league with God, and which is resurrected and remains alive only for and through it. Quite literally the ground had been snatched from beneath the feet of the nation, which was therefore obliged to seek another ground and foundation, and this was necessarily religious. Thus religion became one with this nationality which completely subordinated itself to religion and proposed to be nothing but its body and mouthpiece.

With correct instinct, guided by the prophet Ezekiel, the religious genius of Israel laid its universal mission upon God for the time being, and took up the immediately more urgent task of getting the mastery in its own house, of driving ineradicable roots in Israel itself. And accordingly there is accomplished in the Babylonian exile, and as a consequence of it, that remarkable transformation which makes of the Judean state a Jewish church, of the Israelitish people a Jewish religious congregation. For the history of religion there is perhaps no other period in the history of the people of Israel of equal importance and significance with the half century of the Babylonian exile, from 586 to 537 B. C.

But from the standpoint of secular history we know nothing of Israel in this period : its fortunes are those of the Babylonian Empire. This empire with such a brilliant beginning was not destined to enjoy length of days. It depended on the person of its founder, Nebuchadnezzar. When this mighty monarch died, on the 27th of March, 561 B.C. after a reign of forty-three years, the star of Babylon set. The empire maintained itself only twenty-three years longer, under four short-reigned kings, two of whom died by the hands of assassins, and then the Persian king, Cyrus, put a sudden end to it.

After the overthrow of Assyria, the most extensive empire remaining was Media, to which indeed the lion's share of the spoils of Assyria had fallen. True, the two allies against Assyria had connected themselves by marriage, Nebuchadnezzar marrying Amytis, the daughter of Cyaxares. Nevertheless, Nebuchadnezzar recognized clearly the danger that impended from this neighbor, and the immense fortifications of his capital and of his whole country, constructed by Nebuchadnezzar, could have no other purpose than to protect his empire against Media, as indeed they were called "the Median wall." And when in the year 585 B.C. he made every effort to mediate between his father-in-law and Alyattes of Lydia, and thus to maintain the Lydian kingdom, he was guided by the desire not to let Media become too powerful.

But destiny had already provided that the Median tree should not reach the skies. Nebuchadnezzar's brother-in-law, Astyages, who succeeded his father Cyaxares in 584 B.C., was not the man to give his realm added glory; after he had ruled thirty-four years, Cyrus, the Median vassal king of the powerful and vigorous race of the Persians, made himself independent, defeated the Median army and captured the capital, Ecbatana, in the year 550 B.C.

In Babylon they probably rejoiced at first over the downfall of Media, but they were to learn only too soon what a bad exchange they had made.

As general, king, and man, Cyrus is the greatest personality and the noblest figure in the ancient history of the Orient. In but twelve years, with his handful of Persians, he destroyed forever three great empires, conquered all Asia, and secured to his race for two centuries the dominion of the world: with him the hegemony over Asia passes from the Semitic to the Indo-Germanic races.

The formidableness of the new rival was soon recognized, and in the year 547 B. C. a great coalition was formed between Lydia, Babylonia, and Egypt, which was also joined by Sparta, for the purpose of stifling in its beginnings the ambitious and growing empire of Cyrus. Crœsus of Lydia began operations in the spring of 546 B. C. and made a hostile demonstration toward Persia; but Cyrus fell upon him at the first approach, followed on his heels as he retreated, and captured Sardis, the Lydian capital, in the autumn of the same year taking Crœsus captive: the kingdom of Lydia had ceased to be.

Why Babylon was then given a respite of eight years, and how the quarrel finally broke forth, we do not know; but on the 3rd of November, 538 B. C., Cyrus held his triumphal entry into Babylon, and therewith the empire of Nebuchadnezzar also had ceased to be.

With what enthusiasm the Jewish exiles greeted the victorious Persian king as avenger and liberator, the contemporary Hebrew literature gives the clearest evidence. And in fact, it was one of the first official acts of the new ruler in Babylon to give the Jewish exiles permission to return to their home, and to encourage in every way the restoration of the Jewish commonwealth.

Cyrus could have had in this only political motives. A clash with Egypt was inevitable, and so it was to the interest of the Persians to have on the Egyptian border a commonwealth that was bound to their ruling family by the strongest ties of gratitude, and upon the fidelity of which they could absolutely rely.

In the spring of 537 B. C., forty-nine years

after the destruction of Jerusalem, the exiles set out, about fifty thousand souls all told. And evidently members of all the families and groups participated in the migration. They felt that they were representatives of all Israel, as is shown by the fact that the returning emigrants were under the authority of a council of twelve responsible men, the repeatedly mentioned "elders of the Jews," a number which can have been chosen only with reference to the number of the tribes in the nation. This council evidently had the whole internal control and the guidance of the affairs of the community, for which the Persian government did not concern itself. First among the twelve are named Zerubbabel, grandson of king Jehoiachin, and Jeshua, grandson of Seraiah, the last priest of Solomon's temple, who had been executed by Nebuchadnezzar. Sheshbazzar, who is repeatedly mentioned as Persian governor-general of Judæa, was, by the likeliest supposition, a son of King Jehoiachin born in Babylonia, and hence most probably the oldest, to whom the Persians, as was their custom, entrusted the viceroyalty of his people.

On the site of the great brazen altar in Solomon's temple they forthwith set up a new altar, and had it ready to celebrate the feast of tabernacles in 537 B.C., with an offering to the God of Israel. Voluntary gifts were also received for the expenses of the religious services and for the proper clothing of the priests, but according to the express testimony of contemporary accounts the restoration of the temple was not immediately undertaken. They had indeed enough to do to make the desolate land habitable again and to restore Jerusalem as far as necessity commanded. About one-tenth of the returned emigrants settled in Jerusalem, the remainder in the immediate vicinity of Jerusalem,—the report that the whole territory of the former Kingdom of Judah was occupied at the very beginning is in itself improbable to a high degree, and is entirely contradictory to the impression made upon us by accredited tradition.

The returned exiles held themselves strictly and haughtily aloof from the remnants of the former population that had remained in the country; we read frequently of the value that was put upon pedigrees and the proof of pure stock.

Of the next seventeen years we have no positive knowledge, but must conclude that important events occurred within the priesthood in this period. For in the year 520 B. C. there appears all at once a "high priest" in the person of the before-mentioned Jeshua. Even Ezekiel knows absolutely nothing of a high priest; now on a sudden, he is present and very soon becomes the first personage among the people, crowding into the background even the house of David. We know beyond all doubt that certain things did happen within the priestly class during these years: several families which could not prove their pedigrees were excluded from the priesthood for the time being, and yet we find the descendants of these families mentioned as in important positions in the priesthood eighty years later, whence it appears that they must have secured admission after all. This gives us a significant hint. According to the regulations of Ezekiel only the descendants of Zadok, members of the family of the priests of the temple in Jerusalem, were to have priestly rights after the restoration of the commonwealth and to exercise priestly functions; but it was not possible to carry this out. The very number of the immigrant priests, four thousand two hundred and eighty-nine, that is, one out of every ten free men, puzzles us. These cannot all have been of the family of Zadok, or even in the main so. Whence it appears that it had been necessary to establish the new priesthood on a broader foundation : not the sons of Zadok, but the sons of Aaron are its representatives, and in order to satisfy the claims of the house of Zadok it is probable that the high priesthood was established and reserved exclusively to this house.

Finally in the year 520 B. C. the construction of the temple was begun. Harvest failures and famine burdened the country; the prophet Haggai declared this to be a punishment from God because the people were dwelling in ceiled houses while the house of God lay in ruins. He was supported by another prophet, the priest Zechariah, who worked in the same spirit. So the work was actually begun on the 24th of September, 520 B.C., and on the 24th of December the corner-stone was laid with due solemnities,—laid by the Davidite Zerubbabel, who had succeeded his deceased uncle Sheshbazzar as governor. This was an assumption of privilege on the part of the congregation; but the Persian authority was at the time on a weak footing; almost the whole empire was in revolt against the new king, Darius. The satrap Tattenai, who was Zerubbabel's superior, saw the structure while on a tour of inspection, and demanded an explanation. He reported the circumstance to Darius, but Darius sent reply that the building was really supported by a permit from Cyrus, and that he was therefore desirous to see the work aided in every way. And in fact it was possible on the 3d of March, 515 B. C., after four and a half years' work, to celebrate the completion of the temple and solemnly dedicate the new house of God.

We know nothing about the next fifty-seven years. Only from the descriptions of the book of Malachi we can infer that conditions took a very critical turn. Lukewarmness and indifference, and even frivolous mockery, had taken the place of the old enthusiasm; a painful disappointment had taken possession of men's minds, and they tried to make life as comfortable and agreeable as possible for themselves and to compromise with their religious duties in the easiest and cheapest way. There was, indeed, a little band of the genuinely pious, who labored only the more seriously for their own and the people's spiritual salvation; but they could accomplish nothing. At this crisis aid came to them from Babylon.

The closest connection and the most lively intercourse was maintained between the exiles who had returned to Jerusalem and those who remained in Babylon, so that these received reliable information regarding all occurrences in the old home. The development had proceeded differently in Babylon; the Jews there, without anxiety for their existence, and not compelled to wage a severe struggle for sustenance, had devoted themselves with all zeal and undivided interest to the religious problem; and they, who still lived in a heathen land, were called upon to keep their identity as Jews, and consciously to cultivate and to manifest their Judaism.

Thus there had developed in Babylon, of all places, a regular theological school, which pursued the study of the law and showed also a marked literary activity; the expansion and completion of the law was the work of these circles. One of the most prominent among them was Ezra, likewise a descendant of Zadok and a near relative of the high priest's family in Jerusalem. He determined to take an active interest in this portentous crisis. He succeeded, how we do not know, in interesting King Artaxerxes Longhand in his plans and in securing an autocratic firman which named him as royal commissioner with unlimited authority to reform conditions in Jerusalem.

On the 1st of April, 458 B. C., the caravan assembled; there were seven hundred and seventy-two men, the number of women and children not being given. Ezra had refused a Persian escort. After preparing themselves by fasting and prayer, the train set out on the 12th of April and arrived safely in Jerusalem on the 1st of August. There they celebrated a great thankoffering to God for the happily completed journey.

Ezra proceeded immediately to his work. The most important point was that of the mixed marriages already contracted. In the revival of religion and nationality these presented a great difficulty; if the national identity was dimmed or entirely blotted out the religion also would inevitably perish; then indeed Israel would be swallowed up by the heathen. Therefore it was necessary to apply the knife right here, and to show the most merciless energy. According to what Ezra was told conditions were much more discouraging than he had imagined; even the priests and the Levites turned out to be involved in the abuse and deeply compromised.

And now a scene is played which has been compared not unfairly with the so-called " revivals " of the English Methodists; a deep religious excitement is aroused, and under the pressure of this temporary excitement the participants are led into resolutions which otherwise they would have refused to make. Ezra rends his garments, tears his hair and beard, and as though paralyzed by what he has heard, sits stiff and silent until evening. A great circle of people gathers about him, and finally toward evening he arises, throws himself upon his knees, and speaks in tears a long, loud confession which paints the corruption of the people in the blackest colors.

An even greater circle of men, women and children gathers about him, and all break out into loud weeping. At this point one of Ezra's sympathizers speaks in the name of the assembly: " Yea, we have all sinned grievously! Let us make a solemn vow to put away all our foreign wives and their offspring! Ezra, take thou the matter in hand; we will be with thee." Ezra strikes the iron while it is hot, and puts all those present under a solemn oath straitway. But this did not settle the matter; only when they began to enforce the plan did the whole difficulty of it appear. It is true, every man had by the law the right to put away his wife, and we must take great care not to judge these occurrences from our point of view. But in the case of a marriage prompted by love and blessed with fondly cherished children, it could not but be regarded as a monstrous proposal to put away wife and children absolutely and without condition. And the most serious obstacle was found in the most respected circles of the community. These had formed many alliances with the neighboring aristocracy and with the Persian officials, and to send back to such a father-in-law their daughters and their children was not to be thought of without hesitation.

And so it is almost five months after that prayer-meeting before there is summoned to Jerusalem, on the 20th of December, 458, B. C., a popular assembly at which every male member of the families returned from the captivity was ordered to appear under penalty of excommunication. There sat the whole assembly in the open square before the temple, trembling with excitement, cold, and rain, and when Ezra repeated his demand the matter was treated in dilatory fashion; they said it was too important and weighty a matter to be settled in haste, and asked that a commission under the leadership of Ezra should first ascertain the exact condition of affairs and then deal with the offenders individually. Four adherents of Ezra protested, it is true, against this delay, but the proposal was accepted; the assembly goes home, and Ezra is left to see what he can accomplish with his commission.

Any one who has had the questionable fortune to be chairman of a commission or of a directory can easily imagine himself in Ezra's place. The commission is organized on the 1st of January, 457 B.C. and in three months has so far accomplished its task as to have ascertained and officially identified all the men who are living in mixed marriage. At this point our reports break off suddenly and we have no direct account of the next thirteen years, until April, 444. B. C. Of course the reports of the period were intentionally suppressed because they were too sad and too humiliating. Plainly Ezra accomplished nothing, and an attempt to strengthen his position was a woful failure.

In April, 444 B. C., we suddenly learn that the walls of Jerusalem are torn down and its gates burned with fire. Ezra had probably recognized that he must first of all be master in his own house before he could take any energetic measures. Jerusalem was an exposed and thinly populated city, defenceless against any sudden attack, open to any surprise. Relying, therefore, upon his royal authority, Ezra had proceeded to build city walls and fortify the place.

The neighbors, suspicious and offended most deeply by the recent occurrences in Jerusalem, now publicly denounced this last proceeding to the Persian Government, attributing to Ezra's action a political motive.

We must recall that Egypt had shortly before freed itself from Persian rule. True it had been again subjected, but not by any means pacified; there are still commotions in Egypt as late as 449 and 443 B. C. Accordingly the Persians were naturally very anxious regarding the neighboring countries, and therefore a command actually arrived from Artaxerxes to desist forthwith from the building of the wall. The enemies of the Jews translated this royal command into action and destroyed the work that had been begun. This probably happened in the year 445 B. C.

But just at the moment when Ezra's cause seemed hopelessly lost there came to him unexpected assistance. A Babylonian Jew named Nehemiah had won the favor of King Artaxerxes and his wife, Damaspia, and had become royal cup-bearer. He heard of the depressing occurrences in Jerusalem and could not conceal his distress. The king, whom he was serving at the time, made sympathetic inquiries, and when Nehemiah was directed to ask a royal favor he applied for and received the position of governor in Jerusalem, which was evidently vacant at the time. The king gave him leave of absence for twelve years and actually appointed him Persian governor in Judea.

Well provided with royal privileges and credentials, he sets out in order to assume his new office forthwith. Now the civil arm is at the disposal of the work of reform, and Nehemiah is the man to make use with all energy of the authority given him.

In Nehemiah we have one of the most characteristic and attractive figures in the whole of Israelitish history. He owes his success above all things to the moral nobility of his personality. Entirely unselfish, inspired only by consecrated zeal for the cause, he has the power of carrying all along with him, of encouraging the timid and unenthusiastic by his own belief and confidence, and of lifting plodding and lukewarm souls out of and above themselves by his own idealism and enthusiasm. He is at the same time the soul and arm of the whole work, taking hold everywhere himself and leading. But he proceeds in this openly and honorably, scorning all petty means and evasions : friends and foes alike know where to find him. Even where he uses force he does not cloak his purpose, but meets his man with lifted visor, everywhere throwing his whole personality into the undertaking. And since his energy and practical force were coupled with equally great shrewdness and knowledge of the world—he had not gone through the school of diplomacy at the Persian court for nothing—he was the man of destiny for this difficult task, which demanded a peculiar combination of religious enthusiasm and worldly wisdom, and he accomplished it. What Ezra attempted, Nehemiah achieved ; the establishment and consolidation of the Jewish community is essentially his work and his merit.

The new governor had been but three days in Jerusalem when he undertook, with but a few companions, a night ride about the ruined walls in order to get, by the pale light of the moon, a complete survey of the damage. He had not proceeded far when his animal was checked by rubbish and ruins, and he was obliged to turn back.

Now he called together the whole people and the

priests and elders, painted for them in vivid words the shameful condition of Jerusalem, and presented to them the authority and the privileges which he had received from the king. They proceed to work forthwith and the task is apportioned in an extremely practical way. To each family was assigned a certain part of the wall, which it was to construct, and thus the whole wall rose from the ground at once.

The whole time Nehemiah did not have his clothes off. Day and night he was on the ground, taking hold everywhere himself like the commonest laborer, supervising all and carrying great and small with him by his pattern and example.

The enemies of the Jews, among whom Sanballat the Horonite, Tobiah the Ammonite, and Geshem the Arabian are especially mentioned, behold with wrath and dismay what is going on in Jerusalem, and try in every way to hinder the work. When their ridicule and mockery prove of no avail they try to use force; but Nehemiah makes his arrangements so that the work need not be interrupted, and yet the whole force is at any moment ready for defence. Now the enemy try cunning: they undertake to lure Nehemiah away from the work under pretext of a conference; but Nehemiah, who immediately sees through the clumsy plan, answers with delicate irony that he unfortunately could not leave Jerusalem at the moment, being occupied with an important task which urgently demanded his personal presence.

Then the enemy hit upon the plan of causing him difficulty in his own camp. There were certainly many who had but half a heart in the matter, and to whom any pretext for withdrawing in good order was welcome. And now Nehemiah's enemies hire the pitiful remnants of the prophetic class in Jerusalem, who actually sell themselves for money and work against Nehemiah by means of alleged prophetic oracles, and try to mislead and alienate the people ; but Nehemiah overcomes these difficulties also.

But now he is met by the most dangerous obstacle. By reason of the work upon the wall the common man has been deprived of the opportunity to follow his regular business; moreover the taxes have to be collected afterwards as before, and there seem to have been in addition crop failures and dearth. Thus the poor had become deeply in debt: they had been obliged to mortgage their fields, vineyards, and houses, and even in some cases sell their children into serfdom. Now they bring their complaints before the governor, who forthwith calls a general assembly and with all the pathos of virtuous indignation rebukes the rich usurers for their unfraternal behavior. By referring to his own unselfishness in resigning all the income that belonged to the office of governor in order not to oppress the people, but instead paying for everything out of his own pocket and besides keeping open table daily for a hundred and fifty persons, he brings such a moral pressure to bear upon the rich that they swear solemnly to cancel all their claims and return all property held in pledge.

Now the work advances with giant strides: on the 25th of September, 444 B. C., after fifty-two days' labor, the wall was finished and the gates set in place. A solemn procession, which marched about with psalm-singing and music upon the top of the newly erected wall, expressed thanks to God for the success of the work and proclaimed to all the world its completion.

Thus protected against interference from without, they now proceed to the greater and more important task which Ezra had been obliged to drop. For the very next 1st of October, 444 B. C., the whole people is summoned to Jerusalem. From the midst of the assembly itself comes the proposal that Ezra shall read from the book of the law of Moses. Ezra mounts a pulpit already erected for this purpose; on either side of it stand seven of the most prominent men, and a number of Levites are on hand to explain to the people what Ezra has read. Again the people break out into loud weeping; but Ezra says they are not to weep, but sit down to a joyous meal and give a share to those who have brought nothing, for this day is a sacred jubilee for Israel.

The following day Ezra continues the reading of the law, but only to the heads of families. Then the feast of tabernacles is celebrated on the 15th of October, according to the directions of the law, and on the 24th of October a great and general day of repentance and prayer is held, and there the whole people takes a solemn oath to support the book of the law as read by Ezra; the heads of families sign and seal this obligation with due solemnity: strict observance of the Sabbath, absolute prohibition of mixed marriages, observance of the sabbatical year and the remission of debts, and above all faithful payment of the dues to the temple, are the most important single points of this compact.

The 24th of October is the real birthday of Judaism, one of the most important days in the history of humanity. At last the religion of revelation had succeeded in getting a home of its own, if I may use the expression; it had created for itself a body in and through which it could act and fulfil its lofty mission to the world.

True, not all was accomplished by this one popular assembly. Many had allowed themselves to be carried away by the mass, to whom it now came hard when obligations there assumed were taken in bitter earnest. And the very ones upon whom Nehemiah should have been able to depend, and who were the born promoters and guardians of his work, the priests, stood aside resentful or at least lukewarm. They had by this time developed into a sort of temple nobility, who were now concerned only for the privileges of their position, who fraternized with the civil nobility, but who were not disposed to accept into the bargain heavy obligations. So long as Nehemiah was governor, indeed, he was able with iron hand to suppress all opposition; but at the end of twelve years his leave expired, and in 432 B. C., he was obliged to return to the Persian court. But with a true perception of the needs of the situation he managed to secure the governorship anew and was permitted soon to return to Jerusalem.

How far the whole work depended on him personally became evident immediately. Even this brief absence had sufficed to let everything get at odds and ends. The Sabbath was desecrated boldly, the temple tribute was not paid, mixed marriages began to recur. But the most serious offense had been committed by the high priest, Eliashib. He had given a chamber in the temple to his kinsman, Tobiah the Ammonite, whom we know as an enemy of Nehemiah, and his grandson, Manasseh, had even married Nicaso, the daughter of Sanballat, Nehemiah's chief adversary.

And now Nehemiah adopted rigorous measures. He went about the whole country to hunt out mixed marriages and appeal to the consciences of the guilty parties; he punished severely violations of the command of Sabbath rest; he had the gates of Jerusalem closed on Friday evening and kept closed the whole Sabbath, and when heathen traders tried to set up their market without the walls of Jerusalem on the Sabbath, he had them warned and threatened with violent punishment. The temple tithes, likewise, were systematized carefully and provision made for their correct payment. But Nehemiah took the most energetic measures against Eliashib, the high priest. If he might defy his authority with impunity, it would amount to nothing. Without ceremony Nehemiah had Tobiah's household stuff cast out of the chamber in the temple and had the chamber itself reconsecrated; and when Manasseh refused to put away Nicaso, he expelled him from the people and the congregation.

We have a vague hint that a considerable number of priests, who were dissatisfied with the new conditions, joined Manasseh and left Jerusalem. Manasseh went to the home of his father-in-law, Sanballat, and founded there an Israelitish worship according to the old style, which was adopted by all who were dissatisfied with the reforms. This became the religious community of the Samaritans.

This secession was a decided advantage for the reform in Jerusalem : all the hesitating elements withdrew from the city and only those remained who had firm convictions. Now the Jewish community became an harmonious and homogeneous society in which the strict tendency of the reform party prevailed; whoever was dissatisfied had simply to join the Samaritans. Thus there was a clean division on one side as well as on the other, which however was not accomplished amicably, but planted on both sides a rapidly growing harvest of passionate hatred. For the further history of the development of religion the Samaritans are without consequence ; for a second time, and now for all time, Judah had become Israel, Israel was limited to Judah.

Regarding the length of Nehemiah's second term as governor and his further destinies we know nothing ; but the aftertime shows plainly that he accomplished the work of his life. He impressed the stamp of his spirit upon Judaism for all time and forced it to follow the course he had marked out.

It is one of the greatest ironies of fate known to universal history, or, to speak more correctly, it is one of the most striking evidences of the wonderful ways which divine Providence takes for the attainment of its most important and most significant ends, that the final completion and the permanent consolidation of the exclusive Judaism which sealed itself hermetically against everything non-Jewish and rejected sternly everything heathen, was accomplished and made possible only under the protection and by the aid of a heathen government, that the reformation of Ezra and Nehemiah, to use a modern phrase, hung from the sword-belt of the Persian *gens d'armes*. And yet the work was of God, and only thus could the religion of revelation be preserved. But for the energy of Nehemiah the whole history of humanity would have run an entirely different course. And therefore we too must look up to this man with gratitude and reverence to this day.

For the next two hundred and fifty years only a few scattered dates are transmitted to us. For universal history they are the most important and portentous of all—I need only name the one name, Alexander the Great. Let us examine what we know of this period and sketch the events of the history of the world only in roughest outline, so far as they are indispensable to the understanding of the history of the people of Israel.

Johanan, the grandson of the high priest Eliashib whom we know, had a brother Joshua, who was a friend of Bagoses, the Persian governor. Bagoses wanted to secure the high priesthood for Joshua ; Johanan learns this and murders his brother in the temple during the service. At the news of the crime Bagoses hastens to the temple ; when they beg him not to pollute the temple by his presence he answers scornfully : "Do I, perchance, pollute the temple more than the corpse of the slain man ? " So he goes in, and for atonement fifty silver shekels have to be paid him for every lamb sacrificed throughout a period of seven years,—at least he made a fine stroke of business out of the death of his friend.

Further, we have the wholly disconnected remark that King Ochus destroyed Jericho and deported a great number of Jews to Hyrcania. In the reign of Ochus it is a fact that all Egypt, Phœnicia, and Cœlesyria was in rebellion against the Persians ; it is possible that some scattered Jews took part in this, and so there is at least every inner probability for this report.

But the days of the Persian dominion were numbered. Alexander the Great began his marvelous career of victory in 334 B. C. and the battle of Issus delivered all Syria and Egypt into his hands. Alexander hastens thither immediately in order to make sure of these countries. What Josephus tells of a visit of Alexander in Jerusalem and his meeting with the high priest Jadduah is pure legend; on the other hand it is quite probable that Alexander, who showed all possible consideration for the religious views of the people whom he subdued, may have granted the Jews exemption from tribute in the sabbatical year and permitted to those going with him to war the observance of their own religious customs. When the Samaritans rebelled against him he added a part of Samaria to Judea.

And so the Jews had been transferred from the Persian rule to that of the Greeks.

We pass over the events and confusion of the succeeding years, remembering only that the battle of Ipsus, in the year 301, put an end to the contentions of the immediate successors of Alexander: Palestine and Cœlesyria fell to Ptolemy of Egypt, and until 198 Judea remained an Egyptian province.

This century is the happiest period that Judea experienced after the loss of her independence. The very first Ptolemy favored the Jews in every way. Not only was the Egyptian administration in Judea exceedingly mild and kindly disposed, but Ptolemy endeavored also to persuade the Jews to settle in Egypt proper. It is even reported that Alexander colonized Jews in his newly founded city of Alexandria. Ptolemy pursued this policy with all energy, because, as Josephus informs us, the Jews were the only ones among all his subjects upon whose oath he could absolutely depend ; therefore he preferred to appoint Jews to positions of the highest trust, and granted them in Alexandria complete equality with the Macedonians themselves, "isopolity," as it was called. As the immediate successors of Ptolemy favored the Jews in the same way, Alexandria soon became the second Jewish city in the world, and in Egypt they were numbered by millions.

That this favoring of the Jews by the Ptolemies was based largely on policy, the endeavor to attach to themselves and their family the population of an important and exposed boundary province, is evident from the very fact that Seleucus Nicator, ruler of Syria, the neighbor and rival of Egypt, hastened to grant them in his country and his cities the same privileges : he, too, gave them "isopolity" with Macedonians and Greeks. In the new capital founded by him, Antioch, this right of citizenship even paid something : there were allowances of oil connected with it ; but since the Jews would not accept this heathen oil, as being polluted, Seleucus issued an order that it should be made up to them in money at the prevailing market price.

As Palestine belongs geographically to Asia, nature herself had assigned it to Syria; so long as this province was in possession of Egypt, and the Egyptian boundary was thus advanced to the very gates of the capital, Antioch, the Seleucidæ could not rest nor regard their realm as rounded out and complete. And so, as the result of the inner momentum of circumstances, there soon begin the struggles of the Seleucidæ with the Ptolemies in order to take from them this province which was indispensable to Syria.

It is not our office to pursue these fluctuant events in detail. At first the advantage was decidedly on the side of Egypt. There reigned a series of excellent and highly gifted rulers, while the first Seleucidæ after the mighty Seleucus Nicator present a mournful and lamentable picture.

But soon the leaf is turned. The fourth Ptolemy, a Louis XV. on the Egyptian throne, wholly degenerated in the most shameless excesses, allowed everything to decay and rot, while at the same time in Antiochus III., incorrectly called the Great, the throne of the Seleucidæ had received at least an enterprising and energetic ruler. True, the first attack of Antiochus upon Egypt was repelled; but when in 204 B. C. Ptolemy IV. suddenly died and the kingdom was left to his five-year-old son, the confusion in Egypt was great. Now Antiochus took swift measures. In their helplessness the Egyptian regents offered the guardianship of their youthful king to the Romans ; but the Romans were still occupied with Hannibal, and soon after had Phillip V. of Macedon to look after, and accordingly could not at the time give any attention to their Egyptian ward.

After various chances of war Antiochus succeeded in defeating decisively the Egyptian general, Scopas, at Paneas, and in forcing him to capitulate in Sidon, whither he had retreated with his troops. Thus in the year 198 B. C. Palestine and Cœlesyria became a Syrian province.

The Jews, who had felt the change in condition of the Egyptian state, and who could have no sympathy for such a man as the fourth Ptolemy, received the Syrians with open arms and gave them active support in expelling the Egyptian garrisons, and Antiochus showed his appreciation of their willingness : the whole service in the temple in Jerusalem was put upon the charge of the state treasury, exemption from taxation was granted to everything intended for the temple as well as to the priesthood and all *attachés* of the temple, the entrance into the temple was forbidden to every non-Jew as well as the introduction of unclean animals into Jerusalem, under heavy fines to be paid to the priests of the temple, and all Jews were secured in unconditional religious freedom. Those who had fallen into military captivity and slavery were to be released forthwith. To the population of Jerusalem, and to all who should settle in Jerusalem within a certain period, complete freedom from taxation for three years was granted and after that exemption of one-third.

We see, the new government spares no pains to win the hearts of its Jewish subjects, and these probably looked forward to the future with joyous confidence. But how soon the picture was to be changed! When thirty years had passed over the country Judea was engaged in a desperate struggle with Syria for life and death; and with this we are once more at a turning point in the history of the Jewish people.

CHAPTER VII.

THE MACCABEAN REBELLION TO THE ESTABLISHMENT OF THE HEREDITARY HIGH PRIESTHOOD AND PRINCIPALITY UNDER SIMON.

WE have pursued historical events as far as the point where Judea became a province of the Syrian empire of the Seleucidæ. We must now take a survey partly reminiscent and partly anticipative of the prevailing and rising spiritual forces of the time, since all the succeeding historical development is quite unintelligible without a clear conception of their nature and significance.

The most important of the spiritual forces in question is Hellenism. It lifted the ancient world out of its ruts, while the Orient in particular was entirely transformed by it. With it an absolutely new factor enters the history of the world. Its victories are not merely of the sword, but of the mind. The Assyrians, indeed, aimed at a systematic destruction of nationalities through their wholesale deportations and the resulting mixture of races; but these measures were taken solely with a political purpose: they wished to make other nations defenseless and harmless in order to maintain themselves in unimperiled possession of the supremacy. The Assyrians had no thought of extending the really important and highly developed Assyro-Babylonian civilization, or of propagandizing for Assyro-Babylonian language or religion; if the subjected races were docile and paid their tribute promptly, the aim of the Assyrian diplomacy was attained; they did not ask or desire more.

The conception of the nature of the State as a civilizing power appears first in Nebuchadnezzar; and the Persian kings, continuing and extending his work, gave an admirable organization to their empire; yet even this organization was purely administrative. The Persian Government gave itself absolutely no concern for local and domestic affairs, neither did it ever anywhere attempt a blending of various nationalities; it permitted the Egyptians to be Egyptians undisturbed, the Jews, Jews, and the Greeks, Greeks, provided only they were and remained loyal Persian subjects.

Into these idyllic conditions came suddenly Hellenism. True, Alexander the Great was most scrupulously considerate of the religious views of conquered races, and it would never have occurred to him to put the Greek Zeus, for instance, in the place of the native gods of the Orient; and yet Alexander aimed clearly and consciously not only at conquering the Orient, but at Hellenizing it. The universal empire which rose before his gifted and ardent spirit was to bring an organic blending of all nationalities into a new unity in which of course the Greek was to be the dominant factor fixing the character of the entire combination, but only in order to transmit to the whole world the treasures of the Greek intellect and the benefits of Greek civilization.

In Alexander personally these ambitions were indeed reversed. From a Greek he himself became ever more and more an Oriental, so that the old Macedonian veterans who could not reconcile themselves to altered and un-Greek conditions rebelled against him the year before his death; but his ambition was magnificent and became of incalculable importance in its results.

The successors of Alexander pursued this ambition deliberately; everywhere Greeks streamed in, everywhere there sprang from the soil new cities which, being settled exclusively by Greeks, spread a distinctly Greek net over the whole Orient, in the meshes of which was entangled ever more of the ancient Oriental life. And when we recall what these Hellenes had to offer to the Orient, then only shall we be able to estimate the whole significance of the intellectual process thus initiated and extending its effects ever more swiftly and vigorously. Even to-day our whole culture and civilization is based upon Hellas and what that divinely-favored race gave to mankind. But at the time of which we are speaking, Greece itself had long passed its Golden Age, its intellectual and political meridian.

It is particularly significant, and not at all a matter of accident, that in order to take the aggressive the Greeks themselves had first to be made again presentable in history, if I may be allowed the expression, by the semi-barbarous people of the Macedonians. Hellenism was enabled to enter upon its victorious career of world-conquest only through the Macedonians and under their dominion.

It is just the case of the Greeks which has shown so very clearly whither a civilization leads which lacks religious and moral foundations and is solely a product of unrestrained human spirit. With the intellectual perfection went hand in hand a moral decay whose dreadful depths could not be hidden even by the roses that flourished on the edge of the abyss. Aside from the sole shining figure of Epaminondas, who as a Bœotian was a semi-boor in the eyes of every genuine Hellene, Greek history from the end of the Peloponnesian War to the time of Alexander the Great presents a truly depressing picture of abjectness and worthlessness. Very soon the average Greek had of civilization only the moral decay, of culture only the conceited arrogance. Only recall with what undisguised contempt the Romans looked down upon the Greeks when they first became acquainted with them. The Roman, who still retained the early Roman honesty and thoroughness, regarded every Greek as a mere blackguard, and 'Græculus' became an epithet for the characterization of a windy, puffed-up, characterless, unreliable fellow.

And this ethical dissolution which may be called absolute decay, made rapid progress; they were soon on the verge of complete moral bankruptcy. And so the Greeks became for the Orient the bearers of civilization indeed, but also the the bearers of moral degeneration. Where they really predominated arose frivolity and skepticism and a moral laxity more repulsive under its varnish of culture than undisguised barbarism and untutored license. The result was what we may observe everywhere when differing nationalities are mixed without the mixture being controlled and protected by a strong hand; the good characteristics are lost, while there is a reciprocal exchange of bad qualities, so that the product finally combines in itself all the bad qualities of its constituent elements while the good are dissipated.

Now what was the relation of the Jewish people to this new factor in the world's history? In the first place, Judea was so fortunate as to become acquainted with Hellenism from its best side. Whatever there was good and great in Hellenism and its products is inseparably associated with the name of Alexandria, the capital of the empire at this time and for Judea also. The first three Ptolemies, under whose rule Judea stood for eighty years (from 301 to 221, B. C.), may fairly be designated as the most important historical personages of the entire Hellenistic period; with them and under them Hellenism was solely a civilizing power and put itself at the service of Israel also. At the suggestion of the second Ptolemy, who wished to have in legible form in his model library at Alexandria among others also the sacred writings of his Jewish subjects a beginning was made of translating the Old Testament into the universal language, Greek; and since the religious and national consolidation of the Jewish congregation by Ezra and Nehemiah this is the most important occurrence, perhaps, in the history of the Jewish people.

How well disposed these rulers were towards the Jews, and how they favored them in every way, we have already learned. Accordingly the danger of Hellenization was particularly keen. The Judaism of Ezra and Nehemiah is characterized by an element of gloomy severity and sharp asceticism: that was a soil on which the sunny serenity and merry joyousness of Hellenism was sure to be particularly attractive and to insinuate itself into the heart: it would not have been surprising if the Jews, dazzled by the new light, had deserted in masses. But nothing of the sort took place; religious training prevailed over secular culture, the Jew remained faithful to his God and his law.

The rejection of Hellenism was not at first abrupt and absolute, but there was a sharp and clear perception of the limit where Hellenism must halt. The connexion of the two reached a really touching expression in one of the most remarkable of the books of the Old Testament, the so-called Preacher of Solomon (Ecclesiastes), which was written about the year 200 B. C. by a Jew trained under Hellenistic influence. The author shows himself to be profoundly permeated with Hellenism. He has assimilated it as an element of his culture, he is indubitably influenced by Greek philosophy and Greek science, and expresses views which sound like consummate scepticism; but withal he holds inflexibly true to the faith in a personal God and a moral order of the universe; he gives up the solution of the riddle of existence and falls back resignedly upon the faith of his childhood, although it has shown itself to be inadequate. Truly, Old Testament piety has nowhere had a greater triumph than in this book which at the first glance seems so godless! Yes, Judaism had itself strength and resistance enough to receive the ennobling and illuminating influence of Hellenism without surrendering to it.

About the same time as Ecclesiastes, was written the book Jesus Sirach. In this book genuine Jewish piety shines with such a mild and pure light, purged of all that is sharp and rude; piety and common sense are here combined into such broadly beautiful charity, morality ennobled by religion and religion manifested in morality, that one can see plainly that Judaism is not inherently hostile to culture, but that here too true religion and true culture join in a beautiful union fruitful for both sides.

For the Jewish people it was a vital question what attitude the dominant circles and especially the family of the high priest would take toward the new intellectual force. The influence of the high priest was tremendous. As a result of the central position which religion held in Judaism, whose one and all it was, the highest functionary in the religious congregation was inevitably the first personage in popular life also; besides, the office of high priest was the only permanent national institution which had its foundation within itself, independent of the heathen secular power. We are nowhere informed that the Persian or Egyptian governments interfered in the least with the appointment to the office of high priest, or even made it dependent upon their confirmation; it was evidently regarded as a Jewish local affair.

Thus the people and the heathen secular power grew accustomed to regarding the high priest as the very head and representative of the nation,— we learn from a casual note in Josephus that the Egyptian Government put also the entire financial management into the hands of the high priest, who had to deliver to the Egyptian Government the sum fixed as annual tribute and was held responsible for it. Accordingly it must be regarded as peculiarly fortunate that the office of high priest in the most critical period was in the hands of two worthy and truly pious men: Simon II., of whom his contemporary, Jesus Sirach, gives such a gratifying characterization, and above all his son and successor, Onias III., a really luminous figure, who commanded the respect and admiration of even his enemies and the heathen, and who stood a steadfast rock and a fortress of law and faith in the midst of the surging and foaming flood.

This is perhaps the proper place to consider a local Jewish phenomenon which is suddenly present about the end of the second century without our having any positive reports regarding its origin: this is the Pharisees and Sadducees. It is worthy of note that the first Book of the Maccabees, an historical authority of prime importance for us, nowhere mentions them, although we repeatedly think we have our hands on them. On the other hand they appear in the reign of the third Maccabee as complete and finished phenomena, and from this time on the whole of Jewish history turns about the opposition between these two rival tendencies. It is therefore indispensable for us to form a clear conception of them both.

According to the prevailing view, which has been influenced by the accounts of the Talmud, the Pharisees and the Sadducees are two Jewish sects, and their opposition purely religio-dogmatic but this view cannot stand in the face of the oldest and most reliable accounts.

It is easiest to form an historically correct conception of the Sadducees. The very name is significant: it marks them as Zadokidæ (of the family of Zadok). The Zadokidæ are the family from which the high priest is chosen, and therefore the highest nobility of Israel,—we have in the Sadducees the party of the aristocracy, the Jewish hereditary nobility. The Sadducees are primarily a purely political party; they are the ruling families whose business is the care for public affairs. They do not concern themselves much about heaven, but devote themselves to being comfortable on the earth; they are the officials, the diplomats, the councillors of the secular state, the real support and the most faithful adherents of the Maccabean princes. If the demands of the heavenly king are not reconcilable with those of the earthly king, they decide for the latter; they are not so strict about law and religion if only state and people are maintained and prosper. Improbable as it may sound, they are the real patriots and the national party with the motto: Israel above all! Israel's honor, Israel's dignity, Israel's freedom, are their guiding stars.

Their antipodes, the Pharisees, have accordingly been represented as simple democrats, the popular party, and it is undeniable that their influence upon the people was tremendous and that the people saw in them their intellectual leaders; but they were anything but democratic. The most hidebound aristocrat, the narrowest county squire did not meet the people with the scornful contempt shown by the Pharisees for the "am haarez," which to them were scarcely more than cattle.

It is the Pharisees who constitute an exclusively religious sect, which knows no political interests; their motto is : The law must be fulfilled even if Israel is ruined by it. Utterly blind to the most elementary requirements of an actual state and of political life, they judge everything from a purely theoretical theological standpoint; whatever contradicts the letter of the law is evil and must be combated to the death, even though the most vital interests of Israel are at stake. The very name is highly significant. "Peruschim," or in the Aramaic popular idiom, "perischin," means the "set apart," the separatists. Separation from all that was heathen had been since the time of Ezra and Nehemiah the very vital nerve of Jewish piety, and this is the object of the whole ceremonial law. The Pharisees carried out this purpose with unswerving energy and to its utmost consequences; they are the virtuosi of religion and piety, whose calling it is to fulfil vicariously as it were what God demands of every Israelite, but what the common man under the demands of daily life cannot perform, the most complete, the most rigorous, and the most scrupulous observance of the law, and not simply of the written law, but of all the details derived from it partly by the demands of practise and partly by theoretical subtilizing. The Pharisees are entirely isolated from the world and live exclusively in their ideas; but the fact that they have an idea behind them, which they bear and by which they are borne is their strength, and in it lies the secret of their power; they are the personified genius of Judaism and one of the strongest evidences of the omnipotence of idealism. As opposed to the practical realism of the Sadducees they represent a transcendental idealism, to which facts are nothing, ideas everything. In Pharisaism and the Talmud we have the outcome of the directions which Judaism took under Ezra and Nehemiah,—this fact was realized, and hence the tremendous moral influence of the Pharisees; they destroyed the newly rising Jewish State, but they saved Judaism.

But it is time to return to our history. Young Ptolemy V., from whom Antiochus took Palestine, was, as will be remembered, under Roman guardianship. After Hannibal had been finally subdued, and Philip of Macedon also defeated in the battle of Cynoscephalæ, 197 B. C., Antiochus considered it advisable to make some concession to the Roman demands; therefore he betrothed his daughter Cleopatra to young Ptolemy, and promised to give her the conquered province as dowry. The marriage was performed in the year 193 B. C., but Antiochus had no thought of keeping his word; he did indeed give his daughter the half of the revenues for pin money, but the province remained in Syrian hands. But his hour had come.

In the year 190 B. C., in the murderous battle at Magnesia on the Sipylus, the thoroughly hollow and innerly rotten glory of the Seleucidæ sank in the dust before the Roman swords, and the only care of Antiochus was thenceforth to comply with the enormous demands of Rome. While raising forced loans from the temples for this purpose he was slain in Elymais by the enraged populace. His son and successor, Seleucus IV., a quite insignificant and indolent fellow, accepted as an unfortunate inheritance the obligation to the Romans and fulfilled it in a similar fashion.

And now once more we learn something direct about Judea. Here too Hellenism had made immense progress even among the priests. There were not a few of them who had already adopted Greek names and could scarcely wait for the time when Jerusalem should be a Greek city and they should be free from the troublesome restraint of the law and of Jewish life. Therefore they hated bitterly the pious and loyal high priest Onias and intrigued against him in every possible way. The chief of this Hellenistic party, a priest by the name of Simon, called the attention of the Syrian officials to the treasures of the temple in Jerusalem, and in fact Seleucus sent a certain Heliodorus to Jerusalem to look after things and to materially lighten the temple treasury. The purpose was never accomplished: the second Book of Maccabees tells a marvelous tale of how three angels checked the plundering Heliodorus in his course. Now Simon denounced Onias as a conspirator and traitor, and as the Syrian officials gave him all possible support it came to bloodshed in the streets of Jerusalem. At this Onias himself started upon the way to Antioch in order to represent his and the people's cause in person. Meantime there had been a change of rulers there. Heliodorus had poisoned Seleucus and raised himself to the throne. The rightful heir, Demetrius, the son of Seleucus, had been sent to Rome as a hostage; then the younger brother of Seleucus, Antiochus, overthrew the regicide, but kept the throne for himself, calling himself Antiochus IV. Epiphanes. This took place in the summer of 175 B. C.

Antiochus Epiphanes became a most fateful personage for Jewish history, and there are still disputes as to what his real motives were. Even to his contemporaries this prince was a psychological riddle. The great historian Polybius, who knew him personally, gives a detailed characterization of him, showing forth the most contradictory traits. Popular wit explained the matter by changing his name Epiphanes to Epimanes, that is, the crazy, the fool, and in fact the whole description of Polybius gives the impression that Antiochus was not really malicious and corrupt, but rather afflicted with a mental defect, whimsical and irresponsible and not accustomed to submit to any sort of restraint. There even appears in him a leaning to coarse humor which we may almost characterize as waggishness, and which is indeed very unbecoming in a king. They are regular boys' capers which Antiochus cut for his own royal entertainment. We need not expect to find any more serious thought or any more profound purpose in this thoroughly superficial and flippant character.

Before such a ruler Onias was to plead his case. But he was accompanied to Antioch by his younger brother, Jason. As his Greek name indicates, Jason was a leader of the Hellenistic faction : he promised Antiochus a great sum of money and an energetic Hellenizing of the Jews besides, if he would depose his brother and make him high priest. Antiochus could not resist such a temptation : Onias was detained in Antioch, and Jason returned to Jerusalem as newly appointed high priest.

The work of Hellenization was now begun under high pressure : theaters and gymnasia were built at Jerusalem, so that not even the priests paid any more attention to the altar and its service, but played ball and other games and pursued various physical exercises in the gymnasium. This Jewish high priest went so far in his catholicity as to send a sacrifice to the Tyrian Melkarth. When Antiochus on a certain occasion came to Jerusalem he was received with great rejoicings and welcomed in a wholly Greek fashion, with games and torch dances.

But the glory of Jason was not to last long. Only three years passed when a certain Menelaus outbid him and offered Antiochus still greater sums; forthwith Jason was deposed and the more generous Menelaus appointed. Menelaus was a brother to Simon, who is already known to us as the chief opponent of Onias; he raged like a wild beast against the faithful, according to the drastic expression of the second Book of the Maccabees. But soon he too was in close straits. When Antiochus tried to collect the larger sum promised he was unable to pay, and Antiochus forthwith took action against him in Antioch and deposed him. But Menelaus was not at a loss what to do. When the king had left his capital he bribed the officials who had had the decision in the king's absence, had Onias murdered and was reinstated in his office; a deputation which accused him was simply executed. So Menelaus was again high priest, and pursued his career more shamelessly than before.

But now we must again cast a glance at the political occurrences. Ptolemy V., husband of the Syrian Cleopatra, sister of Antiochus Epiphanes, died in 180 B. C. and his widow seven years later. Antiochus offered himself to his two Egyptian nephews as guardian, but the Egyptians would have none of this, demanding back instead Palestine as the inheritance of the deceased queen.

So there resulted wars between Antiochus and his nephews for four successive years. This was at a time when the Romans were engaged in the second Macedonian War against King Perseus, and could not therefore pay any attention to Oriental affairs.

The fortunes of these Syro-Egyptian wars do not belong here; in the second of them, 170 B. C., Antiochus was reported dead, and the deposed Jason seized the opportunity to recover the high-priesthood by force. He effected a breach in the walls of Jerusalem and inflicted dreadful slaughter, but was unable to capture it; he was obliged to flee and died in Sparta after a fugitive life full of adventure. Antiochus treated this as a rebellion against his authority: returning from Egypt frustrated, he vented his wrath upon the Jews, entered Jerusalem, plundered the temple and played fearful havoc there; Menelaus was more firmly established in his favor than ever. But two years later an end was to be put to his ambition. In the battle of Pydna the Romans had destroyed the Macedonian Empire, and now two words from the Roman ambassador Popilius Lænas were sufficient to make Antiochus resign his Egyptian schemes forever.

Again the Jews had to endure the impotent wrath of the king against fate: a still worse massacre was perpetrated in Jerusalem; the whole city was plundered, its walls razed, and a Syrian garrison put into the city. And now Antiochus

considered the occasion ripe for a master stroke
On the 27th of October, 168 B. C., he issued the
insane decree which was intended to exterminate
Judaism root and branch. All the sacred writings
of the Jews were to be delivered up and destroyed,
the exercise of the Jewish religion was forbidden
on pain of death, all the Jews were to sacrifice to
the Greek gods and the temple at Jerusalem was
to become a sanctuary of Olympian Zeus. The
abomination of desolation was actually established
in the sacred place, and on the 25th of December,
168 B. C., the first sacrifice was offered there to
Zeus—whether by the high priest Menelaus we
do not know. The commands of the king were
executed with unexampled severity and the subordinate functionaries of authority evidently took
fiendish delight in harassing and tormenting in
every imaginable way the Jews who were loyal
to the law; when one reads the accounts in the
Books of Maccabees one is reminded involun-
tarily of the dragonnades under Louis XIV.

Thus the Jews were to be made Greeks by garrisons of occupation and executioners; but now
the measure was full and with elemental power
the rebellion burst forth.

The signal for revolt was given by Mattathias,
an aged and respected priest in the little city of
Modein. He slew the captain who was sent to
Hellenize Modein and tore down the altar of Zeus.
Then he cried with a loud voice: "Whoever is
zealous for the law and will remain faithful to

the covenant, let him follow me!" and marched with those who joined him to the mountains. The example had its effect. Everywhere the pious rebelled and withdrew into the mountains and wastes, a veritable "church of the desert."

Such a band was attacked by Syrian troops on the Sabbath ; faithful to the law, they let themselves be slaughtered without raising a hand on the sacred day of rest. Thereupon Mattathias supported by popular decree promulgated the regulation that they were to defend themselves even on the Sabbath, and must do it when attacked. More and more pious enthusiasts gathered about him as a recognized leader. Now Mattathias marched about the country openly destroying the altars and taking the hostile initiative against heathen and Hellenists. But advanced in years as he was, he died in 167 B. C., in the very first beginnings of the agitation, leaving the leadership to his son Judas.

Judas Maccabæus is probably the greatest warrior whom the people of Israel ever produced ; in him the primitive heroic spirit of Israel is revived. But he achieved more than ever it did. In the course of four hundred years the people had become entirely unused to war and weapons, yet with his volunteers, supported by nothing but their faith in God and in the final victory of His holy cause, Judas scattered the largest armies and won victory after victory. He was in truth a warrior of God, who regarded war as a sacred matter and drew his sword only for God and the oppressed faith; in this his pure and ideal inspiration combined with such genius in tactics and strategy he calls to mind spontaneously the great champion of religion, Gustavus Adolphus. His picture is spotless : he did nothing that could throw an unfavorable light upon his character or tarnish his memory. He must be reckoned among the most ideal figures in all history.

Now that a new element had come into the matter with this youthful and fiery soul, the Syrians too gathered their strength together. The commandant of Jerusalem, Apollonius, collected all the available troops, but was defeated by Judas and himself slain; Judas wore all his life the sword of the defeated opponent. Seron, commandant of Syria, fared no better; despite the superiority of his numbers, the host were scattered at Bethhoron, and Judea was free. This took place in the year 166 B. C.

Now Antiochus realized that earnest measures were necessary against the Jewish rebels ; he himself crossed the Euphrates to plunder the rich temples there ; Lysias, the imperial vicegerent, was to suppress the rebellion with half of the forces of the empire. At first Lysias sent three experienced generals : Ptolemy, Nicanor, and Gorgias, with nearly fifty thousand men to Judea to exterminate the Jews, and so impossible did resistance to this mighty force appear that dealers appeared from all quarters to buy up the captive

Jews at an extraordinarily low price fixed in advance. But Judas did not lose courage nor his faith in God. He was stationed with his forces at Mizpah, the Syrians at Emmaus. Gorgias planned to surprise the Jewish camp by night with a small force, but Judas anticipated him and undertook the initiative with an attack on the Syrian camp which resulted in a total defeat for the Syrians and the great army fled in a lamentable condition.

Then the imperial regent Lysias himself undertook the command and invaded Judea from the south with sixty-five thousand men. Judas had only ten thousand with which to oppose him, but again the victory was to the death-defying army; at Bethsura, southward of Jerusalem, Lysias too was defeated and had to seek safety in flight.

After this victory Judas considered the time come to wipe out the insult done the sanctuary : he marched to Jerusalem, and beneath the very eyes of the Syrian garrison, whom Judas held in check, the temple was consecrated anew, all the abominations of idolatry were removed, and on the 25th of December, 165 B. C., that is just three years after the first sacrifice had been offered to Olympian Zeus, once more a burnt offering was smoking according to the regulations of the law of Moses, a sweet savor to God, and this day became a fixed festival for Israel.

Judas restored the overthrown walls of Jerusalem and fortified also Bethsura, where he had won that magnificent victory, in order to block the approach to Jerusalem from the south. But this great success had serious results: everywhere in the surrounding districts began persecutions of the Jews, the Syrians attacking and slaying them. Accordingly Judas with his two brothers, Jonathan and Simon, marched about chastising the heathen and bringing the persecuted Jews to Judea and Jerusalem, where they were received with rejoicings.

But there was still a sharp thorn in their flesh: the citadel of Jerusalem was still in the hands of the Syrians, and the garrison did the Jews much damage. So Judas set about besieging them. At this there came urgent calls for help to Antioch especially from the Hellenistic Jews, and Lysias determined to use all his forces to suppress the rebellion. He gathered 100,000 infantry, 20,000 cavalry, and 32 elephants, and took to the war with him the young king, Antiochus V., who had succeeded his recently deceased father. Again the attack was made from the south. The Syrians besieged Bethsura, and Judas was therefore obliged to leave Jerusalem and hasten to the aid of the hard-pressed fortress.

The forces met at Bethzachariah. Although the Jews again performed marvels of bravery—Eleazar, a brother of Judas, fighting his way through the whole host to a particularly large elephant upon which he supposed the young king

to be, killed the elephant and was himself crushed
to death by the animal in its fall—they were
utterly defeated and themselves besieged in Jerusalem. Bethsura fell, and Jerusalem also was
in great straits, when events in the Syrian Empire
brought relief.

Antiochus Epiphanes on his death-bed had
formally bequeathed to his general Philip the
guardianship of his son together with the regency.
Accordingly Lysias made peace with the Jews in
the name of the young king. They were granted
free exit from the city and perfectly unrestricted
exercise of their religion for all time, but the walls
of Jerusalem were razed to the ground; the fortresses, of course, remained in the hands of the
Syrians. In addition, Lysias executed the high
priest Menelaus as the real instigator of the whole
troublesome affair, and then marched upon Antioch where he quickly conquered Philip. This
was in the year 163 B. C.

With this event we are at a turning-point in
affairs. The object for which the sword had been
drawn was attained, and religious freedom for
all times recognized. In fact, there was one
group, the "pious" as they have been especially
called, standing for exclusively religious interests,
who were satisfied with this and wished nothing
further. If the Syrians had proceeded with moderation and good sense, all would probably have
remained in *statu quo*, and Judea would not have
thought of shaking off the Syrian yoke. But

shortsightedness and infatuation threw everything into confusion again.

In the year 162 B. C., Demetrius, the son of Seleucus IV., the rightful heir, returned to his country, and soon Lysias and Antiochus V. ended their careers under the ax. Now came the question of appointing a successor in the high-priesthood. An Aaronite named Alcimus, accordingly in this respect qualified for the office, applied for the tiara to Demetrius as sovereign; Demetrius conferred it upon him and sent Bacchides with some troops to Judea.

The "pious" were the very ones who met Alcimus with confidence; but Alcimus was a Hellenist through and through, and began his official career with an immoderate attack upon the "pious," so that Judas Maccabæus was compelled to resort to the sword again in self-defense. Alcimus did not feel secure and asked Demetrius for reinforcements. Nicanor was sent to Judea with a large army. He tried first to get possession of Judas by cunning, but Judas did not go into the trap, and so they met in the battle at Caphar-salama. Once more victory was favorable to Judas; Nicanor was obliged to retreat, and on his transit through Jerusalem uttered the most terrible threats against city and temple.

Strengthened by new forces, Nicanor took position at Bethhoron. Judas had but three thousand men at his disposal, but full of confidence in God he threw himself upon the superior force of the enemy. On the 13th of March there was a battle at Adasar; at the very beginning of it Nicanor fell, and the whole army poured out of the country in wild flight. So marvelous was this victory, so evidently was the hand of God in it, that the day was celebrated as the day of Nicanor.

By this time Judas was convinced that only separation from the Syrian Empire could give to the people peace and permanence to religion, and this, political and national independence, but only as a guaranty and indispensable condition of religious freedom, becomes henceforth the conscious object of his struggle and contention.

Immediately after the battle of Adasar, Judas entered into negotiations with Rome, sending two ambassadors to the senate who were to establish a friendly alliance with Rome; the senate, to which any weakening of the Syrian power was welcome, gladly agreed to this. But when the ambassadors returned from Rome all was lost for the time being.

Scarcely had Demetrius received the news of the defeat at Adasar when in the very next month he sent Bacchides with a new and powerful army after Judas. Now the case seemed so hopeless that Judas's troops dwindled to 800 men. But Judas preferred an honorable death to a life in disgrace. With his little band of desperate men he undertook the death struggle at Elasa; all day long the heroic band held its own and even won some points of advantage, but toward evening Judas fell, and with that the fate of the day was determined. His supporters were able to carry off in safety the corpse of the fallen hero and to bury him honorably in the tomb of his fathers at Modein; so even this last battle of Judas was not a real defeat, but his followers could not hide from themselves the fact that they were beaten and defenseless.

Now Alcimus continued his reign of terror, and the Syrian troops and commandants gave him hearty assistance in hunting down and murdering those of the national party. The latter chose Jonathan, the younger brother of Judas, as their leader and withdrew into the desert of Judah and to the east side of the Jordan. A third brother, John, was indeed slain by treachery, but Bacchides could win no permanent advantages in this guerilla war; therefore he had a number of cities fortified and occupied by strong Syrian garrisons and the children of the most prominent Jewish families taken as hostages to the citadel of Jerusalem. And when finally Alcimus died suddenly of apoplexy during the execution of some alteration on the temple, Bacchides left the country in May, 160 B. C.

Jonathan, who of course continued the struggle against the Hellenists with all the means at his disposal, must have made great progress in the next two years, for in 158 B. C. the Hellenists again apply to Demetrius, who again sends Bacchides into the country.

Again Jonathan and Simon withdrew to the desert and carried on a guerilla warfare so successfully and so skilfully that Bacchides caused the leaders of the Hellenistic party, who had persuaded him to undertake the hopeless task, to be executed, and concluded with Jonathan a peace which gave the latter quite his own way in local affairs.

The Hellenistic administration in Jerusalem, indeed, remained under the wing of the Syrian garrison, but 12 miles from Jerusalem, at Michmas, Jonathan set up a regular rival government and was soon *de facto* ruler of the country. And his highest hopes were to be surpassed by the favor of circumstances.

Demetrius was an energetic monarch, and a thorn in the flesh of his neighbors. And now an unparalleled comedy was played. In Smyrna lived an obscure young man, named Alexander Balas, who bore a striking resemblance to Antiochus Epiphanes, and claimed to be his son. The kings of Egypt, Cappadocia and Pergamon actually backed this young man and set him up as claimant to the throne, and the disreputable combination took the field against Demetrius in the summer of 153 B. C.

Now Jonathan was a welcome ally. First Demetrius courted him, appointed him Syrian prefect and returned the hostages. Jonathan immediately appeared before Jerusalem, received the hostages, expelled the Hellenists and began directly to rebuild the walls torn down by Antiochus and

Lysias ; only Bethsura remained in the hands of his opponents.

But Balas too made promises, appointed Jonathan high priest, and sent him the purple robe and golden crown. Jonathan had no hesitation at receiving the pallium from such besmirched hands ; at the feast of tabernacles, in the year 153 B. C., he appeared in public for the first time as high priest, and from this day the office of high priest was reserved to the family of the Maccabees until its extinction.

Thus Jonathan was recognized in fact as ruler of Judea. He remained faithful to Alexander and had no occasion to regret it ; in the year 150 B. C. Demetrius fell and Alexander Balas was king in the empire of the Seleucidæ. The lucky swindler had the presumption to sue to Ptolemy for the hand of his daughter Cleopatra, and actually received it. When the marriage was celebrated, Jonathan too was invited and was overwhelmed with honors by Alexander.

From this weakling, who spent his reign in the most vulgar excesses, there was no danger to be expected ; but in the year 147 B. C. Demetrius II., son of the preceding Demetrius, appeared as claimant to the throne against Alexander. Jonathan remained on the side of Alexander and rendered him important aid : but in the year 145 B. C. the adventurer met a disgraceful death and Demetrius II. became king.

Jonathan had meantime ventured to besiege the

citadel of Jerusalem, when he was summoned to appear before Demetrius. He actually presented himself, but did not immediately raise the siege ; on the contrary, he managed to frighten Demetrius into fulfilling all previous concessions to him and received considerable extensions of his territory and freedom from taxation. Only the citadel of Jerusalem and a few fortresses remained in Syrian hands.

Soon Jonathan was able to show his gratitude. Demetrius had quickly made himself odious, and a general rebellion broke out against him. Trypho, a general of Alexander Balas, set up the latter's little son as anti-king ; even the troops in Antioch deserted Demetrius, who was in such straits that he appealed to Jonathan for help and promised him in return the evacuation of all the remaining places held by Syrian garrisons. Jonathan immediately marched to his aid, and his troops succeeded in suppressing the rebellion and in establishing Demetrius upon his throne. But now that the danger was past, Demetrius had no mind to keep his word. Thereat Jonathan espoused the cause of Trypho, and waged war upon Demetrius so successfully that Jewish arms carried victory beyond Damascus, while his brother Simon finally captured Bethsura, so that the only Syrian garrison remaining was that in Jerusalem.

Jonathan sent an embassy to Rome to renew his alliance, and also made a treaty with Sparta.

Trypho was grateful of course for the help he had received, confirmed the previous concessions and added new ones. But as the advantage turned more and more to his side he became suspicious of the growing power of his Jewish friend and ally. Trypho managed to persuade Jonathan that the maintenance of so large an army was unnecessary in view of their tried friendship. Jonathan actually allowed himself to be deceived, dismissed his troops, and with only one thousand men went to Trypho at Ptolemais. Trypho had the thousand men cut down, took Jonathan prisoner, and moved immediately upon Jerusalem. Simon, the sole surviving brother, came out to meet him; Trypho told him that he had a financial claim against Jonathan, and that he would release Jonathan directly if the money were paid and Jonathan's sons given as hostages. The money and the hostages were actually given up to him, but he did not release Jonathan ; on the contrary, he attempted to take Jerusalem by surprise, but this could not be carried out because of a sudden great snowfall. Thereupon he had Jonathan and his sons murdered, and returned to Syria. This happened in the winter of 143-142 B. C.

In Jonathan we have the real founder of the Maccabean state. He is not to be compared with his brother Judas in moral greatness, but he is a gifted statesman, who understood how to reach his ends by a shrewd use of circumstances, an important character and decidedly a great man.

After the death of Jonathan and his sons, Simon was his recognized successor. Simon naturally put himself into touch with Demetrius, and received from him the confirmation of all previous concessions and in future entire freedom from tribute, which was the recognition in fact of the independence of the Jews from the Syrian dominion. Simon captured the important fortress of Gazara, and finally, on the 23d of May, 142 B. C., the citadel of Jerusalem also capitulated, and Simon celebrated his triumphal entry with great pomp.

Thus the last trace of the Syrian overlordship was extinguished, and Simon was the sovereign ecclesiastical and secular prince of the Jews. And this fact did not fail to receive formal and legal sanction. On the 18th of September, 141 B. C., took place a great popular assembly in which Simon was solemnly confirmed as permanent prince and high priest, and the office declared hereditary in his family. From that day there is again a national Jewish state, and the Jews now reckon dates from the high-priesthood of Simon. Rome, too, whither Simon immediately turned, formally and solemnly recognized him in his offices.

When Simon's father, Mattathias, took the sword twenty-six years before certainly no one could have foreseen the outcome. Will not the fact that the movement ended otherwise than it began finally bring down a judgment upon it?

The spirit is not to be mocked, and nothing can hope for permanence which contains an inner and inherent contradiction. Soon the Maccabees found themselves compelled to combat the very spirit which had carried them and lifted them to the throne; but the idea was superior to violence, and the state of the Maccabees was wrecked upon this inner contradiction.

CHAPTER VIII.

FROM SIMON THE MACCABEAN TO HEROD THE GREAT.

IN the year 141 B. C. the Maccabeans had accomplished all that could be accomplished. Judea was actually independent of the Syrian Empire and this independence was formally acknowledged also by the Syrians, King Antiochus VII. Sidetes having conceded to Simon even the right to coin money, the outward sign of sovereignty. Simon, the last of the five heroic brothers, had become hereditary prince and high priest, the clerical revolt had finally led to the establishment of a secular state. If the incongruity in this was not felt at first it was due to the personality of Simon.

Simon was a genuinely pontifical and at the same time a genuinely royal figure. Upon his venerable gray head tiara and crown could be joined without any evident impropriety. Of absolutely pure character and genuine piety, he exercised his sway in an episcopal spirit as the protector of right and faith, of law and justice : one recalls spontaneously the ideal figures of the clerical princes of the early Middle Ages before the Church had grown worldly. But Simon also conducted his civil rule with circumspection and on a large scale, as is proved by the fact that he conquered Joppa and developed and improved the harbor there with great pains and expense, in order thus to open for his people a direct outlet to the sea. True, Antiochus VII., the last vigorous ruler on the throne of the Seleucidæ, tried again, with shameful disregard of his royal promise, to force Judea into the former subjection to the Syrian Empire; but his general, Kendebeus, was so decisively defeated by Simon's sons at Modein, the birthplace of the Maccabean family, that Simon was left unmolested.

Among the Maccabean rulers Simon is the most brilliant figure and the noblest personality, and his reign one of the happiest periods ever experienced by Israel. And yet it was to close with a harsh dissonance, and Simon, like all four of his brothers, was to die a violent death.

Simon had given to a certain Ptolemy, commandant of the fortress of Dok, near Jericho, one of his daughters in marriage; while on an inspection trip he visited his son-in-law, accompanied by his two sons, and during a banquet which Ptolemy gave for their reception he had his father-in-law and his two brothers-in-law assassinated, in February, 135 B. C.

Ptolemy also sent out assassins against Simon's other son, John, surnamed Hyrcanus; but news of the murder had already reached him; he immediately threw himself with all his troops into

Jerusalem and thus saved the dominion of his house. His first enterprise was of course to avenge the murder of his father and his brothers. He marched to Dok ; but his aged mother was also there, and upon this fact Ptolemy based a fiendish scheme.

When Hyrcanus opened the siege, this monster brought his mother-in-law upon the walls, half naked, had her scourged before the eyes of her son till the blood ran, and threatened to throw her from the wall unless Hyrcanus immediately desisted from the siege. The mother, indeed, conjured her son to ignore her torment : she would gladly endure the most terrible death if only the deserved punishment might overtake the murderer of her husband and her sons ; but Hyrcanus desisted from the siege and contented himself with investing the fortress. And as the sabbatical year began soon after, he raised the siege entirely and withdrew.

Ptolemy now slew the mother also and fled the land of Judea, where of course he was no longer safe. But Hyrcanus was to suffer an even heavier visitation and keener sorrow. Antiochus Sidetes had only deferred his plans, not given them up ; in the very first year of Hyrcanus's rule, 135, B. C., he began a war against him which must have lasted several years and brought Judea to the verge of the abyss.

As far as we can conclude from incidental allusions, Antiochus reconquered the whole country

and finally besieged Jerusalem for more than a
year. A terrible famine ensued and all was given
up for lost when Hyrcanus determined to treat,
and obtained reasonable terms. Such moderation
toward one utterly vanquished is always suspicious : indeed it is not difficult to infer that it was
an utterance from Rome that saved the Jews.
Hyrcanus in his great straits had turned toward
Rome, and Rome did not wish to let Antiochus
grow too mighty; he had to renounce the anticipated prize of his victory, but Hyrcanus became
again wholly subject to the Syrian empire ; the
walls of Jerusalem were razed and Hyrcanus had
to pay tribute and furnish troops.

Thus we see that he accompanied Antiochus in
the year 129 on his great campaign against the
Parthians, and Antiochus, out of consideration
for his Jewish troops, had his whole army rest
for two days because Pentecost and a Sabbath
came that year in immediate succession and the
Jews refused to march on these two days. But
Antiochus fell the following year, 128 B. C., and
from that moment Hyrcanus is again practically
independent.

The last sixty years of Syrian history offer a
disgusting picture of contemptible tricks and
crimes, of quarrels over the succession and of
civil wars ; these degenerate kings were no longer
a real danger for Judea. Hyrcanus now became
a victorious aggressor. He was convinced that
the mere popular militia was no longer sufficient ;

therefore he kept a standing army of mercenaries who, obedient to his every nod, were an ever ready tool in his hand. Plainly he contemplated renewing the kingdom of David. First he advanced victoriously upon the east bank of the Jordan and in the ancient land of Moab; next he captured Shechem and destroyed the Samaritan sanctuary upon Mount Gerizim; then he turned southward against the old land of Edom, subdued this too, and compelled the Idumeans to receive circumcision and the Jewish law.

Finally he advanced upon Samaria. The Samaritans appealed for aid to the neighboring Seleucid, Antiochus IX. Cyzicenus, and Judea was laid waste by Syrian and Egyptian troops; but at last Hyrcanus prevailed, advanced victoriously as far as Scythopolis, and took Samaria after a long and hard siege; the city was razed to the ground and the neighboring brooks diverted across the site.

This is all that we know of the thirty years' reign of Hyrcanus, and we cannot refuse our admiration and recognition for what he accomplished: after the days of Solomon no Israelite ruled over so great and powerful a state as John Hyrcanus.

But what of the high priest? is the involuntary question. The answer is found in the fact, reported by Josephus and the Talmud alike, that under him the conflict with the Pharisees arose. We are told that Hyrcanus at first favored the Pharisees in every way, and sought their favor. On one occasion when he had them all at his table he begged them to remind him openly and honestly when he did anything contrary to the law. Thereupon all the Pharisees were full of his praise; only one *enfant terrible*, Eleazar, said: "If you wish to know the truth, be content with the principality, and give up the high-priesthood." At the suggestion of a Sadducee named Jonathan, Hyrcanus asked the Pharisees what punishment Eleazar deserved for that utterance, and the Pharisees replied: "Forty stripes less one." Hyrcanus, who had expected that they would condemn him to death for blasphemy against his prince, conceived from this moment a deep distrust of the Pharisees, renounced them utterly, and threw himself into the arms of the Sadducees.

Even though the anecdote form of the tradition betray it as unhistorical, the fact itself is beyond question, and results with absolute necessity from the circumstances. The inner incongruity which the extraordinary personality of Simon had hidden was revealed even under his son. In the whole nature of Jewish conditions the priesthood was the capital matter. But for Hyrcanus the tiara had fallen to the rank of a mere decoration; he was a secular prince just like the neighboring heathen kings, his state was a purely secular realm which was no longer able to pursue spiritual aims, no longer had spiritual concerns.

But the most awkward self-contradiction lay in the point which Eleazar had ruthlessly laid bare. The Maccabeans were the champions and pioneers of the law: zeal for the law of Moses had impelled and advanced them; even their political aims and objects found in the law and religion not a pretext, but their real foundation. And now they themselves were violating the law: the very pinnacle of the structure which was founded on the law was a violation of the law. Inasmuch as the Maccabees were not Aaronites, hence not eligible to the high-priesthood, their whole occupancy of the office was illegal, a perpetual violation and mockery of the law, which could be made endurable only by extraordinary ethical merit and personal qualities. As soon as these failed, the dilemma was precipitated.

The Pharisees, wholly proof against all political or national opportunism, remained true to the foundation principles, and on this basis antagonized the Maccabean state and the Maccabean princes, and so these in sheer self-defense were constrained to suppress the spirit which had created and elevated them. Hyrcanus, indeed, was a ruler of such force that he remained master of the situation; but it was a "mene tekel" for the future. The conflict was inevitably to become more violent and burst forth more tremendously just in proportion as the Maccabean rulers developed fewer priestly qualities, and the more baldly and undisguisedly the secular sway became their sole aim and ambition.

And indeed the degeneration of the family that had begun so gloriously made colossal progress ; dominion had demoralized and poisoned them. While the contrast between Hyrcanus and his great father Simon is immense, we find in his two sons and successors personages who remind us of the most corrupt popes of the Renaissance period, of Sixtus IV., Innocent VIII., and Alexander VI.

Hyrcanus died in the year 105 B. C. By will he left the rule to his widow ; the oldest of his two sons, Judas Aristobulus (all the Maccabeans henceforth bear double names, one Jewish and the other Greek) was to succeed him in the high-priesthood only. But Aristobulus let his mother die of hunger in prison, and was the first to adopt with the rule also the royal title, calling himself "King of the Jews." Three of his brothers he had imprisoned ; the fourth he at first trusted blindly, but later, as his distrust was aroused, had him murdered.

In the face of these reports of the Jewish historian Josephus, it strikes us as very strange when a Greek historian calls Aristobulus a humane man and a good ruler. But the puzzle can be explained. Aristobulus called himself officially "Phil-Hellene," the friend of the Greeks, thus boldly denying the principles and the traditions of his family : this explains the partiality of the Greek as well as the dislike of the Jew.

The chief event of his short reign is the conquest and Judaizing of Galilee, whereby he rounded out the realm of the Maccabees and reunited under his scepter all the territories formerly belonging to Israel. But after one short year he died of a hemorrhage. As he left no children, his widow, Alexandra-Salome, merely observed the law in bestowing her hand after her husband's death upon the eldest of his brothers, Jonathan-Alexander or Alexander Jannæus. Thus Alexander Jannæus, the third son of Hyrcanus, became king and high priest, 104 B. C. One brother who was said to be striving for the throne was immediately executed; the fifth, who was quite harmless, was honored as a prince of the blood.

Alexander Jannæus is perhaps the most unattractive and worthless personage in all Jewish history. Even his father, Hyrcanus, despised him, and there was nothing great or good about him to reconcile us to him: his entire reign of twenty-six years was one succession of raids and wars in which he did not even manifest strategic gifts, and of outrages which rank him with the most reprobate characters in history.

He first made a campaign of conquest toward the sea-coast. There Ptolemais, Gaza, and Strato's Tower, ruled over by a certain Zoilus, had not yet been incorporated with the Jewish kingdom. Alexander first attacked Ptolemais. The inhabitants in their need turned for aid to the Egyptian prince, Ptolemy Lathyros, who, expelled from Egypt by his mother, Cleopatra, had established a dominion in Cyprus, and Alexander was obliged to raise the siege. But soon he made friends with Ptolemy, who was a fellow-spirit, and promised him a large sum if he would slay Zoilus and turn the latter's little coast realm over to him. But at the same time Alexander opened negotiations with Cleopatra whereby she was to drive his new bosom friend out of the country. Ptolemy learned of this and began a fearful persecution of unhappy Judea. Alexander was utterly defeated, and Ptolemy gave his troops orders to butcher and cook in the camp-kettles the captive Jewish women and children, in order that the Jews might believe them to be cannibals and have a proper fear of them. But mother Cleopatra actually did come upon the scene and expelled her son from Palestine, compelling him to withdraw to Cyprus. But then Cleopatra wished to confiscate the former Egyptian province, and could be dissuaded from this purpose only by her Jewish general Ananias. Scarcely was Alexander fairly relieved from this danger when he undertook new conquests toward the north, the south, the east, and the west, the details of which are of no interest to us.

Rather is our gaze attracted to the deep domestic difficulties. That this man who passed his whole life in camp among harlots and rowdies was high priest and actually officiated as such on high holidays was too cruel a mockery of every religious sentiment to continue any length of time; the contradiction between ideal and reality had become so sharp that it could no longer be ignored. While officiating at the feast of tabernacles the king even went so far as to express a blasphemous ridicule of the sacred ceremony, whereupon the patience of the people gave out and they threw at the contemptible high priest the lemons which they were carrying for the celebration; the king gave command to his troops to use their swords, and six thousand people perished in the temple on the sacred holiday. Alexander then had a wooden barrier built about the altar to secure him in the future against such material testimonials of the sentiments of his subjects.

The heaped-up tinder needed only a spark to flash out into vivid flames. Alexander began a quarrel with an Arab sheik named Obedas, and in the course of time fell into an ambush from which he barely saved his life. When he arrived in Jerusalem thus, a deserted fugitive, an open rebellion broke out and a six years' war resulted, in which fifty thousand Jews are said to have perished.

Now Alexander thought the time had come to offer the hand of peace, and he asked what was wanted of him, whereupon the Pharisees answered: "Your head." At the same time they appealed for help to the neighboring Seleucid, Demetrius III. Eucairus. Matters came to an issue at Shechem. On the one side stood the Pharisees and the national party in alliance with the Syrians, on the other side the Jewish king and high priest with an army consisting almost exclusively of Greek mercenaries ; Alexander was totally defeated, his army was scattered, and he himself wandered about in the mountains a hunted fugitive.

But now there came a reaction. The Pharisees were ready to accept again subjection to the Syrian Empire. Against this, however, the national instinct rebelled : they deserted to Alexander in troops, Demetrius withdrew from the country, and now the Pharisees were exposed defenseless to the vengeance of the tyrant. They threw themselves into the fortress of Bethome, which, however, was soon captured. Now Alexander led his captives in triumph to Jerusalem, where a terrible judgment awaited them. Eight hundred crosses were set up and all the chiefs of the party were crucified ; before their eyes as they were dying Alexander's executioners butchered their wives and children, while the tyrant, carousing and feasting in the midst of his harlots and dancers, looked on at the horrible spectacle. And this was the Jewish high priest !

Now all who were in any way compromised left the country, and for the remainder of his reign Alexander had domestic peace.

But wars did not cease ; however, we shall pass over their shifting issues. When Alexander had

succeeded in conquering the whole of the country
east of the Jordan he was received in triumph
by the people at Jerusalem. The regions and
cities conquered there were almost wholly Greek,
and this is the only point in which Alexander
manifested his Judaism ; he compelled the conquered Greek cities to submit to circumcision and
the Jewish religion ; if they refused to submit he
destroyed them, as we have evidence in a large
number of cases.

But soon his wild and dissolute life brought
upon him a severe illness. Even then he did not
rest, until at last at the siege of Ragaba his fate
overtook him ; only forty-eight years old, he died
in the year 78 B. C., and is said on his dying bed
to have given his widow the advice to make peace
with the Pharisees and be guided by them.

If this tradition is correct it means that Alexander himself perceived that the work of his life
squandered in adventures was in vain. True, at
the close there was no lack of outward success :
the kingdom which Alexander left at his death
equalled in extent the kingdom of David, but it
is easy to understand that a glory acquired by
such means bore within itself no guaranty of per-
manency. There were two ways of maintaining
it : either the whole must be placed upon an ethical basis and thus be conquered morally after the
physical conquest, or what had been acquired by
violence must be maintained by violence.

At first they tried the first way. Alexander

left two youthful sons : the elder, Hyrcanus, was an indolent, narrow, and incompetent person, the younger, Aristobulus, shrewd, impetuous, and energetic, the image of his father. Alexander had provided in his will that Hyrcanus should succeed him only in the high-priesthood, while the government was to be in the hands of his widow, and this provision was obeyed : Alexandra-Salome was in uncontested possession of the royal power for nine years until her death (78–69 B. C.). She is said to have been a sister of the celebrated Simon ben Shetach, the head at the time of the Pharisees, and there is no question that she was a really pious woman and a sincere adherent of the Pharisaic party.

Thus a complete change of system came about : she had only the name of ruler, the Pharisees the actual rule. For this reason this queen is celebrated and praised by Jewish tradition more than any member of the house of the Maccabees ; her reign is said to have been outwardly a truly Golden Age for Judea.

But now the Pharisees began a reign of terror, and held such bloody reckoning with their ancient enemies that finally a deputation of the Saducean nobility, led by the queen's own son Aristobulus went to her to remonstrate and declare that things could not continue thus, and Alexandra actually checked the vengeance of her friends. Aristobulus and his friends asked for an honorable exile from court in such a form that they might serve their fatherland in the army, and Alexandra turned over to them all the fortresses of the country save three. Moreover Aristobulus waged in her name a war against Damascus, in which, however, he won no laurels.

The great danger to which Judea was exposed from Tigranes, king of the Armenians, who had conquered the shadowy empire of the Seleucidæ, was happily averted. After nine years Alexandra was taken mortally ill. Now Aristobulus thought that the moment for action had come: he withdrew secretly from Jerusalem, made a league with his Sadducean friends and prepared to secure by force the succession to his mother. Before there was any outbreak Alexandra died. Hyrcanus now assumed the crown, but was decisively beaten by Aristobulus at Jericho and compelled to retreat to Jerusalem. Here he had the wife and children of his brother in his power, and thus a compromise was finally concluded by which Hyrcanus retained all his revenues but formally resigned the high-priesthood and the crown to Aristobulus; to seal the compact Alexandra, the only child of Hyrcanus, was betrothed to Alexander, the eldest son of Aristobulus.

Hyrcanus was satisfied with the settlement and would probably have led a life of peace and quiet until his end if fate had not destined him to be forever the plaything of others' passions, a dummy for the intrigues and plans of others. In spite of his abdication he was after all and remained the legitimate heir of the house of the Maccabees, and that was his doom.

The Jewish general who served as prefect in Idumea was a certain Antipater, whose father, of the same name, had enjoyed the especial confidence of Alexander Jannæus. This man, for whose ambitious plans the weakling Hyrcanus was better adapted than the energetic Aristobulus, devoted himself to a systematic instigation of the abdicated ruler and to making sentiment for him among the people. At first Hyrcanus would not hear of the matter, but finally Antipater represented so persistently that his life was in danger at the hands of his brother, that he actually permitted himself to be persuaded to flee from Jerusalem to the Arab sheik Aretas, who proposed, in consideration of a promise to restore the Arabian territory conquered by Alexander Jannæus, to reëstablish him in his kingdom. In fact a war resulted and Aristobulus was utterly defeated, being compelled to take refuge in the temple at Jerusalem, where Aretas and Hyrcanus besieged him.

In this connexion Josephus reports two characteristic details. There lived at that time an especially pious man named Onias, to whose prayers miraculous efficacy was attributed. He was brought before the temple to pronounce a curse upon Aristobulus. But Onias said: "Almighty God! Those beside me are thy people, the besieged are thy priests; therefore neither hear those nor help these." But this conciliatory mood was not in accord with the wishes of his employers, and Onias was forthwith stoned to death.

But now Pascha came on. The beleaguered priests wished most urgently to celebrate Pascha, and begged the besiegers humbly to admit to them the necessary animals for sacrifice. For each separate animal the immense sum of one thousand silver shekels was demanded, and the requisite sum was actually let down over the walls. The besiegers pocketed the money but did not furnish the animals.

But the last word already belonged to Rome, which was just preparing to give the "sick man" in Syria the finishing stroke. Pompey had conquered Mithradates and subdued Tigranes of Armenia, and was now making a clean sweep of Asia. He first sent a legate, Scaurus, into Syria to look after things. The legate went also into Judea. Aristobulus, who well knew how to treat the Romans of that day, promised Scaurus a large sum of money; Hyrcanus could not fall behind his brother, and promised a like sum. But Scaurus decided in favor of Aristobulus and commanded the Arabian king to raise the siege of Jerusalem forthwith. Aretas ventured no opposition, and on his retreat Aristobulus inflicted upon him a severe defeat.

This was a great temporary success for Aristobulus, but the final decision still lay in the hands of Pompey. Next year he came in person. Aristobulus tried to win his favor by a valuable present; in Damascus the two brothers appeared before his tribunal, and at the same time a Jewish delegation which urged Pompey to abolish the royal dignity altogether and to restore the old sacerdotal constitution in accordance with the law. Pompey was dilatory in the matter and directed all parties for the present to keep the peace; but Aristobulus had no confidence in the truce and prepared for resistance. Now Pompey marched into Judea; when the Romans appeared before Jerusalem Aristobulus lost courage; he surrendered to Pompey and promised also to turn the city over to him, but the lieutenant-general, Gabinius, who was to make the entry, found the gates closed. Although there was no evidence of a breach of faith on the part of Aristobulus, Pompey, angered by this, threw him into chains and prepared to take the city by force.

In Jerusalem the parties were not harmonious. The adherents of Hyrcanus saw in the Romans allies, while the adherents of Aristobulus were determined to resist to the utmost; they withdrew into the temple, while the city surrendered to the Romans. Three months the siege of the temple lasted; finally, on the Day of Atonement in the year 63 B. C., the younger Sulla, a son of the dictator, led the scaling of the wall, and then began a frightful massacre; the priests, who refused to desist from their ceremonies, were cut down at the altar, and twelve thousand persons met their death in the temple.

Pompey held his entry, and, despite the most urgent protests, entered the Holy of Holies, though he left the treasures of the temple untouched. The leaders of the war party were executed, the walls of Jerusalem razed, and all lands not hereditary Jewish possessions were sequestrated and added to the new Roman province of Syria ; over what remained was placed the reappointed high priest Hyrcanus, as tributary Roman vassal without the royal title.

Aristobulus and his four children were taken to Rome ; the eldest son, Alexander, succeeded in escaping on the way ; the other three, together with their father, were compelled to walk in front of the chariot of the "imperator" as a spectacle for the Roman populace on the occasion of the great triumph of Pompey in the year 61.

In Judea the all-powerful man was now Antipater, who managed to make himself ever more indispensable to Hyrcanus, and actually exercised whatever authority the Romans thought best to leave in Jewish hands. The sole ambition of both these men was to make themselves popular with their new lords and useful to them.

We have little positive knowledge of the whole succeeding period. In the year 57 B. C. Alexander, the son of Aristobulus, who had escaped, undertook a revolutionary incursion into Judea, and actually gained some successes at first ; but when the Romans took the matter seriously he had to surrender. The fortresses were razed, but Alexander himself got off easily, probably, because he treated the Roman general in the right way, that is, with clinking arguments.

In order to repress any new disposition to revolt Gabinius divided the country into five independent districts, each of which had its own sanhedrin like that at Jerusalem; all that was now left to Hyrcanus was the high-priesthood. But in the very next year, 56, Aristobulus himself with his younger son Antigonus, succeeded in escaping from Rome and raising the standard of revolt. He was received with rejoicings, but was soon once more a Roman prisoner; he was sent to Rome and kept now in close confinement, while his children were liberated. The following year young Alexander tried his fortune again, but accomplished nothing, despite the enthusiastic support which he found.

The next year, 54 B. C., was to show the Jews what they might expect from the Romans. The triumvir Crassus visited Jerusalem and actually sacked the temple: he is said to have carried off partly in coin, partly in other valuables, ten thousand talents, that is, about nine million dollars. Now there broke out under the lead of a certain Pithalaus a new rebellion, the only results of which were that the ringleader was executed and thirty thousand Jews sold into slavery.

With the year 49 B. C. begins the great crisis

in ancient history marked by the Roman civil wars. The fate of Judea is henceforth dependent on the destinies of Rome, and is the mere echo of the latter's fluctuant events. Cæsar, in order to make trouble for Pompey in the Orient, released the captive Aristobulus and was about to send him to Judea at the head of two legions, but the adherents of Pompey poisoned him ; his body was embalmed and deposited later in the tomb of the Maccabees. Now his son, the old enemy of Rome, became an object of suspicion, although he had made no move as yet ; at the express command of Pompey he was prosecuted and beheaded at Antioch on account of his former crimes against the Roman people.

When the destiny of Rome was decided at Pharsalia, Hyrcanus and Antipater immediately went over to the victor, and were able to render him such material service on his Egyptian campaign that the full favor of Cæsar rested upon them in the rearrangement of Syrian affairs. True Antigonus, the younger son of Aristobulus, appeared and called attention to the fact that his father and his elder brother had lost their lives in the service of Cæsar ; but Cæsar was too practical a politician to be accessible to the suggestions of sentiment. Antigonus withdrew with empty hands.

Cæsar abolished the division of the country introduced by Gabinius, confirmed Hyrcanus in the high-priesthood, and appointed him ethnarch of the whole country ; Antipater received the title of procurator, as well as Roman citizenship and exemption from taxation. Cæsar also permitted the restoration of the walls of Jerusalem which had been destroyed by Pompey, and in general showed the Jews especial favor in order to attach to himself and his cause this race which was already an international power. Thus it is expressly reported that the death of Cæsar was mourned by no other people so sincerely as by the Jews.

Who the actual ruler was in Judea was soon to appear through a striking instance. Antipater had appointed his two sons, Phasael and Herod, as generals. In this capacity Herod had defeated and captured in Galilee, Hezekiah, a so-called robber chief, that is, a volunteer soldier hostile to Rome, and had executed the whole band in short order. The sanhedrin saw in this an infringement of its rights. Herod was summoned to Jerusalem. He came, indeed, but at the head of a strong military force, and appeared defiantly before the sanhedrin. For Hyrcanus, who presided over the sanhedrin, had received from Sextus Cæsar, the legate of Syria, an explicit command to acquit Herod. But the Pharisee Shammai, the most distinguished member of the sanhedrin, was not to be intimidated; he declared openly that Herod deserved death, and that the sanhedrin, if it acquitted him, would incur a heavy guilt which Herod himself would some day severely punish. After this speech, which made a deep impression upon the sanhedrin, Hyrcanus adjourned the session and advised Herod to withdraw secretly from Jerusalem. Herod did so, but soon returned with a still greater force, and could be dissuaded from an attack upon Jerusalem only with the greatest difficulty.

At this point the death of Cæsar changed the whole situation instantly. One of the murderers of Cæsar, Cassius, went to Asia, and soon all the Roman troops there swore allegiance to him. Then Antipater and Herod made haste to show the new master their devotion, and were especially steadfast in satisfying the financial wants of the ever impecunious Cassius. Suddenly Antipater died of poison. A certain Malichus had been endeavoring to acquire the same influence over Hyrcanus that Antipater exercised, and so had the latter poisoned ; but he was not to reap the reward of his deed, for soon assassins hired by Herod put an end to him.

In the midst of this general confusion there were again new disturbances in Judea. In Jerusalem a certain Helix rebelled against Phasael, and in the north Antigonus, the youngest surviving son of Aristobulus, made an incursion into Galilee ; both uprisings were suppressed only with difficulty. Then came the day of Philippi : the glory of Cassius was past and Antony was ruler of Asia. The position of Herod, who owed everything to Cæsar, was critical, and made worse by the fact that a delegation of Jews was marching to meet Antony, bearing most serious charges against Herod and Phasael. But Antony had known Herod personally in earlier days, and in them were two congenial souls who could not fail to please each other. Antony dismissed the accusers and appointed Herod and Phasael as tetrarchs, thereby merely legalizing the actual situation ; Hyrcanus retired altogether into his high-priesthood.

But soon a remarkable chain of circumstances was to call once more a Maccabee to the throne of Judea. In the year 40 occurred that fearful invasion of the Parthians which brought all Asia into their hands. Antigonus now entered into negotiations with the Parthians and promised them a thousand talents of gold and five hundred of the fairest Jewish maidens if they would restore him to the kingdom of his father, Aristobulus. Against these hosts all resistance was in vain. Herod found safety in a daring flight, Phasael and Hyrcanus fell into the power of the Parthians. Phasael dashed out his brains in prison ; Hyrcanus, after his ears had been cut off at the command of his nephew in order to permanently disqualify him for the high-priesthood, was dragged away into captivity by the Parthians.

Thus Antigonus was king and high priest by the grace of the Parthians, and maintained himself in this position for three years, from 40 to 37 B. C. His Hebrew name was Mattathias, so that this last degenerate descendant bore the same name as the glorious founder of the family. The history of his reign is really only the history of its loss.

Herod had succeeded in escaping to his friend Antony in Rome. Antony managed also to interest Octavius in him, and thus there was issued in the year 39 B. C. a decree of the senate appointing Herod king of Judea. True, he had first to conquer his kingdom. He immediately went thither, and would probably have taken Jerusalem directly had not the Roman generals, who by Antony's direction were to support him, been bribed by Antigonus to hinder him in every way. Not even in the year 38 B. C. had he attained entire success. But now Antony himself went to Asia and sent his legate, Sosius, with explicit commands to Judea, where meantime a great massacre had taken place among the adherents of Herod. Aided by Sosius, Herod overcame all opposition, and only the approach of winter gave Antigonus a brief respite.

In the spring of 37 B. C. the siege of Jerusalem was undertaken with all vigor. While it was going on Herod married Mariamne, the grandchild of both Hyrcanus and Aristobulus, thus uniting in himself the claims of both brothers and their families. After a siege of forty days the first wall was taken, after fifteen days more the second; but Antigonus still maintained himself in the temple. Finally in the third month, on a Sabbath, the temple was stormed and a fearful slaughter began, for the Romans, embittered by the long resistance, spared neither age nor sex.

Thus King Herod entered his capital. In womanish distress Antigonus threw himself at the feet of the Roman legate, begging for his life; Sosius exclaimed in scorn: "Arise, Antigona," using the feminine form of the name, and had him put into chains. At Antioch his head fell under the ax of the Roman lictor—it was the first captive ruling monarch whom the Romans had ever executed like a common criminal.

Herod's first care was to get rid of his friends and assistants without trouble; he actually bribed Sosius and the Roman troops, at great personal sacrifice, to abstain from the plundering of Jerusalem and the entering and desecration of the temple, and so they marched away leaving Herod behind in his kingdom.

First Herod made a clean sweep of his enemies and opponents, and sought to keep the people, who feared and hated him, in terror and subjection. In order to show that he did not shrink from the memories of the Maccabees, he recalled to Jerusalem old Hyrcanus, who was honored as a prince of the Jews in Babylon, and at the same time selected a Jew of the race of the high priests, Ananiel by name, then living in Babylon, in order that the high priesthood should be conferred upon him.* But Herod's mother-in-law, Alexandra, demanded this office for her son Aristobulus, although he was as yet very young. She managed to work every lever, especially with the Egyptian Cleopatra, who completely dominated the all-powerful Antony, and so Herod was obliged to remove Ananiel and appointed in his place as high priest his own seventeen-year-old brother-in-law, Aristobulus. This was in the year 35, B. C.

But when Aristobulus, on the occasion of his first appearance as high priest, at the feast of tabernacles, was received by the people with demonstrative rejoicing, Herod had him stifled in his bath. True, Antony called him to account for this; but Herod knew how to manage Antony, and again they parted the best of friends. It was a less agreeable matter when Antony made a present to Cleopatra of the best part of Herod's land, and Herod was obliged to rent it of her at a high rate. Soon after this Cleopatra paid a visit to Herod in Jerusalem, and planned to snare him in her net in order thus through the resulting jealousy of Antony to destroy him; but Herod saw through the fine plan and acted toward his guest like a perfect cavalier indeed, but with such reserve and propriety as to afford not the least ground for suspicion.

In the year 32 B. C. the war between Antony

* Hyrcanus had been disqualified from filling the office by the mutilation described p. 230.—*Trans.*

and Octavius broke out. Fortune spared Herod from participation, for he was compelled by the command of Antony to wage a war in the interest of Cleopatra against the Arabian king Malchus, and when this war was over it was also all over with Antony : the battle of Actium was fought on the 2nd of September, 31 B. C., and Antony was a dead man.

Now the game was to win the new ruler, and in this again Herod showed his whole cunning and knowledge of men : he visited Augustus in person at Rhodes, having first, to meet contingencies, put old Hyrcanus out of the way. And thus the last Maccabee was gone, and the family that had begun so gloriously less than a hundred and forty years before had perished most ignobly at least as much by the fault of its younger and unworthy members as by what we must admit was a harsh destiny. Herod managed to win over Augustus entirely, and returned to Jerusalem confirmed as king ; he held the throne without opposition until his death in the year 4 before the birth of Christ.

The history of the reign of Herod is a history of palace details. Events of universal importance did not occur, and Herod followed his single principle— the favor and friendship of the Romans at any cost—so successfully and skilfully that not even the slightest cloud threatened him. But the history of his court is such a bottomless sea of filth and blood that I spare myself and the reader the narration of things at which the guardian genius of humanity can only veil his face. A wife who was passionately loved, his mother-in-law and three sons fell victims to his suspicion and tyranny, and in the country as well every hint or motion of opposition was suppressed with barbarous severity.

Herod was certainly an extraordinary man, decidedly the first really important personage in Jewish history since Simon. He was a born ruler, and his rule might and indeed must have been a blessing for his land and people if there had not been a lack of mutual confidence and love. Even in the best acts and undertakings of the hated monarch the Jews saw only evil intentions and selfish motives, and they hampered him in every possible way. He was simply the Idumean semi-Jew, the friend of the Romans, whose heart was on the side of the heathen anyway, and who would gladly have made them all heathen. Herod in turn repaid this hatred with the fiercest hostility and the most implacable vengeance ; he knew that his own subjects were his worst enemies, and he acted accordingly.

It would be folly to deny that the outward condition of Judea under his rule was fortunate : he secured peace within and without, commerce flourished, prosperity increased visibly, and the great popularity which the king enjoyed everywhere else cast also a ray upon the people he ruled, and Herod used his very considerable influence everywhere for their benefit : wherever a wrong was done the Jews, he interfered in their behalf and protected them in their rights and privileges.

So there would have been every outward reason for content ; Judea under the government of Herod enjoyed in abundance what in the common view constitutes the happiness of nations—but he received no thanks for this because the people could not believe that it came from pure motives, and because they did not wish to accept, or at least to acknowledge, benefits from the hand of the friend of the heathen. Even repeated remission of taxes and extravagant aid in cases of public misfortune could bring forth no love where none had been sown ; not even by the splendid restoration of the temple could he win the hearts of the Jewish people, because they were convinced that he would much rather have built in Jerusalem a heathen temple.

Aftertimes called Herod "the Great." He had the making of a great man ; he was of the wood from which great men are carved, and in more favorable circumstances he would have been one perhaps ; but as it was he wore out his strength and his life upon a hopeless task and thus brought upon his people and himself indescribable misery.

The reign of Herod is perhaps the most convincing evidence that there are powers which are stronger than crown and sword, and that violence avails nothing against the spirit. When Herod died in the spring of the year 4 before the birth of Christ, unlamented by his own, cursed by his people, a far-seeing eye could already perceive unmistakable signs of the end.

At home a mass of hatred and hostility had accumulated which only the iron hand of the old king had been able to restrain, and the real ambition of his life, to make the Roman rule tolerable to the Jews and to absorb them into the Greco-Roman world, had been an utter failure; contempt and loathing of everything Roman and Greek had become deeper seated than ever—when these two opposites clashed, the result could not fail to be a life and death struggle. Could it have been avoided? To do so would in any case have required on the part of the Romans more than human wisdom and moderation, and on the part of the Jews more than angelic patience and self-denial. But neither side wished to avoid it. We shall see how arbitrary injustice and wicked arrogance made the already difficult situation absolutely intolerable, so that at last the hopelessly tangled knot had to be cut by the sword.

CHAPTER IX.

THE HOUSE OF HEROD—JUDEA AS A ROMAN PROVINCE.

IT was a moment of intense interest at which we closed our last chapter. Everywhere there was ferment and repressed excitement; the peace established by the iron hand of Herod was but the peace of the churchyard. Even in the last days of the tyrant the flames began to shoot up. While he was still wrestling with death upon his bed of suffering at Jericho the report was spread that he was dead, and straightway open rebellion broke forth against him and his system.

Over the chief entrance to the temple Herod had had placed a golden eagle as a sign of the Roman sovereignty. Some forty young pupils of the highly respected Pharisees Judas and Matthias climbed up and with axes cut the golden eagle to pieces. The perpetrators were at once seized by the guard and, together with their two teachers, dragged to Jericho, where Herod condemned them and had them all burned alive. Soon after this, in the spring of the year 4 before the birth of Christ, he himself died.

I assume that my esteemed readers are already aware of the fact that Abbot Dionysius Exiguus, who in the sixth century calculated the Christian era according to which we still universally reckon time, erred in his establishment of the year of Christ's birth, placing it several years, probably five, if not seven, too late. It is positively certain that Herod died in the year 4 before our era; if, therefore, Jesus was born during his reign—and there is no reason for doubting this tradition—the conclusion is unavoidable that the date commonly assigned for the birth of Christ is wrong. The place of Jesus' birth is just as much a matter of uncertainty as the time; and so is the year of his death,—in this latter point reports and estimates vary a matter of seven years, from 29 to 36 A.D.

It is downright providential that we know so little from the historical and biographical point of view concerning this greatest life that was ever lived on earth. Thus every possibility is to be precluded of our falling into the delusion that we know him in knowing the date of his birth and of his death and the outward circumstances of his life; he is to stand before us simply in his work.

The life and activity of Jesus fell into the period of Jewish history which is to occupy our attention in this chapter, and his activity was possible only on the soil of Israel and among the Jewish people; but yet a history of the people of

Israel is not the place in which to speak of him.
He swept across the hopelessly darkened sky of
Israel like a meteor, flashing and vanishing; he
had no effect upon the history of the Jewish
people, and the fact that he did not do this, that
he deliberately refused to do so, became, humanly
speaking, his doom. His people and his time
demanded a Messiah with the sword of Gideon,
one who would break the dominion of Rome
and re-establish the ardently longed-for kingdom of Israel. Jesus regarded it as his mission
to break the power of sin and to establish the
Kingdom of God, which is not accomplished with
the sword of outward power but through the inward regeneration of the spirit. In the invincible faith that this Kingdom of God would and
must come, Jesus went to his death. But on his
way to death he had for his people only this affecting farewell: "Daughters of Jerusalem, weep
not for me, but weep for yourselves and for your
children" (Luke xxiii. 28).

Herod had a numerous family—nine wives and
nine sons and five daughters. He had himself
caused his three oldest sons to be executed, and
had frequently altered his will; the last form of
it, composed shortly before his death, divided the
kingdom among three of the surviving sons.
Archelaus was to receive the royal title together
with Judea, Samaria, and Idumea; Herod Antipas, Galilee and Perea; and Philip the northern
districts, the two latter with the title of tetrarch.

The confirmation of the will was of course dependent on Augustus, and Herod by testamentary provision had commissioned Archelaus and Antipas to carry his seal-ring and the sealed documents to Rome immediately after his death. But before attending to this Archelaus was saluted as king by the troops and the people and celebrated his father's obsequies with a pompous, seven days' ceremony. Then he addressed the people and promised to be a good ruler, and especially to be more clement than his father. They immediately took him at his word, and demanded that he remove the unworthy high priest last appointed by his father and put a worthier one in his place, and likewise that he should punish those councillors of his father who had condemned the two Pharisees and their pupils to such a terrible death for destroying the golden eagle over the temple gate. Archelaus wanted to avoid a conflict before his journey to Rome, and sent delegates to the people to pacify them, but these delegates were received with showers of stones and sent back with scoffs and jeers.

They were in the midst of preparations for Pascha, and for this reason there was an immense concourse in Jerusalem; the dissatisfied multitude took possession of the temple in order to compel compliance with their demands. Now Archelaus sent a tribune with a cohort to the temple to establish order, but almost the entire cohort was stoned to death by the excited popu-

lace; the tribune barely saved his life with a
few of his followers. Now of course the whole
available military force had to be called out to
storm and purge the temple. Three thousand
corpses covered the floor of the sanctuary. All
pilgrims from without the city received peremptory
orders to return home straightway.
Order being thus restored, Archelaus started
upon his journey to Rome. In Cæsarea he met a
Roman official, Sabinus, who purposed to take
present charge of Herod's heritage. Archelaus
tried to restrain him, but of course Sabinus pursued
his way, and to make him secure Quintilius
Varus, at that time legate in Syria, the same
who attained such a melancholy renown by his
defeat in our Teutoburg forest, gave him one of
his three legions.

Sabinus treated the country after the usual
fashion of Roman provincial officials; this aroused
such bitterness that an unusually large number
of pilgrims came to Jerusalem for the celebration
of Pentecost and actually besieged Sabinus. The
Jews having taken possession of the porches of
the temple and thrown thence weapons and stones
upon the heads of the Romans, Sabinus set fire to
the porches so that the Jews perished miserably
in the flames. The temple was stormed and of
course plundered; Sabinus is said to have stolen
for his own treasury four hundred talents, that
is considerably over $500,000.

Now open rebellion broke forth throughout the

country. Everywhere there gathered bands which slaughtered all the Romans and all the adherents of Herod whom they could capture. Sabinus sent to Varus for help, and the latter entered the rebellious country with all the troops at his disposal. How he conducted himself can be imagined. Plundered and burned cities whose inhabitants had been slaughtered or sold into slavery marked the route of the victorious Roman army. Varus entered Jerusalem and there had two thousand of the ringleaders crucified at one time ; after these valiant deeds he left the pacified country and returned to Antioch.

Meanwhile the two brothers had presented a very discreditable scene in Rome. Each sought to exclude the other and to get possession of as great a share as possible of his father's heritage, while at the same time there appeared a delegation of the Jewish people praying for the removal of the whole Herodian family in order that they might live according to their own laws under immediate Roman overlordship. Now Augustus was obliged to come to a decision. He confirmed the last testament of Herod in its main features, merely denying Archelaus the royal title for the time being and requiring him to be satisfied with that of ethnarch.

The destinies of the three brothers developed in great divergence. The only attractive figure in the whole Herodian family, a genuine white raven, is Philip. And it is to be remembered in this connection that the portions of the country over which he ruled were almost entirely heathen and the Jews in a great minority, a fact which made government much easier. According to Josephus he carried on a search for the sources of the Jordan which lie in his territory. He rebuilt Paneas and Bethsaida; thenceforth the former was called Cæsarea Philippi, the latter Julias. Josephus gives the following sketch of him: "He was well-disposed and kind toward his subjects, without ambition, and never left his country his whole life long. He always went about with a small retinue and had a tribunal-seat carried about after him in order to be able to pass forthwith upon any petition which might be presented by whoever met him." He died in the year 33 A. D., after a reign of thirty-seven years, leaving no children; thereupon Tiberius sequestered his country and added it to the province of Syria.

The second son, Herod Antipas, is the sovereign of Jesus, and is characterized by him as a fox; it was he that had John the Baptist executed. We know of him only by his architectural constructions, his founding of cities, and the serious scandal in his domestic relations which cost the Baptist his life. The most important city founded by him is Tiberias, on the west shore of the Sea of Galilee, named in honor of the Emperor Tiberius. In laying the foundations it turned out that there had been on the spot an ancient burial-place with quantities of skeletons. This made the spot unclean, and pious Jews refused to dwell there, so that Antipas was finally constrained to settle the city with the most questionable elements. It had a wholly heathen character, and at the outbreak of war the wrath of the people was directed first of all against these edifices and they were destroyed. The final complications and the close of his forty-three years' reign, which all arose from his sinful union with his brother's wife, Herodias, will receive our attention hereafter in another connection.

Of briefest endurance was the reign of Archelaus, who exercised his authority almost exclusively in the appointment and removal of high priests, incidentally erecting some edifices. He too gave deep offense by his marriage with Glaphyra, the widow of his half-brother Alexander. Besides this a false Alexander soon made his appearance. Alexander, the eldest son of Herod and Mariamne the Maccabee, would have been the regular heir to the throne. So a young man with a striking resemblance to him claimed to be Alexander, reporting that the executioner, moved by pity, had failed to carry out the command of Herod, but had substituted a corpse that looked like him. This youth was received everywhere with shouts of rejoicing by the Jews, and even had the impudence to go to Rome in order to demand his inheritance at the hands of Augustus ; but Augustus, who had been personally acquainted with the real Alexander, saw through the fraud directly and sent the adventurer to the galleys.

After Archelaus had ruled for nine years in barbarity and tyranny, as Josephus puts it, his subjects made charges against him to Augustus, who immediately summoned him to Rome. The charges were so serious that Augustus deposed him without ceremony and banished him to Vienne in Gaul, where he had time, far from Jerusalem, to meditate upon the duties of a ruler. The principality of Archelaus was sequestered and put under immediate Roman government; a procurator of noble rank was to rule it subject to the legate for the province of Syria.

Thus the people had attained what they had themselves requested ten years earlier, but they were soon to realize with terror what a yoke they had thereby brought upon their own necks. The moment when Judea came under immediate Roman government, in the year 6 A. D., is the beginning of the end. While Herod and his sons from mere shrewdness and for self-preservation had shown all possible consideration for the religious convictions of the Jews, they were now exposed without rights or defense to the whims of Roman subaltern officials who regarded their office first of all as a gold mine, had absolutely no appreciation of the character and position of the Jews, but on the contrary regarded them with dislike and contempt and took a fiendish delight in making the unfortunate race feel their power and in offending and mocking them in every conceivable manner.

When we read of the actions and tyrannical usurpations of these "stewards," who almost without exception were pests, it seems often incomprehensible that the Jews endured such conditions for sixty years. The procurator had his official residence in the city of Cæsarea, which had been splendidly built up and beautified by Herod. Only on the occasion of the great religious festivals were they accustomed to come to Jerusalem in order to keep an eye on the multitudes gathered there; then they occupied the palace of Herod, which served as prætorium. They had control of all military and financial matters and were referees in affairs of justice: capital sentences, especially, pronounced by the sanhedrin, required their confirmation. As a token of the heathen overlordship which was felt by the Jews to be especially hard and oppressive, the Romans had taken under their charge the high priest's robe; it was kept in the prætorium which was occupied by a cohort that served as permanent garrison of Jerusalem, and was brought out for use in the temple only four times a year, at the three high feasts and on the day of atonement, but had to be returned every time immediately after it had been used.

The very first experience of the Roman rule showed what was to be expected on both sides.

Augustus caused a census of the new province to be taken by the Syrian legate P. Sulpicius Quirinus, thereon to base a readjustment of the taxes. At this, open rebellion broke forth on every side. The high priest Joazar, indeed, by shrewd and conciliatory management, succeeded in avoiding the worst consequences and in bringing the people to reason; but the irreconcilables now formed a regular faction, the enthusiasts or Zealots, whose only aim was to oppose the Roman dominion by every possible means and never to permit a compromise between Israel and Rome; the leaders of the party are reported to have been the Galilean Judas (very probably a son of Hezekiah, the judicial execution of whom had once brought Herod into conflict with the sanhedrin at Jerusalem) and a Pharisee named Shadduck. Thus from the start, civil war was latent and revolution was declared as a standing condition.

Under such trying circumstances it would of course have required persons of extraordinary tact to avoid adding new stores to the already great mass of tinder. But these procurators were no better, rather worse if possible, than they generally were at that period. Of the first four we know scarcely more than their names. From the time of Coponius, the first of them, Josephus tells us how some Samaritans slipped into the temple during the Pascha period and strewed all about the temple human bones which they had carried hidden under their cloaks; thus the temple was made unclean for seven days, and Pascha could not be celebrated at all. The fourth of them, Valerius Gratus, appointed and removed not less than five high priests during his eleven years of office. We have more details concerning only the fifth of the series, Pontius Pilate, who tormented the Jews from 26 to 36 A. D., and earned a melancholy immortality through the destiny which, supported by his uneasy conscience, condemned him to pronounce upon Jesus the sentence of death and have it executed.

Up to this time the religious views of the Jews had been treated with the utmost possible consideration, and at least all wanton conflicts had been avoided ; in particular the military standards with the image of the emperor, which were especially offensive to the Jews, had been kept away from Jerusalem. This seemed to Pilate a lamentable weakness, and one night he caused some of these images to be brought to Jerusalem. When the Jews saw the abomination the next morning there set out for Cæsarea a deputation en masse, thousands of men, women and children who beset the procurator for five days and nights with their cries and lamentations. Pilate declared that the honor of the emperor would not permit the revocation of the order ; finally he invited them to gather in the stadium at the end of six days, when he would give them his decision. He caused the whole stadium to be surrounded by soldiers who awaited only his nod to fall upon the defenseless host. After they were all assembled in the stadium he announced that the standards would and must remain in Jerusalem ; and when a loud outcry and lamentation answered him he ordered the soldiers to advance. Then the Jews of their own accord bared their necks and breasts, begging Pilate to kill them all in order that they might not be constrained to witness such a sacrilege. This persistence and desperation moved Pilate to recede from his position : he dismissed the Jews and the standards were in fact quietly removed from Jerusalem.

But Pilate hoped to gain his end indirectly. He caused to be hung up on the walls of the prætorium in Jerusalem votive tablets with only the name of the emperor and of himself as the one offering them. Again the Jews beset Pilate to recall the offensive order, but this time he was inexorable. Thereupon they appealed directly to Tiberius, who, seeing that Pilate cared less to honor him than to offend the Jews, commanded the tablets to be removed and hung up in the temple of Augustus which Herod had built at Paneas. Encouraged by this success, the Jews opposed Pilate even where religious scruples were not so distinctly involved. Pilate recognized the need of a water system for Jerusalem, and for this public labor demanded a contribution from the treasury of the temple. When he came to Jerusalem to inspect the construction he was again surrounded by a screaming and groaning mob ; but Pilate had known or foreseen what was to come, and had given orders to his soldiers to mingle with the multitude dressed in civilians' garb and with clubs under their cloaks. At a sign from him they burst forth and with their clubs slew a great number of people. The construction was completed without further disturbance.

In an official document addressed to the Emperor Caligula, Pilate is described as inflexible and unsparingly harsh in character, and his administration as an unbroken series of outrages and crimes of every sort : venality, violence, plunder, abuse, insults, continual executions without sentence, and infinite and unbearable cruelties.

Thus we can understand well when we are told that Barabbas, a notorious murderer familiar to us in connection with the Passion of Jesus, was captured in an uprising, and that Pilate mingled the blood of Galileans with their sacrifices, that is to say, evidently had to suppress an insurrection of Galileans that had broken out in the temple. But finally the unhappy people were to be released from their tormentor. The Samaritans believed that the ancient and sacred vessels of the tabernacle were buried on Mount Gerizim and that they would appear again at the approach of the Messianic period. A zealot or a fraud invited the people to gather at Mount Gerizim with a promise to show them there the sacred vessels. Pilate had heard of the affair, and had the whole multitude of innocent people incontinently hacked to pieces. For this the Samaritans brought charges against him before the Syrian legate, Vitellius, who suspended him from his office immediately and sent him to Rome to answer to the charges. Of the two successors of Pilate we know only the names.

At Pascha in the year 36 A. D. the legate Vitellius came himself to Jerusalem and took the hearts of the Jewish people by storm by giving back the high priest's robe and having it taken back to the temple for free use on all occasions. This same Vitellius shows how easy it was with even a modicum of good will to avoid conflicts. Herod Antipas, in order to marry his sister-in-law, Herodias, had put away his first wife, a daughter of the Arab sheik Aretas, and as a result got into a war with his former father-in-law, which was turning out very unfortunately for himself. Accordingly he applied to Rome for aid and Tiberius commanded Vitellius to punish the Arab sheik. Vitellius, who had no liking at all for Antipas, was not eager to do this, but of course was obliged to obey the imperial command. He set out upon his expedition from Antioch. At the border of the Holy Land he was met by a Jewish deputation with the urgent petition not to conduct his army with the imperial images through Jewish territory. Vitellius, being a humane and considerate man, actually had his troops go around the Jewish country and went alone to Jerusalem, where he was received with tremendous enthusiasm. Here he received the news of the death of Tiberius and returned in haste to Antioch without having taken the field against Aretas.

With the death of Tiberius begins a troublous time for Judea; for now ascends the throne of the Cæsars that horrible combination of fool and tyrant which continues to be known in history under the nickname of Caligula. Caligula was completely in earnest in demanding divine worship of his person, and the servile heathen populace made haste to show its fidelity by the erection of altars and images of the emperor. Such an altar was erected in Jamnia, but was immediately torn down by the Jews. When the emperor heard of this he commanded that his image be set up in the Holy of Holies of the temple at Jerusalem, and the legate in Syria, Petronius, was directed to march forthwith to Jerusalem with all the troops at his disposal in order to carry out the imperial command. Petronius was a man of sense; the genuine despair of the Jews made such an impression upon him that he made every effort to postpone the affair. But as nothing came of these efforts and the emperor insisted on his order, Petronius risked the anger of the emperor, withdrew his troops from the country and reported to Caligula that the execution of his order was impossible, wherefore he must beg him to rescind it. Who knows what would have happened if the Jews had not had in King Agrippa, of whom we shall soon speak more at length, a powerful advocate with the emperor. Caligula decreed that all should remain as of old in the temple at Jerusalem, but that no one should be prevented from erecting altars and images to the emperor in the rest of the country. As punishment for his insubordination Petronius received orders to take his own life. But before this order arrived the good legate had received the news of the assassination of the tyrant, and thus the danger for Petronius and the Jewish people was past.

And now Judea was destined once more to become an independent realm and a Jewish king once more to unite under his scepter the whole territory of Herod. Agrippa was the son of Aristobulus, the second son of Herod and Mariamne, and consequently a scion of the Maccabees. In his youth he lived at Rome, like all young princes at that time. He followed the instincts of youth and incurred grudges and debts until the soil of Rome became too warm for him. He arrived in his native country absolutely without means of subsistence. His sister Herodias appealed on his behalf to her husband, Antipas, who gave him the position of market prefect at Tiberias. But Antipas, on an occasion when he was under the influence of liquor, having reproached his brother-in-law at the public table with living wholly at his expense, Agrippa had sufficient sense of honor to resign the position of market prefect. He went to Antioch, to the legate Flaccus, whom he had known at Rome, but

was soon obliged to leave this place also when
Flaccus learned that Agrippa was making capital
out of his friendship and receiving payment for
his interference in government affairs. After an
adventurous journey, on which he barely escaped
from his creditors, he finally landed in Rome,
paid his respects to the old emperor at Capri and
formed a close friendship with the heir to the
throne, Gaius Cæsar, the later Caligula. An incautious expression of Agrippa's having come to
the ears of Tiberius, he had him imprisoned ; but
only six months after this Agrippa's boon com-
panion, Caligula, ascended the throne, released
his friend from prison, presented him with a
chain of gold as heavy as the iron chain which he
had worn, and in addition gave him the tetrar-
chate of his deceased uncle Philip with the title
of king.

For a time the newly appointed king remained
in Rome, and did not start upon the journey into
his kingdom for a year and a half. Then he
went by way of Alexandria. There lived in Alexandria at that time a Jewish man whom not even
the briefest history of the people of Israel can
pass over in silence, the philosopher Philo. The
importance and influence of this man are almost
incalculable. He was the first who succeeded in
completely and harmoniously uniting Shem and
Japhet. He is a Jew by conviction and at the
same time a perfect Greek, who makes it the task
of his life to combine into a higher unity revela-

tion and philosophy, to establish religion upon a philosophical basis and to transfigure philosophy with the spirit of religion. Only in this does the Jew appear : that the religious element is decidedly predominant and that his ultimate aim is not philosophical but religious.

The unique significance of this man lies in the fact that, while his people refused to follow him and under the pressure of circumstances soon entered upon a course exactly the opposite of his own, the Christian Church walked in his footsteps. It adopted Philo's especial conception and treatment of the Old Testament and his philosophical method : the whole theology and dogmatics of the early church, especially of the church of Alexandria and the Orient, which laid the foundation of dogmatics, is inconceivable without Philo. We owe to him also the account of the terrible events that took place in Alexandria at that time. Although Agrippa avoided any offensive action on the occasion of his visit, nevertheless the king of the Jews was most rudely insulted by the populace of Alexandria, and from this resulted one of the most shocking persecutions of the Jews that is reported in history.

Fresh from the impression of such occurrences, Agrippa entered his kingdom. Now he outranked his neighbor, the uncle and brother-in-law upon whose bounty he had shortly before been dependent. The pride of Herodias could not endure this ; she did not rest until her husband had gone to Rome in order to beg the royal title for himself. But Agrippa had already prepared his friend Caligula to give him a fitting reception ; Antipas was simply deposed and exiled to Lyons, and Agrippa received his kingdom in addition to his own. Herodias remained faithful to her husband even in the misfortune into which she had plunged him, and accompanied him on his exile into Gaul ; there they both died.

Agrippa happened to be in Rome just at the time when his friend and patron, Caligula, was murdered ; and to him chiefly the weak and contemptible Claudius owed his elevation to the throne of the Cæsars. Now Claudius showed his gratitude : he conferred upon Agrippa in addition the whilom Roman province of Judea, so that in the year 41 A. D. there was once more a Jewish kingdom under a native ruler. As a king of united Judea, Agrippa made earnest efforts to atone for his former graceless life. The three years of dominion which were vouchsafed him are the last bright spot in the history of the people of Israel.

As is often the case with flippant and dissolute people, Agrippa seems to have been personally very good-natured, attractive and amiable ; along with this he observed most strictly and conscientiously all the laws and commandments, and endeavored in all respects to be a faithful and pious Jew. Once more under his rule the Pharisees had things their own way, and the people were attached to him with affectionate ardor, while his heathen subjects felt for him an equally great hatred and contempt. Withal, he used his great personal influence with Claudius everywhere for the advantage of the Jews, just as his grandfather Herod had done. In order to please the Jews he persecuted the rising Christian Church and had the apostle James beheaded.

He also looked after the outward welfare of his people and his kingdom, and was on the point of building new fortifications about Jerusalem when the Syrian legate, Marsus, reported the matter to Rome, whereupon the Roman government forbade the continuation of the work. A council of princes which he called to meet at Tiberias, at which five Roman vassal-princes were present, was dispersed by Marsus, who went in person to Tiberias and simply sent the members home.

But this last happy period for the Jewish people was not to last long. After a reign of but three years Agrippa died at Cæsarea a sudden death, the remarkable circumstances of which are related in substantial agreement by Josephus and the Acts of the Apostles. The heathen inhabitants of Cæsarea gave unrestrained expression to their joy at the death of the Jewish king and insulted most obscenely the statues of his daughters. What was likely to be the result when this hatred could flame out unchecked, or even if possible be stirred up?

Agrippa left three daughters, and a son of seventeen years bearing his own name. The Roman government considered it dangerous to entrust the Jewish people to the hands of so young a ruler. And the hesitation was certainly well founded. Josephus reports the remarkable fact that about this time two Jewish brothers from Nehardea in Mesopotamia, by name Asinæus and Anilæus, had placed themselves at the head of a great troop of Jews there and were keeping all Mesopotamia in excitement and terror. Accordingly the youthful Agrippa remained for the time being as a private citizen in Rome, where indeed he took every opportunity to be of use to his countrymen; the whole kingdom of his father was sequestered as a Roman province and again placed under the administration of a procurator subordinate to the legate in Syria. The supervision over the temple and the right to appoint and remove high priests were conferred upon a younger brother of the deceased Agrippa, Herod by name, who through the intervention of his brother had received the little kingdom of Chalcis at the foot of Lebanon.

With the return of Judea to a Roman administration begins the prelude of the destruction of Jerusalem and the Jewish people—perhaps the most shocking tragedy known to the history of the world. The seven procurators who had the administration of the unhappy land from 44 to 66 A. D. seemed to act as if in concert in order to drive the people to despair and revolt. The very first, Cuspius Fadus, began his official career with an act of petty spite by demanding back the high priest's robe. The Jews appealed first to the Syrian legate, Cassius Longinus, and, this being without result, directly to the emperor; here young Agrippa, by his personal connections, managed to secure a decision that all should remain as of old. Josephus characterizes the activity of Fadus in the words: "With the greatest discretion and energy he purged all Judea of highwaymen." We already know what to think of that. One detail has been transmitted to us. A certain Theudas, who is also mentioned in the Acts of the Apostles, had summoned the people to the Jordan where at his command the miracle of Joshua was to be repeated. Fadus sent thither a company of cavalry, who simply cut the people down and brought the head of Theudas to Jerusalem.

Tiberius Alexander, the successor of Fadus, was himself a Jew and a nephew of the philosopher Philo. But Alexander was a renegade who had no feeling for his people; he even served Titus later at the siege of Jerusalem as chief counselor. Under him Judea was visited by a severe famine. Furthermore he crucified two sons of Judas, the founder of the faction of the Zealots, by name James and Simon.

But these were innocent trifles compared with what took place under the third procurator, Ventidius Cumanus, from 48 to 52 A. D. On the great holidays the procurator was always present in Jerusalem, and a guard was stationed in the temple. On the day of Pascha a soldier of the temple guard indulged in an unmentionable obscene insult of the ceremonial procession. The people hastened to Cumanus in order to demand the punishment of the offender. When Cumanus failed to satisfy their demands, he himself was assailed with abusive epithets and stones were thrown at the guards. Then Cumanus gave the word to attack, and there resulted such a butchery and such a fearful riot that ten thousand, according to another report twenty thousand, persons perished.

It is no wonder that such occurrences kindled anew the hatred against the Romans. Thus an imperial official, Stephanus, was attacked shortly after this upon the open highway not far from Jerusalem and robbed of all he had. As the perpetrators could not be found out, Cumanus for punishment had all the adjacent villages plundered by his soldiers. On this occasion a roll of the Thora fell into the hands of the soldiery, and one of them could not refrain from tearing the sacred book to pieces before the eyes of the horror-stricken Jews and throwing the fragments with rude jests into the fire. Again the people resorted to one of those popular demonstrations en masse and went to Cumanus at Cæsarea. The excitement was so tremendous that Cumanus found it advisable to give in. He had the perpetrator of the outrage led forth and decapitated before the eyes of the Jews, whereupon they dispersed and returned home.

A third instance was still worse. Some Samaritans had murdered a Galilean on his way to the celebration in Jerusalem; the Jews complained, but Cumanus, bribed by the Samaritans, paid no attention to the complaint. Now the Jews took redress into their own hands; great troops armed themselves and attacked the Samaritans, and, as Josephus himself relates, cut down all without regard for age or sex, and laid the villages in ashes. Now Cumanus sent his tribune, Celer, against the insurgents, and the Roman soldiers of course made easy work of the undisciplined hordes. It need not be added that they took merciless advantage of their victory. Now the Jews complained to the Syrian legate, Ummidius Quadratus. He investigated the affair and crucified all whom Cumanus had taken alive, besides arresting and decapitating eighteen others who were deeply compromised; but Cumanus himself he suspended from office, and sent him, together with the tribune, Celer, to Rome, there to give account of themselves before the emperor.

Again the influence of Agrippa was felt; Cumanus was exiled and the tribune Celer taken back to Jerusalem, where he was dragged through the streets and executed; even the guilty Samaritans were executed. The ex-high priest Jonathan, the successor of the Caiaphas of the New Testament, who headed the Jewish delegation which had accused Cumanus and the Samaritans in Rome, asked of Claudius as an especial favor that Felix, the brother of the all-powerful freedman of the emperor, be made Roman procurator. The emperor willingly granted this request, and thus a man of the most fateful destiny enters upon the soil of Palestine. His administration is the turning-point; from that time on the revolution became established.

The great historian Tacitus characterizes Felix as a man who exercised the authority of a king with the temper of a slave through every sort of cruelty and license, and who, as brother of the all-powerful Pallas, thought himself able to practise all his outrages with impunity. We can still recognize clearly the various stages through which events developed. First Felix attacked the Zealots. He succeeded by treacherous violation of his word in capturing alive their leader, Eleazar, whom he sent to Rome in chains: "The number of highwaymen who were crucified, and of those who were executed in other ways on suspicion of making common cause with highwaymen, cannot be calculated," says Josephus, with blood-curdling brevity.

The answer to this Roman policy of extreme brutal violence was not long lacking. Now was formed the party of the so-called Sicarii, whose maxim was to put Romans and Roman sympathizers out of the way by assassination. With short daggers, called "sica," under their cloaks, they mingled with the multitude, crowded upon their victims and stabbed them unseen. One of their first victims was the high priest Jonathan, whom they murdered at the direction of the procurator. Jonathan, who had secured the position for Felix, was an inconvenient monitor, and kept urging him to endeavor to give a more just administration. Thereupon Felix paid to the Scarii through a go-between a large sum of money to have them put his troublesome friend out of the way. The wretches actually went to Jerusalem in the disguise of pilgrims and stabbed the high priest in the temple. Of course the perpetrators of the infamous deed instigated by the procurator himself remained undiscovered and unpunished. The evil increased to such an extent that soon no one felt his life to be safe, and people suspected an assassin in every one they chanced to meet.

There were religious as well as political fanatics, false prophets and Messiahs who stirred up the people and promised miracles and signs. When Felix proceeded against these also with barbarous severity, and when even the more conservative Jews helped him in suppressing the particularly dangerous uprising led by the Egyptian who is mentioned in the Acts of the Apostles, the fanatics went through the country in troops with the watchword that those who chose voluntarily to be slaves must be forced into freedom. Everywhere they murdered those friendly to Rome, pillaged their houses and their villages and then gave them to the flames. Besides all this there was a regular civil war between the Jewish and non-Jewish population in Cæsarea, the residence of the procurator himself. The Jews claimed that Cæsarea, having been built by a Jewish king, was a Jewish city, which the heathen of course would not admit. The Jews were in the majority, but the heathen had the Roman soldiers on their side. Once when the Jews were getting the best of it in such an encounter, Felix ordered the soldiers to use their swords and plunder the houses of the richest Jews, and when the disturbances did not cease sent the leaders of both parties to Rome to advocate their cause before Nero. By bribing Nero's secretary the heathen secured a decision adverse to the Jews and recognizing themselves as masters of the city. During these scenes of violence the Apostle Paul lay in prison in Cæsarea.

However, Felix did not live to hear the decision. After a rule of eight years he was recalled, probably in the year 60 A. D., and barely managed to escape being sentenced at Rome. A searching side-light is thrown upon Jewish conditions at that time by the report of Josephus, that the high priest Ishmael, through his servants, appropriated to himself alone the tithes due to all the other priests and Levites, so that even priests died of starvation.

At last they seemed to understand at Rome that they had obligations toward Judea ; Felix was succeeded by Porcius Festus, a really upright man with good intentions and a sense of justice. Festus too had to deal with highwaymen and Sicarii and false prophets, but even now the worst might have been avoided had not Festus died after two short years. The high priest Ananos used the interval between the death of Festus and the arrival of his successor to have James, the brother of Jesus, stoned to death. This next procurator, Albinus,—I now quote from Josephus,—"conducted affairs in an entirely different spirit from his predecessors; there was no wickedness that he did not practise. Not only did he embezzle public moneys and rob a multitude of private citizens of their property and burden the whole people with imposts, but he released captive highwaymen for ransoms from their relatives; those that could not pay remained in prison. Every villain gathered a band of his own, and Albinus towered among them like a robber-chief, using his adherents to plunder honest citizens. The victims remained silent; others, still exempt, flattered the wretch in order to secure immunity. Nevertheless Albinus appeared honorable in comparison with his successor, Gessius Florus. For while the former had practised his villainies in secret, and with a certain degree of caution, Gessius Florus made an open boast of his crimes against the people; he practised every sort of robbery and abuse precisely as though he had been sent to punish condemned criminals. His cruelty was pitiless, his infamies shameless; never before did any one so veil truth with deceit, or discover more cunning ways of accomplishing his knaveries. To enrich himself at the expense of individuals was not enough for him; he robbed whole cities and ruined whole communities; things could not have been worse had he made public proclamation throughout the land that every one might plunder where and what he would, provided only that he himself received his share of the booty. Whole districts were depopulated by his greed, multitudes left their homes and fled into foreign provinces." A single syllable added would destroy the impression made by these words of Josephus.

When the legate in Syria, Cestius Gallus, was in Jerusalem on the occasion of the Easter celebration he was surrounded by three million Jews who besought him with tears and lamentations to take pity on their unspeakable misery. Florus stood beside the legate and listened to the complaints with a scornful smile. Gallus promised to persuade Florus to be milder, and the two left Jerusalem, the latter with the firm intention of forcing the Jews into rebellion as the only means of concealing his own crimes and infamies.

Soon there were new troubles in Cæsarea. The most prominent Jews endeavored to approach Florus on his own footing, offering him eight talents, about $7,500, if he would check the arrogant encroachments of the heathen. Florus took the money and left Cæsarea, of course without doing anything. The following Sabbath the heathen went so far as to publicly ridicule and disturb the Jewish worship. From this arose such a fearful riot that even the Roman troops in Cæsarea were unable to restore order. When a delegation of Jews went to Florus and referred plainly to the eight talents, Florus simply imprisoned them.

Then came the drop which filled the brimming cup to overflowing. On the pretense that the emperor needed the money Florus demanded from the treasury of the temple seventeen talents (that is, about $15,000). At this their rage burst forth like flames; with dreadful outcries and uttering imprecations upon Florus, the multitude gathered in the temple, and some waggish fellows passed a plate to take up a collection for poor, distressed Florus. To avenge this insult he marched upon Jerusalem with his troops. A respectful deputation went forth to meet him; but Florus challenged them through fifty horsemen sent in advance to mock him to his face, and the horsemen charged upon them and scattered them in fright. The next morning Florus established his tribunal and demanded the surrender of those that had mocked him. But when they calmly represented to him the impossibility of this, since those persons were not known and not to be discovered, Florus commanded his troops to pillage Jerusalem and cut down every one they met. Florus even scourged and crucified Jews who possessed the rank of Roman knighthood, and on this one day three thousand six hundred persons perished.

Berenice, the sister of King Agrippa, happening to be in Jerusalem at the time, went barefoot to Florus and implored mercy for her people : but she was treated roughly and driven away with insult and abuse. This occurred on the 16th of May of the year 66 A. D.

But even now the more prudent succeeded in calming the rebellious people. This was very unwelcome to Florus, and he declared that he could not regard their desire for peace as sincere unless they would formally meet and salute two cohorts which were approaching from Cæsarea. At the urgent entreaty of the priests the people consented even to this. But Florus had commanded the cohorts not to return the greeting of the Jews, and to attack them the moment a word of resentment was heard. The result was actually as he anticipated : the soldiers were saluted with respect but did not return the greeting of the Jews ; the latter were at first surprised, and then when some began to murmur the soldiers drew their swords and began the slaughter. At the same time Florus started out from Jerusalem with his remaining troops and thus attacked the people from both sides. But the latter held their ground and the small force of troops were insufficient to prevail against the population of Jerusalem. During the night all the bridges and approaches to the temple were destroyed. When Florus, who had intended to plunder the temple, found this plan frustrated, he departed from Jerusalem, leaving in charge a Roman cohort and making the priests and leaders of the people responsible for keeping the peace.

Both Florus and the Jews reported this occurrence to the legate, Cestius Gallus; but as these reports, were naturally contradictory, Cestius sent the tribune Neapolitanus to Jerusalem to ascertain the facts. Neapolitanus was received with much ceremony, and the Jews poured forth their woes in eloquent words, saying that they were opposed only to Florus and not to the Romans. To show him how peaceably disposed the people were Neapolitanus was invited to walk about the entire city with but a single guide and see whether the slightest harm would befall him. In fact Neapolitanus made the experiment and was soon so sure of the situation that he summoned the people together, praised their loyal and faithful conduct and admonished them urgently once more to keep the peace, and all might turn out well. With this he returned to Antioch to make his report to the legate.

Now the people requested Agrippa, who had accompanied Neapolitanus to Jerusalem, to denounce Florus to Nero. Agrippa demanded that they first restore the broken connections between the fortress and the temple and pay the forty talents of taxes still in arrears (about \$38,000). Both demands were complied with; they began at once to build up what had been destroyed and the large sum was soon raised by voluntary contributions. But when Agrippa further demanded that pending the emperor's decision they should recognize Florus as procurator, and honor and obey him, he was greeted with a shower of stones and speedily left Jerusalem. In accordance with a formal decision the daily sacrifice in the temple for the emperor and the empire was now discontinued, and thus war was declared—henceforth there was no return for either side.

CHAPTER X.

THE WAR IN JUDEA AND THE DESTRUCTION OF JERUSALEM.

WE are about to view the final act of the terrible drama. Our inclinations would bid us turn away in mournful silence and close our eyes to the frightful things we shall behold; perhaps more shocking things have never happened on earth than in this last desperate life-and-death struggle of the people of Israel. But the duty of the historian compels us to look matters in the face, and, what is still sadder, it compels the spectator to act as judge. Even though our hearts should break over all this misery and suffering, there is no atoning feature; the genuine tragic sympathy is wanting. We behold only a mad riot of all the passions, which blindly assail one another; the most shocking deeds were committed by Jews against Jews, and the most victims fell not by the sword of the Romans, but by that of the infatuated nation itself. The most frightful terrors of the Thirty Years' War combined with the most frightful terrors of the French Revolution will come before our reluctant gaze.

It seems as though all the fiends of hell were released in order to destroy the people to whom God had spoken aforetime often and in many different ways through his prophets. Scarcely on another occasion in history has the spectator the same feeling of irredeemable ruin, of inevitable destruction, as in the case of the fall of Jerusalem in the year 70 A. D.

Eleazar, the son of the high priest Ananias, first becomes the leader of the war party. The stronghold Massada, built by Herod, was taken by a sudden assault, and in Jerusalem all preparations were made for the impending war. But there was still a strong peace party who foresaw certain ruin in a conflict with Rome, and even yet wanted peace at any price. They applied for assistance to King Agrippa, who actually sent them three thousand soldiers. The war party had their headquarters in the temple, which by its position was an almost impregnable fortress ; the peace party in the citadel. Blood flowed daily, and civil war was raging in the streets of Jerusalem when the war party received reinforcements. Menahem, a grandson of the old rebel and Roman-hater, Judas the Galilean, broke open the arsenals of Masada and armed a large force of Sicarii, with whom he marched to Jerusalem. At this the peace party saw the impossibility of further opposition ; the troops of Agrippa were allowed to depart, but the Roman cohort was expressly refused permission to do so. They took refuge in a particularly strong tower, while the leaders of the peace party concealed themselves. At their head stood the high priest Ananias; he was murdered, together with his brother, and the torch applied to his palace as well as to that of Agrippa and Berenice, and the portion of the citadel, already taken, in which were all the archives, including the tax accounts and the records of loans. This was on the 6th of September, 66 A. D. But scarcely had the war party obtained the upper hand in Jerusalem when Eleazar and Menahem began to make war on each other. The men of Jerusalem did not propose to accept commands from the foreign adventurer; Menahem and his troop were attacked in the temple, and overpowered, he himself executed under torture and his troops massacred. Finally, the Roman cohort also had to surrender. They were promised free retreat on the delivery of their arms; but scarcely had they actually laid them down when the Jews fell upon the defenseless men and butchered them to the last one. Only the tribune, Metilius, was so contemptible as to purchase his life by submitting to circumcision. Josephus calls especial attention to the fact that this incredible infamy was perpetrated on a Sabbath.

The fortresses of Cyprus and Machærus also fell into the hands of the Jews, so that very soon there was not a Roman left in the country.

Now the war extended into all quarters and

assumed altogether the nature of a race-conflict : where the Jews were in the majority they massacred the heathen, and where the heathen were in the majority the Jews met a like fate. Thus in Cæsarea alone more than twenty thousand Jews were slaughtered in one hour, in Damascus ten thousand, and in this connection Josephus makes the characteristic observation that the heathen in Damascus must needs have kept this plan a close secret from their women, since the women were almost without exception proselytes.

At last the Syrian legate, Cestius Gallus, approached the scene, and marched directly upon Jerusalem ; at Gibeon there was a battle in which the Jews fought heroically, but could not prevent Gallus from marching to Jerusalem, taking and setting fire to a part of the city. Now the peace party, which still had numerous and influential secret adherents, wanted to surrender the city to the Romans ; but this plan was betrayed, and all who had embraced it or even known of it were thrown over the temple walls before the very eyes of the Romans. Cestius perceived that he could accomplish nothing with his troops against the city and its desperate defenders, and accordingly withdrew. But on the retreat he was surrounded in the gorge of Beth-horon, and suffered a disastrous defeat. Only by sacrificing a small force did he succeed in saving at least the remainder of his troops, but the rest of the retreat was a wild flight : nearly all the arms and all of the engines of war belonging to the Romans fell into the hands of the Jews. The battle at Beth-horon was on the 8th of November, and the continuation of the war was prevented by the approach of winter.

After these occurrences of course all hope of a peaceful settlement was gone. Those who still did not wish war left Jerusalem, while in the city preparations were made with all energy for the impending crisis. The first requisite was seen to be the organization of the opposition; accordingly commanders were appointed who were to draft and drill men in all the provinces, and in short make all ready for war with Rome.

It is a characteristic fact that those selected were without exception members of the nobility eligible to the high-priesthood; the historian Josephus was one of them. Thus far the movement has, in accordance with the inherent nature of the Jewish people, an aristocratic character; in Jerusalem the high priest Ananos and a certain Joseph, son of Gorion, are at the head of the whole. It is a tragi-comic thought to imagine these men who had never in their lives had a sword in their hands, and had done nothing but study the Thora, now suddenly transformed into generals and drill-masters with the task of creating an army equal to a contest with the Romans. Moreover, a part of them had only half a heart in the matter, and very likely had themselves no real confidence in their success.

Young Josephus, to whom was assigned the most difficult territory, Galilee, was confronted at the very start with fierce opposition on the part of a popular hero, John of Gish-chala, who had taken part in the battle against Cestus at Bethhoron. He stirred up the people against the traitor and friend of the Romans, and would have killed him if Josephus had not managed to reach a boat at the right moment. In other places there were probably similar results, for people could not long fail to recognize that the whole affair was in the most incompetent hands conceivable, so patent was the incompetence.

The Romans proceeded very differently. The command was conferred upon the best general of his time, Vespasian, a veteran warrior and victor, and sixty thousand of the best Roman troops put at his disposal. Hostilities were begun by the Jews in the year 67 A. D. There was but a weak Roman garrison in Ascalon. The Jews attacked the city twice, but were repelled with a total loss of eighteen thousand men.

At this point Vespasian appeared upon the scene of war. He clearly pursued the policy of localizing the war in Jerusalem, first subjecting the country and then with his whole force crushing the city. To begin with, he marched into Galilee, where Josephus was in command. The important border fortress, Sepphoris, surrendered to the Romans without drawing a sword. Josephus approached with his forces, but at the first sight of the Romans they dispersed without ever venturing a battle.

Now there remained in the province only a series of fortified cities and points to be taken. Josephus himself had withdrawn into the fortress of Jotapata, the defense of which he narrates with complacent diffuseness; and in fact Vespasian required forty-seven days for its reduction, while more than forty thousand men lost their lives in the siege. Josephus managed to make his peace with the Romans, and was honorably received and well treated by Vespasian, whose future elevation to the office of emperor he claims to have foretold. At the same time the fortress of Japha fell, and fifteen thousand men lost their lives there. Some troops of fugitives had established themselves in the maritime city of Joppa—they too perished miserably. Tiberias, in which the peace party was strong, surrendered to the Romans and was therefore spared.

The real home of the rebellion in Galilee was the city of Tarichæa, on the Sea of Genezareth; against it was sent Titus, the son of Vespasian, who took it by a bold assault, by plunging into the lake with his cavalry and storming the city from the wholly unprotected water side. Vespasian now executed stern judgment. In the assault six thousand and five hundred people had perished; the old men and invalids who no longer had a value as human property he slew; from the remainder he picked out six thousand of the strongest and sent them to Nero at Corinth, where the latter was having a canal cut across the isthmus ; all the rest, thirty thousand and four hundred in number, were sold into slavery.

There now remained in the hands of the Jews only Gamala, Gish-chala and Mount Tabor. Vespasian first advanced against Gamala. When King Agrippa summoned the city to surrender he was wounded by a sling, and then the attack began. The first assault of the Romans was repulsed with such enormous loss that Vespasian had to use his whole authority to maintain any kind of order. A regular siege was begun, and a second assault brought the city into the power of the Romans. Four thousand fell by the swords of the victors, more than five thousand had cast themselves down and been dashed to pieces on the rocks below ; only two women remained alive of the whole population of the city.

Mount Tabor was taken through the perjury of the Roman commander, and Titus himself proceeded against Gish-chala. John, who was in command there, managed to elude Titus. He slipped through the Roman lines in the night with his forces and hastened to Jerusalem, while the city itself surrendered the following day. Thus all Galilee was in the hands of the Romans at the close of the autumn of the year 67 A. D.

It is easy to understand how these defeats stirred passions to the highest pitch. They were rightly ascribed to the wholly incompetent existing leadership, which was in no respect equal to its task. John of Gish-chala, especially, who had taken part in the war in Galilee, could not say enough of the shameful treason of the leaders. By degrees all those who had been fighting and murdering during the summer had gathered in Jerusalem, and now they could undertake to overthrow the party of the alleged traitors and friends of Rome, and bring the Zealots to the helm.

First a few of the foremost men were imprisoned and assassinated. In order to gain some sort of moral support the Zealots appointed a new high priest, an obscure and uneducated person named Phannias, chosen by lot,—he was to be the last to wear the sacred garment in Jerusalem. At this point two former high priests, Ananos and Jesus, placed themselves at the head of the conservative portion of the people and roused them to energetic measures against the Zealots; once more actual civil war raged in Jerusalem until the party of order succeeded in getting into the temple. The Zealots would have been irretrievably lost if Ananos had not hesitated to desecrate the temple by battle and bloodshed; he contented himself with isolating the Zealots in the temple. Thereupon they called for help from without. The wild, marauding, semi-Jewish Idumeans were always ready for plunder and murder: twenty thousand reckless fellows responded to the call of the Zealots, whose request had been wrapped in the cloak of patriotism, alleging that

Ananos and his party intended to deliver the city to the Romans. These Idumeans marched to Jerusalem, where of course the gates were shut against them. But in the night a storm arose, under the protection of which the Zealots succeeded in opening the gates to their allies; the rising sun looked upon eight thousand five hundred murdered victims.

Now they began to make a clean sweep of the traitors. The naked bodies of the two high priests, Ananos and Jesus, were thrown into the street horribly mutilated, and within a few days twelve thousand men of the party of order were executed amid terrible tortures. Even the comedy of a court was introduced. Once when this court ventured to acquit an especially venerated and respected man, two Zealots rushed upon him and thrust their daggers into his breast with the words: "Here hast thou our vote also."

But now it was growing too bad for even the Idumeans, who must have perceived for some time that the Zealots were merely cheating them and using them for their own lawless purposes; they released two thousand persons who had been imprisoned for execution, and left Jerusalem, where John of Gish-chala then instituted an unrestricted reign of terror; soon, as Josephus relates, all the respectable people in Jerusalem had fallen victims to—I had almost said, the guillotine; only those escaped death whom humble birth or poverty made already humble enough. The Zealots went so far as to forbid, on penalty of death, the burial of the bodies of those executed, which were left to rot in the sun. The Sicarii who occupied Masada carried on from that point marauding incursions throughout all Southern Judea, where they had their terrible will, pillaging and murdering whole villages and towns.

All this was known in the Roman headquarters, and the officers advised Vespasian to march forthwith upon Jerusalem and capture the city, which was wasting away in civil strife. But Vespasian considered it more profitable to let the Jews destroy one another, and calmly continued his methodical warfare. In the spring of 68 A. D. he began by subduing the whole country east of the Jordan excepting the fortress of Machærus, where a generation before had fallen the head of John the Baptist, and then the South and West. He was just preparing for a decisive blow against Jerusalem when the news arrived of the death of Nero and the elevation of Galba. Vespasian sent his son Titus to the new emperor to receive his orders; but on the way Titus learned of the death of Galba also, and accordingly returned to his father. A whole year the Roman arms rested, but the unhappy people was destined to have no repose.

A certain Simon bar Giora succeeded in rising to power and authority among the Sicarii in Masada. Soon this fortress was too small for his ambition and he gathered great troops about him, whose number increased in a short time to twenty thousand men. The people of Jerusalem regarded this as a menace, and a battle resulted between Simon and John, in which the latter was defeated; but Simon felt too weak to assail Jerusalem and turned his attack upon Idumea. Soon his host had increased to forty thousand, who of course had to live, and accordingly wasted and pillaged the whole land unmercifully. At this point the Zealots by a treacherous attack succeeded in capturing Simon's wife and taking her to Jerusalem. Now Simon again marched to Jerusalem, killed with the most terrible tortures all whom he could seize, or sent them back to Jerusalem minus their hands, until finally they returned his wife to him.

Meantime in Jerusalem all the bonds of decency and order were loosed. The savage soldiery of John had complete control of the city, and soon ceased to obey John; they were no longer content with plunder and murder, but gave themselves up to the most shocking excesses. This prompted the desperate suggestion of driving out the devil by Beelzebub; a solemn deputation besought Simon bar Giora to free the city from the tyrant and in April, 69, A. D. he entered the city, greeted with loud acclaim. John was shut up in the temple, but the attempt to take it was unsuccessful. Simon established himself in the city, and now Jerusalem had two tyrants instead of one, for Simon's sway was no less atrocious than that of John.

In June, 69, A. D., Vespasian resumed his activity and completed the conquest of the South; only Jerusalem, Herodeion, Masada, and Machærus, remained in the hands of the Jews. But now the legions proclaimed their commander emperor. Of course this was a more important matter for Vespasian than the war in Judea; therefore he turned this over to his son Titus and set out for Rome by the way of Alexandria; Josephus, his prophecy having been thus fulfilled, was released from his chains, and, together with Tiberius Alexander, the sole remaining Jewish procurator, he was the chief adviser of Titus at the siege of Jerusalem.

Meantime in Jerusalem the mutual destruction and anarchy had progressed. Even in the ranks of the Zealots the dissatisfaction with the tyrannical and cruel rule of John was growing strong. A certain Eleazar, son of Simon, who at the very beginning of the war had won distinction by the great victory over Cestius Gallus at Beth-horon, but had since been pushed aside by the patrician party and entrusted with no office, now made use of this dissatisfaction. He formed a new faction among the Zealots which made fierce war upon John, and finally got possession of the temple itself. Thus there were now three camps in the wretched city: Simon held the city, John the mount of the temple, and Eleazar the temple itself, so that John was now beset from two sides. In the course of this constant civil war all the immense stores of grain within the city went up in smoke. In the language of Josephus, these three were united only in murdering those who deserved to live longer, and they outdid themselves in the torture and cruel execution of their enemies.

Finally, in the spring of the year 70, Titus marched upon Jerusalem, arriving shortly before the Paschal celebration. As Titus, with six hundred horsemen, was making a reconnaissance about Jerusalem, he came very near being captured and his troop just escaped annihilation; with a few supporters left he managed to cut his way through. The next day they began to make camp, the tenth legion occupying the Mount of Olives. But as they were going at the work the Jews made a sortie in force, which was executed with such daring spirit that the legion dashed up the Mount in wild flight : only by the personal action of Titus was it possible to check them and save the honor of the day.

But not even yet did the civil war within the walls of Jerusalem cease. Eleazar had opened the temple to worshipers : those who wished to offer sacrifice were admitted after close inspection by Eleazar's guards. On account of the great number of pilgrims at the feast of Pascha this inspection could not of course be thorough : John took advantage of this fact and had the most daring of his followers slip into the temple ; here they attacked Eleazar, and finally, with the shedding of streams of blood, captured the temple.

Now once more there were but two parties in Jerusalem, and John was in control of the entire temple. Josephus reports the number of able-bodied defenders of Jerusalem at twenty-three thousand four hundred all told.

Now Titus moved his lines nearer to the city, and was again met with a sortie which caused his troops to waver and led to a retreat. Every prospect of taking Jerusalem by storm being thus excluded, a systematic siege was begun on the 23rd of April; soon the engines were constructed and the battering-ram began its dismal activity against the outer walls. Only now, amid the dull thuds of the battering-ram, did internecine war cease, and Simon and John joined forces to combat the enemy from without. The first united sortie was made with such violence that they succeeded in setting fire to the Roman works; the entire destruction of the badly damaged works was prevented only by the personal participation of Titus, who with his own hands shot down twelve Jews. The one Jew who was taken alive was crucified in sight of the walls.

On the 7th of May the Romans had effected a breach in the outer wall, the Jews withdrew behind the second, and the Romans were masters of the New City. Five days later, on the 12th of May, the second wall also was stormed, and Titus was one of the first to force an entrance; but now there arose such a desperate hand-to-hand struggle that the Romans were finally forced out. For four days the Jewish defenders covered the breach with their bodies, when their resistance weakened, and the Romans again entered on the 16th of May, and now held their own in the suburb and razed the second wall.

Already the defenders were short of provisions and people were dying of hunger in Jerusalem, but no one thought of surrender; the resistance only became the more stubborn and desperate. Once more Titus tried peaceful measures. The troops were about to be paid, and Titus commanded them all to appear in parade uniform at a point visible from the city. In fact all Jerusalem hastened to the roofs and walls to enjoy the rare military spectacle. But if Titus had expected thus to intimidate the besieged he had miscalculated. When Josephus was sent out to summon them to surrender he was met with abuse and missiles.

In the city, meantime, famine was increasing. In order to provision the troops, soldiers were sent into the houses to search for food ; where they brought nothing to light, the unhappy occupants were put to terrible tortures in order, by indescribably exquisite torment, to force from them a confession of their hidden stores. Driven to desperation by this, the people sought the mercy of the Romans. They stole out of the city ; but Titus had all the deserters, as many as five hundred in one day, crucified after inhuman tortures, and when, as Josephus says, crosses enough could not be obtained, he cut off their hands and drove them back into the city, where Simon and John were competing in the work of hunting down traitors and friends of the Romans in order to reduce the number of superfluous mouths to be fed.

On the 29th of May the Romans had moved four ramparts up against the inner wall. John succeeded in destroying two of these by digging mines beneath, supported by timbers, and then burning the timbers; the other two were burned by Simon two days later. Thus the laborious achievement of weeks was undone, and matters were just where they had been before. Now the Romans held a council of war, the conclusion of which was that, the engines being destroyed, famine should be left to complete the work of destruction. Titus had a wall with thirteen watchtowers built around the entire city, thus to make a complete blockade: the Romans are reported to have built this wall of more than three miles in length in three days.

I pass over the scenes of horror that follow: suffice it to say that, according to the declaration of a captive taken by the Romans, whose business it was to count the dead in order to pay from the public treasury the burial fee, there were carried out through one gate under his charge one hundred and fifteen thousand eight hundred and eighty corpses, in the period from April 14 to July 1, that is, in two and a half months. Unfortunately the beginning of the siege had fallen in the Paschal week, so that all the pilgrims from without were shut up in the city.

Now Titus's humanity was touched, and he permitted the Romans to receive fugitives; the starved wretches were even cared for—to be sold afterwards as slaves, of course. But it came to light that one of these unfortunates had swallowed a few gold pieces, his last possession, and from that time on the Syrian and Arabian troops ripped open the bodies of the fugitives and tore out their bowels in order to hunt for gold. In this brutal fashion two thousand were slaughtered in one night. Titus learned of the monstrous deed, but could not punish it, because there were too many implicated in it; despite his severest prohibition the abominable performance was continued, only more secretly and more cautiously— and so at last it seemed preferable to starve in Jerusalem than to perish thus.

Now Titus undertook to restore the ramparts that had been destroyed. The whole region for ten miles around was stripped of timber, and after untold labor the ramparts were completed at the expiration of twenty-one days. This time everything was hazarded. If these structures were destroyed the Romans could not renew them because of the entire lack of timber; on the other hand the city was lost if it did not succeed in destroying them. On the 1st of July the Jews made a desperate sortie under John; but the Romans had learned wisdom from the previous sorties,

while as a matter of course the strength of the
Jews, who were emaciated by famine, was less.
The sortie was repulsed and in the following night
the inner wall fell under the blows of the battering-ram ; but to their astonishment and dismay
the Romans found back of this a new one ; John
had anticipated the case and made his arrangements accordingly. After repeated failures this
new temporary wall was scaled on the 5th of July,
and the Romans poured in. In the confusion
Titus undertook to storm the temple forthwith,
but met there such desperate resistance that he
retreated ; however, the Lower City remained in
his possession, and he proceeded to raze the last
wall and prepare for a regular assault upon the
temple. Wood had to be fetched from twelve
miles away, but the Romans, despite all obstacles,
pushed their work persistently and once more the
ramparts rose from the earth.

On the 17th of July the daily morning and evening sacrifice in the temple was finally suspended.
We are filled with a feeling of shuddering admiration when we read this report. For three months
the most terrible famine had prevailed ; thousands
and hundreds of thousands had succumbed to it,
and yet day after day they burned upon the altar
the sacrificial animals prescribed by the law, and
only a short time before had John ventured to
touch the stores of sacred wine and sacred oil and
distribute them among the starving people.

Meanwhile, Titus having once more made

through Josephus a fruitless demand for surrender, fighting had been going on all the while about the temple and with incomparable bravery on both sides. Once more, on the 27th of July, the Jews were able to inflict heavy losses on the Romans. They filled the west porch of the temple with combustibles and lured the Romans thither by a sham retreat; then it was fired, and the whole force of Roman soldiers perished miserably in the flames before the very eyes of their comrades, who were unable to succor them.

On the 8th of August the ramparts were at last finished and the battering-ram began to operate ; but it was ineffective against the massive foundations of the temple. The scaling-ladders were run up for an assault, but in this attempt the Romans even lost several standards without accomplishing anything. Then another method was tried. Next day the Romans set fire to the gates. Titus had the fire put out in the night and the final assault was to be made on the 10th of August.

Titus had given strict orders to spare the temple, but after the Jews had twice in succession made desperate attacks upon the assailants the Romans lost patience. To hasten matters a soldier hurled a torch through an open window into the temple building proper, which straightway burst forth in flames. Titus galloped up to check the work of destruction, but even the iron discipline of the Romans weakened in the fire of passions roused to madness. There was no stopping them. More and more torches and firebrands flew into the temple, within whose walls Romans and Jews were fighting for life breast to breast in inextricable confusion. With the crackling of the darting flames and the crash of falling timbers were mingled the heartrending screams of the dying and the triumphant yells of the victorious Romans.

Titus had barely time to secure the sacred vessels of the temple and to enter the Holy of Holies; then the temple of the God of Israel went down never to rise again. Upon its smoking ruins the legions hailed the son of their emperor as "imperator" and offered a sacrifice to the Roman Jupiter. Then fire and murder continued their sway. The conflagration became general, neither age nor sex was spared. The priests had succeeded in hiding themselves; on the fifth day, driven by hunger, they came forth and begged for their lives, but Titus replied: "It is fitting for priests to perish with their temple," and had them beheaded.

But not even yet was Jerusalem subdued. Simon still held the Upper City, and John too had been able to make his way thither with the remnants of his troops. They asked for a conference, and Titus consented. He with his troops was on the east side of the Tyropöon valley, Simon and John, surrounded by the Jews, on the west side. They said they had sworn never to surrender to the Romans, and begged therefore for permission to withdraw, promising to leave the country. Titus felt unable to permit this, and now the formal siege of the Upper City began.

Not even now were passions subdued. Simon and John still fought each other, and suspected Roman sympathizers and traitors were still being killed. Josephus gives the number of such at eight thousand four hundred. With incalculable labor and difficulty the Romans began on the 20th of August the erection of ramparts against the Upper City; on the 7th of September they were completed and the engines were moved up; the worn-out defenders were no longer able to offer resistance, and with a rush the walls were scaled. The Romans, grown suspicious, feared a ruse; but they were soon convinced that all that were left in the city were dead or nearly so. Simon and John, with their last troops, had hidden in subterranean passages; Jerusalem was finally and completely conquered. Everywhere fire was set, the houses having first been plundered and the occupants murdered: on the 8th of September the rising sun shone down upon what was no longer a city—the smoldering ruins of Jerusalem. Only three towers were left standing as memorials of the prowess of the Romans in the conquest, together with a part of the wall to shelter the garrison that was left to guard the ruins. Aside from this the city was so nearly leveled to the ground that, as Josephus said, no one who visited the place would have believed that a city ever stood there.

Driven by hunger, John came forth from his hiding place and begged for mercy; Titus put him into heavy chains and let him live. In Rome he perished forsaken in prison. Simon tried to escape by an underground passage, but failing in this he suddenly appeared in a white garment with a purple cloak on the spot where the temple had stood, rising out of the earth like a specter. But the Roman guards seized him; confessing his identity, he also was cast into chains.

The total number of those who perished in the siege and capture of Jerusalem is estimated by Josephus at one million one hundred thousand persons; ninety-seven thousand were taken captive by the Romans. Of these seven hundred of the finest and strongest were selected to grace the triumphal procession of Titus. The old and the weak, who could not be used, the Romans had butchered in cold blood; those over seventeen years of age were part of them sent into the Egyptian mines, part of them forced to appear in battle with wild beasts and be torn to pieces by them, or to fight as gladiators with one another to delight the eyes of the heathen populace. In Cæsarea Philippi alone, at the celebration of the birthday of Domitian, more than two thousand five hundred Jews shed their blood in the arena. The males under seventeen years of age and the women were sold directly into slavery. Titus, with all his prisoners and all his booty, marched to Rome, where he had a brilliant triumph in the year 71, A. D.; the sacred vessels of the temple were carried before the "imperator" and Simon and John, for the first time shoulder to shoulder, were obliged to march before the chariot of the victor with the seven hundred chosen captives. Simon, being the real leader, was first scourged and then throttled at the stake, in accordance with Roman custom; John finished his career in prison.

But although Titus had thus celebrated his triumph, Judea was not yet wholly subdued. The three fortresses Herodeion, Machærus, and Masada, still stood unconquered, held by all that were left of the rebels. The legate, Lucilius Bassus, was commissioned to complete the pacification of the country. Herodeion seems to have surrendered immediately, but Machærus, trusting to its exceptionally strong position, took the risk of a siege. Both sides fought with the greatest bravery and desperation, a certain noble youth named Eleazar distinguishing himself particularly among the Jews; but in a sortie he advanced too far and was captured by the Romans. Bassus had him scourged in sight of the besieged and erected a cross as though to crucify him; at this the garrison promised to surrender the fortress in return for the liberty of Eleazar and free retreat for themselves. Of course Bassus accepted these terms and actually kept them, but the inhabitants of the city were partly slaughtered and partly sold into slavery. The retiring garrison united with various stragglers who had succeeded in escaping from the underground passages of Jerusalem and found a hiding-place in the forests east of the Jordan ; Bassus had the whole region surrounded by cavalry and then cut down the forests, so that every man of them perished, three thousand in number.

Now only Masada was left. Here Eleazar was in command, a descendant of Judas the Galilean and a near kinsman of that Menahem who had fought in Jerusalem as leader of the Sicarii. Eleazar too had fought under his banner, but when disaster befell Menahem he had been able to escape from Jerusalem and take refuge in Masada. By its location the place was almost impregnable. Flavius Silva, now commanding in place of Lucilius Bassus, who had died meanwhile, had a wall built about the whole place to make the escape of the garrison impossible ; then with tremendous exertion he built a rampart at the only vulnerable spot, and thereupon had the engines approach the walls. They succeeded in destroying the wall ; but behind it Eleazar had constructed a new one of wood and earth, against which the battering-ram was powerless. Accordingly they tried fire against the new wall, and the whole wooden structure went up in flames. This sealed the fate of Masada. The assault was planned for the next day, and the watchfulness of the guards was doubled in the intervening night in order that no victim might escape. That night,—it was the night of Pascha—Eleazar took a desperate resolution. Nobody should fall into the hands of the Romans ; all preferred death to captivity. Ten were selected by lot who were to kill all the others, and of these ten one, who in turn should first kill the other nine and finally himself. The horrible plan was actually carried out. The sole survivor went about once more to all the corpses to make sure that no life was left. When he was convinced of this he hurled the torch into the house and thrust his sword into his own breast. Only an old woman and a mother with five children had hidden themselves in an aqueduct. Nine hundred and sixty corpses covered the ground which they could no longer defend.

The next morning when the Romans advanced they were met with a deathlike silence ; they suspected a ruse and raised a loud battle-cry. Then the seven survivors came forth and told the Romans what had happened. On the 15th of Nisan, i. e., of April, in the year 73 A. D., the first day of the Easter festival, the same day on which, according to tradition, the God of Israel had led his people out of Egyptian bondage into freedom, the last bulwark of Israel's liberty had fallen, and Israel was delivered into Roman bondage. Fifty years later, indeed, it made once more an attempt to conquer its freedom from Rome with the sword, but God had decreed otherwise : this attempt led only to more wretched slavery. Israel as a people, as a nation, was dead, and was destined to remain dead.

Rome was rude and heartless in letting the conquered nation feel the *vœ victis*. Innumerable are the medals and memorial coins of the three Flavian emperors : Vespasian, Titus, and Domitian, on the obverse of which appears beneath a palm-tree a woman sitting on the ground in inconsolable grief, with the legend, "Conquered Judea." The whole country became a Roman province, and the soil was declared the personal property of the emperor ; perhaps no provision seemed to the Jews so much like bitter mockery as this, that they were now compelled to pay to the imperial treasury and deliver upon the Capitol the tithes which formerly, in accordance with the law, they had paid annually to the temple ; the Capitoline Jupiter was to take the place of the God of Israel. As a picture which touches the depths of the heart, I quote a passage from a Jewish writing composed under the fresh impression of these awful blows of fate :

"Well for him that is unborn, or if born, has died. But woe to us who live, that we must see the afflictions of Judah and the fate of Jerusalem. Arise and prepare to lament, begin to mourn with me and lament along with me. Ye husbandmen, scatter seed no more, and thou earth, why givest thou thy fruit ? Keep back the sweetness of thy nourishment. Thou grape, why givest thou still thy wine when it shall no longer be offered in Zion and no firstlings be sacrificed? And thou heaven, withhold thy dew, neither open the storehouses of the rain. And thou sun, hold back thy shining light, and thou moon, quench thy clear beams; for to what end shall any longer lights arise after the light of Zion is sunken in darkness? And ye young men, go not into the bridal-chamber, and ye virgins, deck not yourselves with bridal wreaths, and ye wives pray not to become mothers; for the barren shall rejoice, and those who have no children be glad; and those who have children shall lament. For wherefore shall they bring forth with pain and bury with groans? Wherefore shall they have sons henceforth, and their names be kept alive, when the mother of all is desolate and her children dragged into bondage? Therefore speak no more of ornaments, neither think how ye shall deck yourselves. But ye priests, take the keys of the sanctuary and cast them up to heaven, giving them back to God, and say: Do Thou guard Thy house, we could not do it! And ye maidens who weave byssus and silk with the gold of Ophir, take it all swiftly and cast it into the fire, that the fire may give it back to Him that made it, and the enemy obtain it not. Our fathers rest without griefs, and the righteous slumber in the earth in peace: for they know nothing of this distress and have not heard of the fate that is come upon us. O that thou haddest ears, thou earth, and thou a mouth, thou dust, to go and proclaim it in the under world and say to the dead: Blessed are ye above us who still live."

Our eyes fill with tears as we see the curtain go down upon all this misery and woe. The tragedy is over. We are at the end of the History of Israel. Dreadful as this end has been, we cannot refuse our admiration. The Jewish people fell like a man and a hero, and even in its fall it triumphed over the victor. All-powerful Rome could destroy Israel but not pervert it. Israel did not give way to Rome to the extent of even a single thought; it remained what it was, and all its misfortunes served only to confirm and strengthen it in its essential character. While Rome has long since passed away, and only ruins tell us of its glory, Israel is still, after two thousand years, what it was. It has survived all the vicissitudes of history, all the changes of ages, ever consistent, comparable in the life of nations to one of those erratic boulders, which wear out the tooth of time and mock at eternity, a strange yet imposing spectacle, a living witness of long-vanished millenniums.

Indeed, in a certain sense we may say that Israel has become the heir of Rome. To this day there stands in Rome the arch of Titus with the sculptured representation of the sacred vessels of the temple at Jerusalem, which were carried before the wondering eyes of the Roman populace in that triumphal procession; this arch tells us still in its mighty stone language what happened at Jerusalem eighteen hundred years ago. But what a change in Rome itself! When the glory of the Cæsars had fallen into the dust and Rome had become a provincial city, there arose in Rome a new universal dominion, a dominion so powerful and extensive that even the empire of the ancient Roman emperors grows pale in comparison. And the wielder of this new Roman dominion was the man with the triple crown, the successor of the Jewish high priest. The new spiritual power, which originated on Jewish soil, has overcome the whole world and triumphed over Rome. To it even Rome was compelled to bow, confessing the supremacy of Jerusalem. For empire passes away, but the spirit endures. It is the only imperishable thing on earth and in history.

APPENDIX.

QUESTIONS AND ANSWERS ON "THE HISTORY OF THE PEOPLE OF ISRAEL."

A reader of *The Open Court* has proposed a number of questions on "The History of the People of Israel" which Professor Cornill has answered one by one. We publish the following condensed statement referring to this subject:

On page 8 occurs the remark: The composer of the Book of Kings had before him the official annals of the ancient kings of Israel and Judah. The frequent reference in the Book of Kings for wanting matter to "the book of the chronicles of the kings of Israel" or "the book of the chronicles of the kings of Judah" is probably supposed by uncritical readers to mean the Bible Book of Chronicles, as on the other hand the references in the latter book to "the book of the kings of Israel" or sometimes "the book of the kings of Israel and Judah" are supposed to be to the Biblical Book of Kings.

Professor Cornill explains: "The chronicles of the kings of Israel, or of Judah, to which the author of the Biblical Book of Kings constantly refers cannot be the Biblical Book of Chronicles, since the latter comes at the earliest from the Persian period and is in any case much younger than the Book of Kings. How thus could it be possible for the Book of Kings to refer to the Book of Chronicles, and *vice versa?* For the evidence on the latter statement, and the probabilities regarding the actual "chronicle of the kings of Judah" which constituted the authority of the writer of our Book of Kings, see Cornill's *Einleitung in das alte Testament*, pp. 108-128."

In the description of the Holy Land (p. 13) occur the statements: "the land is almost entirely shut off from the world outside," and on the following page, "at the same time it is a bridge and highway of world-commerce without parallel." How are these two statements to be reconciled? Professor Cornill's answer is: "The characterization is derived from no less an authority than the great geographer Karl Ritter. As an explanatory illustration the reader is referred to Switzerland and the Tyrol. By virtue of the passes through the Gotthard and St. Bernard, in the case of Switzerland, and of the Brenner Pass in the case of the Tyrol, these two lands constitute 'a bridge for the commerce of the world without a parallel' and were formerly the highways for the entire commerce between Italy and the North, while nevertheless both countries are shut off by themselves and secluded."

The characterization (p. 16) of Tacitus's description of Palestine as "notoriously unjust" (*berüchtigt*) seems severe, and in explanation Professor Cornill refers to the passage in Tacitus's History, V., 2–9, "in which all the anti-Semitic slander of the world seems to be collected."

Professor Cornill accepts Abraham as a real historical person, but rejects all the other patriarchs, saying, "However plastic and distinct the individualities of Ishmael and Edom Israel and Joseph may seem to us, they are all only personifications and representations of the races or tribes whose names they bear." "Races never adopt the names of individuals, but the patronymic tribal ancestor is first and ever a composite, a personification of the people." (p. 30.) When asked on what ground he rejects Isaac, for instance, Professor Cornill explains that "Isaac too is only a patronymic, and that the name is plainly a synonym of Israel (just as Jacob is used in parallelism to Israel), in the only two passages in which it occurs outside the Pentateuch. (Amos vii. 9, 16.)" Moreover, Professor Cornill does not regard Isaac as an imposing personality, but on the contrary strikingly subordinate and painted in dull colors; he is merely the son of his father and the father of his own children.

The curious shifting of the names Gideon and Jerubbaal in

Judges viii. 29 to ix. 1, led to some confusion, which is cleared up by the observation that Gideon and Jerubbaal are two names for one and the same person. He had taken into his harem, from purely political considerations as tribal king of Manasseh, a noble woman from the important Canaanite city of Shechem, and her son, with the help of his kinsmen of Shechem, set himself up as king after the death of his father. This story of Abimelech is especially well and reliably transmitted and is an historical genre-piece of first quality.

The seeming conflict of characteristics in Saul (pp. 63 and 65), who is spoken of as having a noble and chivalrous nature, a strong and yet sensitive nature, but of whom Professor Cornill also says that his whole character has a rude and commonplace cast (*spiessbürgerlich*), is explained on the ground that *spiessbürgerlich* is not of itself a reproach: "the *Spiessbürger* is thoroughly honest and honorable, an honest man in the fullest sense of the word, and generally an excellent fellow; the application of the epithet only implies that Saul was entirely without genius. This is the tragic feature of the situation. It is no reproach to be without genius, but in Saul's circumstances genius was needed."

It will be observed that Professor Cornill entirely ignores the Goliath episode. In reply to a request for his reasons, he states: "The episode of Goliath is pure legend, inasmuch as the giant Goliath, according to the indisputable testimony of 2 Samuel xxi. 19, was killed in David's wars with the Philistines, and by the Bethlehemite Elhanan." The phrase "the brother of," preceding "Goliath," is not in the original. The corresponding passage 1 Chronicles xx. 5, is corrupt. The writer of Chronicles, which is much later, or some copyist, misunderstood the word Beth-lehemite (-lechemi) in 2 Samuel xxi. 19, and brought out of it "Lachmi" as the name of the person slain, which is not to be found in the source, and then to make this harmonize with the legend of David he inserted the words "brother of" before Goliath. Older translators then adopted this phrase into the original passage in 2 Samuel.

In the first book of Samuel, as is well known, in the chapters from xviii. to xxvi., there are apparently two occasions on which Saul hurls a javelin at David while he is with him in his house, and two occasions on which David approaches Saul, while the latter is pursuing him, and leaves evidence that he might have taken Saul's life but spared it out of consideration for the royal office, and perhaps for the sake of Jonathan. Professor Cornill speaks of but one of the first incidents because there are two parallel accounts involved and rather clumsily woven together. He entirely passes over the other incident, the duplication of which is to be explained in the same way, not because he questions the verity of the incident, but because it is relatively insignificant; it may be an important testimonial for David's character, but has no particular influence upon the political development of the people of Israel.

Our history (p. 123), after mentioning the accession to the throne of Israel of the usurper Pekah, adds: "In Jerusalem the crown had just been assumed by Ahaz, the grandson of Azariah," whereas 2 Kings xvi. 1, says that this occurred in "the seventeenth year of Pekah." Moreover Professor Cornill entirely ignores King Jotham, to whom 2 Kings, xv. 32 gives a reign of sixteen years. Of this and the general confusion in the dates of these two chapters Professor Cornill says: "The chronology of the period in Israelitish history from the accession of Jehu to the siege of Jerusalem by Sennacherib is extremely uncertain. It is conceded and undeniable that the chronology of the Bible is inconsistent here and objectively incorrect. We are forced to depend here upon the chronology of the Assyrians which is at our disposal and which we have to use as a basis. According to the accounts of the Assyrians it is beyond doubt that Jehu occupied the throne of Samaria in the year 842, wherefore the murder of Ahaziah had already taken place, while by Assyrian records Ahaz must have reigned in Jerusalem in 735. Since Ahab of Israel was still ruling in 854, we must accept 842 as the first year of Jehu, and consequently of Athaliah also. Now the Bible reckons: Athaliah 6 years, Joash 40, Amaziah 29, Azariah-Uzziah 52, and Jotham 16 years, that is altogether 143 years, whereas according to Assyrian chronology there can have been but

107. Since therefore the Judean series must be shortened it will be simplest to either strike entirely from the list or reduce to a minimum the reign of Jotham, who according to the express declaration of 2 Kings xv. 5, was regent for his leper father. But after all we must give up the attempt to entirely reconcile the "synchronisms" of the Book of Kings.

The victory at Raphiah, referred to on page 130, of Sargon the Assyrian over the combined Egyptians and Canaanites, is not referred to by the Hebrew Scriptures, but it is attested by the Assyrian monuments of Sargon himself. Raphiah is the same place where in 217 occurred the famous battle between Ptolemy IV. and Antiochus III.

In reply to a question regarding the seeming confusion in the account of the deeds of King Hezekiah, Professor Cornill says: "The only explanation that can be offered for the statement, 2 Kings xviii. 8, that Hezekiah smote the Philistines even to Gaza, coming where it does, is that Hezekiah actually succeeded in regaining some parts of his country which Sennacherib had taken from him. It signifies nothing that this statement occurs in the Bible before the account of the invasion of Sennacherib. and since Isaiah as well as Sargon and Sennacherib, there seems to be no other way but to assume that 2 Kings xviii. 8, belongs in fact after chapter xix., just as the last half of chapter xx. plainly belongs after chapter xviii., verse 8.

The History of Israel states that Elijah (1 Kings xviii. 21) was advocating the calves of Dan and Bethel. On the surface this seems quite contrary to the fact, and Elijah's address beginning with this verse is commonly quoted as an evidence for the purely monotheistic zeal of Elijah. Professor Cornill's statement and his reasons can be understood only in connection with 1 Kings xii. 28–33, and what follows up to the passage in question. He says: "It is implied in 1 Kings xviii. 21, that Elijah advocated 'the calves of Dan and Bethel.'" (p. 127.) The "calf-worship" was the official religious service of Israel's Jahveh cult. (1 Kings xii. 28–33.) Not a word of criticism of this is reported to us on the part of Elijah. Consequently when he grows zealous for the national Israelitish worship as against the Tyrian Baal, he is "advocating" the calves of Dan and Bethel. It is not to be overlooked that these "calves" were not idols in the technical sense, but merely symbolical representations of Jahveh, the god of Israel; Hosea was the first who regarded them as idols.

INDEX.

ABIATHAR, opposes Solomon's claim, 82; is banished, 83.
Abijah, son of Rehoboam, alliance with Damascus, 97.
Abimelech, succeeds Gideon, 52; slain at Thebez, 53.
Abishai, brother of Joab, in David's wars, 77.
Abner, Saul's cousin and general, establishes Ish-bosheth at Mahanaim, defeated by Joab, deserts to David, 72; murdered by Joab, 73.
Abraham, an historical personage, 21; compared with Lycurgus, 29.
Absalom, slays Amnon, cultivates insurrection, 79; defeated and slain by Joab, 80.
Achish, of Gath, receives David, 69.
Adonijah, David's heir, supplanted by Solomon, 82; is executed, 83.
Agrippa, a friend at the Roman court, 253; his youth, 254; a friend of Caligula, made successor to Philip, 255; succeeds Antipas, receives Judea, 257; favors the Jews, persecutes the Christians, 258.
Agrippa (II.), serves his people at Rome, 259; his vain attempt at conciliation, 270; supports the peace party, 273; with the Roman forces, 279.
Agu-kak-rimi, Cossæic King, 24.
Ahab, marries Jezebel, 101; undeserved ill repute, makes peace with Judah, 102; wars with Damascus, 103-4; peace, 105; renewed war, death, 106; the curse upon his house, 108.
Ahaz, King of Judah, assailed by Israel and Damascus, 123, sacrifices his son, calls in the Assyrians, 124; dies, 130.
Ahaziah, a weak king of Israel, 107.
Ahaziah, King of Judah, 108.
Ahmes, Pharaoh, expels the Hyksos, 25.
Aijalon, occupied by Elon of the tribe of Zebulon, 50.
Albinus, procurator in Judea, 266.
Alcimus, a Hellenist, appointed high priest by Demetrius, 198; persecutes pious Jews, 200.
Alexander the Great, his relation to the Jews, 170-171; his policy, 176.
Alexander Jannæus (Jonathan-Alexander) high priest and king, 215; wars with Ptolemy and Cleopatra, 216; his desecration of the sacred office, his people rebel,

217; massacres the Pharisees, 218; his achievements, 219.

Alexander (II.), captured by Pompey, escapes, invades Judea, 225; fails and tries again, 226; executed, 227.

Alexandra-Salome, wife of Aristobulus and of Alexander Jannæus, 215; her rule, 220; her death, 221.

Alexander Balas, pretender, opposes Demetrius King of Syria, 201; courts Jonathan, appoints him high priest, succeeds, and is then defeated, 202.

Alexander, a pretender to the throne of Archelaus, 245.

Amalekites, defeated by Saul, 64.

Amasa, supplants Joab as David's general, is slain by Joab, 81.

Amaziah, war with Joash of Israel, 120–121; is slain, 121.

Amenhotep IV. the Heretic King, 26.

Ammonites, assail the Israelites east of the Jordan, 55.

Amnon, David's eldest son, forces his sister Thamar, 78; murdered by Absalom, 79.

Amon, King of Judah, murdered, 136.

Amos, though a Judean, worked in Israel, 128.

Ananias, high priest, 273; murdered, 274.

Ananiel, high priest, 232; removed by Herod, 233.

Ananos, high priest, 266, 276, 280; slain, 281.

Antigonus (Mattathias), escapes from Roman imprisonment, 226; seeks in vain the support of Cæsar, 227; makes incursion in Galilee, 229; seeks aid of the Parthians and takes Judea, 230; besieged by Sosius, 231; taken and executed, 232.

Antioch, founded by Seleucus Nicator, Jews in, 171.

Antiochus III. takes Palestine from Egypt, 173; gives his daughter to Ptolemy V., 186; slain, 187.

Antiochus Epiphanes, 188–196; sacks Jerusalem, 191; offers sacrifices to Zeus in the temple, 192.

Antiochus VII. recognizes the independence of Judea, 207; tries to overthrow it, 208; conquers it, 209; dies, 210.

Antiochus IX. fails to subdue Hyrcanus, 211.

Antipater, prefect in Idumea, takes up the cause of Hyrcanus II., 222, 225; procurator, 228; appoints his sons Phasael and Herod generals, 228; goes over to Cassius, is poisoned, 229.

Antony, ruler of Asia, 229; supports Herod, 230–231; gives much of Herod's territory to Cleopatra, 233.

Apuriu, of Egyptian monuments, not the Hebrews, 40.

Apollonius, commandant of Jerusalem, defeated by Judas Maccabæus, 194.

Aramæans, the Hebrew patriarchs were, 20; defeated by David at Helam, 77; establish a kingdom at Damascus, 91. (See Damascus and Syria.)

Aretas, an Arab sheik, aids Hyrcanus II., 222, 223; war with Herod Antipas, 252.

Archelaus, son of Herod, 240; saluted as king by the troops, 241; begins his reign with a massacre in the

INDEX. 311

temple, goes to Rome for confirmation, 242; trouble with a pretender, 245; is removed and banished to Gaul, 246.

Aristobulus (Judas A.), adopts royal title, murders his relatives, a Hellenist, 214; Judaizes Galilee, dies, 215.

Aristobulus (II.), 220; overthrows Hyrcanus II. 221; defeated by him, 222; aided by Scaurus, 223; overthrown by Pompey, 224; taken prisoner to Rome, 225; escapes, rebels, and is reimprisoned, 226; released by Cæsar, but is poisoned, 227.

Aristobulus, high priest, murdered by Herod, 233.

Artaxerxes Longhand, favors the Jews, 155, 160.

Asa, King of Judah, son of Abijah, punishes his mother for idolatry, 98; is beset by Baasha of Israel, 98; fortifies Judah, 99.

Asinæus and Anilæus, two Jews, cause disturbance in Mesopotamia, 259.

Assyria, rise of, 24; revival of under Asurnazirpal, 101; intimate connection of her history with that of Israel, 117.

Asurnazirpal, King of Assyria, receives tribute from Omri, 101.

Asurbanipal, decay of Assyria under, 138.

Athaliah, daughter of Ahab, marries Jehoram, 103; murders her grandchildren, 112; institutes worship of Baal at Jerusalem; explanation of her course, 113; death, 116

Augustus, favors Herod, 234; confirms Herod's will, 243; takes a new census of Judea, 248.

BAAL, worship of, suppressed in Israel by Jehu, 111; established in Judah by Athaliah, 113.

Baasha, murders Nadab, 98; blockades Judah, 98–99; end of reign, 99.

Babylon, fall of, 148, 150.

Babylonia, primitive inhabitants of, Sumerians, 22; conquered by Semites, 22; conquered by Elamites, 23.

Babylonian civilization, our debt to it, 22.

Babylonian captivity, see Captivity.

Babylonian Jews, their conditions and relations with those returned from exile, 155.

Bacchides, Syrian general, defeats Judas Maccabæus, 199; makes peace with Jonathan, 201.

Bagoses, Persian governor, 169.

Barak, resists and overthrows Sisera, 50.

Bath-sheba, 78; controls David, 82; has Solomon declared successor to David, 82.

Benaiah, captain of the guard, supports Solomon's claims, 82.

Ben-hadad, King of Damascus, makes war on Israel, defeated by Ahab, 104; breaks forth with Ahab, 106; defeats him, 107; dies, 108.

Ben-hadad II. besieges Samaria, 119; defeated by Joash of Israel, 120.

Benjamin, united with Joseph in trying to rule, 37; separated from Joseph after the conquest of Canaan, 49.

Bethsura, scene of a victory of Judas Maccabæus, 195; besieged by Lysias, 196; taken, 197.

Bethzachariah, scene of defeat of Judas Maccabæus, 196.

Beth-horon, scene of defeat of Cestius Gallus, 275.

Bible History, weakness of as commonly taught, 4.

CÆSAR, releases Aristobulus, 227; favors the Jews, 228.

Cæsarea Philippi, founded by Philip, son of Herod, 244; insurrection in, 265; terrible slaughter in, 275.

Caligula, 253–254; intimate with Agrippa, 255.

Canaan, origin of name, 10.

Canaanites, expelled from Palestine by Philistines, 45; conquest of, a slow process, 47; enslaved by Solomon, 91.

Captivity, Babylonian, beginning of, 141–144; influence of, on the mission of Israel, 145–148; return from, first expedition, 150–152; second expedition, 156.

Cassius, courted by Antipater, 229.

Cassius Longinus, legate in Syria, 260.

Celer, a Roman tribune, butchers Jews, is executed, 262.

Cestius Gallus, legate in Syria, 267; burns part of Jerusalem, and suffers defeat, 275.

Chabiri, the, possibly the Hebrews, 34–35.

Chatti, see Cheta, 39.

Chedorlaomer, King of Elam, 24.

Cheta, invade Syria, 39; rule Northern Palestine, 40; their rule overthrown, 45.

Chetasar, King of the Cheta, his war with Rameses II., 39.

Christian era not coincident with the birth of Christ, 239.

Chu-en-aten, see Amenhotep.

Claudius, aided to the throne by Agrippa, gives him Judea, 257.

leopatra, invades Palestine, 216.

Cœlesyria, invaded by Shalmaneser II., 105, 108, 117, 118; invaded by Semiramis, 119, 120; falls to Egypt, 170; taken by Syria, 172.

Coponius, Roman procurator in Palestine, 248.

Cossæans, conquer northeast Mesopotamia, 24.

Crassus, sacks Jerusalem, 226.

Cuneiform characters, used by Pharaoh Amenhotep, 27.

Cuspius Fadus, Roman procurator in Judea, 260.

Cyaxares, 139.

Cyprus, important fortress in last stand against Rome, 274.

Cyrus, King of Persia, 148; conquers Babylon, reason for his release of the Jews, 150.

DAMASCUS, capital of Aramæan Kingdom, 91; wars with Ahab of Israel, 103–106; besieged by Shalmaneser II., 118; taken by Assyrians, 122; the kingdom obliterated, 124; slaughter of Jews in, 275.

Dan, settles in the north, conquers and renames Laish, 49.

David, 8; called in to soothe Saul, characterization of, loved by Jonathan, marries Michal, 66; suspected by Saul, 67; assailed by Saul, 68; flees to Judah; his affair

INDEX. 313

with Nabal, 68; relieves Keilah, becomes a Philistine vassal, resides at Ziklag, 69; becomes the avenger of Saul and the finisher of his work, tribal King of Judah, resides at Hebron, 71; attacked by Abner, receives Abner to favor, 72; punishes the murderers of Ishbosheth, 73; chosen successor to Ish-bosheth, subdues the Philistines, defeats the Moabites, 74; moves his capital to Jerusalem, contrasted with Saul, 75; brings the ark of the covenant to Jerusalem, 76; chastises the Ammonites and the Aramæans, takes the Ammonite capital, 77; his wars all defensive, his sin with Bathsheba, 78; banishes Absalom, receives him back, 79; flees before his revolt, laments his death, 80; returns to Jerusalem, recalls Joab, suppresses the rebellion of Sheba the Benjaminite, 81; controlled by Bath-sheba, makes Solomon heir to the throne, 82; summary, 83–85; created the people of Israel, 83.

Darius, permits work on temple to continue, 154.

Dead Sea, 11.

Deborah, 50.

Demetrius, King of Syria, defeats and slays Antiochus V. and Lysias, appoints Alcimus high priest, 198; wars with the Maccabees, 199–201; opposed by a pretender Alexander Balas, 201.

Demetrius II., defeats Alexander Balas, 202; makes concessions to Jonathan, is overthrown by Trypho, 203.

Demetrius III., supports the Pharisees against Alexander, 218.

Dionysius Exiguus, calculator of the Christian era, 239.

Division of David's kingdom, 96.

Ecclesiastes, a product of Hellenism, 181.

Edom, foundation of nation of, 34; frees itself from Solomon, 90; successful revolt from Judah, 108; conquered by Hyrcanus, 211.

Edomites, assail David and are punished, 77.

Ehud, stabs Eglon, king of Moab, 51.

Elah, of Israel, son of Baasha, murdered by Zimri, 99.

Elamites, the, their conquest of Babylonia, 23; overcome by Semitic Babylonians, 24.

Elasa, scene of the death of Judas Maccabæus, 199.

Elath, Edomite seaport, taken by Uzziah, 121; restored by Israel, 123.

Eleazar, a Pharisee, rebukes Hyrcanus, 212.

Eleazar, leader of the Zealots, taken treacherously by Felix, 263.

Eleazar, son of Ananias, a leader of opposition to Rome, 273; engages in civil strife, 274.

Eleazar, son of Simon, one of the leaders in Jerusalem, 284; defeated by John of Gish-Chala, 285.

Eleazar, a noble Jew, at the siege of Machærus, 295.

Eleazar, his desperate defence of Masada, 296–297.

Eliashib, high priest, allied

with the enemies of Nehemiah, 166.
Elijah, religious conflict with Ahab pure legend, 102; does not condemn the Baal worship, 127.
Elisha, selects Jehu to exterminate the house of Ahab, 108; connected with Jehoahaz of Israel, 119.
Emmaus, scene of victory of Judas Maccabæus, 195.
Esarhaddon, conquers Egypt, 137.
Ethbaal, king of Tyre, father of Jezebel, 101.
Exodus, from Egypt, History of Israel begins with, 16; time of, 27–41; why it tarried in Sinai, 43.
Ezra, his influence with Artaxerxes, 155; arrival in Jerusalem, 156; his zeal against mixed marriages, 156–159; assisted by Nehemiah, 160; produces and reads the law, 164.

FELIX, Roman procurator, attacks the Zealots, 263; suppresses Messiahs, 264; plunders Jews in Cæsarea, recalled, 265.
Festus (Porcius), procurator in Judea, 265.
Flavius Silva, takes Masada, 296.
Frederick William IV. of Prussia, compared to Saul, 65.

GABINIUS, general under Pompey, 224, 226.
Galilee, physical features of, 12; Judaized by Aristobulus, 215; conquest of, by the Romans, 277–279.
Gedaliah, Babylonian prefect over Jerusalem, 143.

Gessius Florus, procurator in Judea, 266; his extortions and outrages, 268–269.
Geshem the Arabian, opponent of Nehemiah, 162.
Gibbethon, besieged by Israelites, 98, 99.
Gibeonites, a Canaanitish alliance, 64.
Gideon, defeats the Midianites, 52; establishes kingdom, 52.
Gilboa, scene of defeat and death of Saul, 70.
Gilead, location of, 10.
Gish-chala, taken by the Romans, 279.
Gad, assailed by Ephraim and Manasseh, 51.
Gorgias, Syrian general, defeated by Judas Maccabæus, 195.
Goshen, Land of, has monuments of bricks made of mud and straw, 40.
Greece, influence of on modern civilization, 2; decay of before the Macedonian conquest, 178–179.
Gudea of Sirgurla, Babylonian prince, 23.

HADAD, frees Edom from Israel, 90,
Hagen of Tronje, compared with Joab, 73.
Hammurabi, founder of Babylonian Empire, 24.
Hanum, son of Nahash, insults David's messengers, 76; is punished, 77.
Haran (Carrhæ) the initial point of Israel's emigration, 20.
Hazael, King of Damascus, murders Ben-hadad, 108. defeated by Shalmaneser II., 171; overruns Israel, 118.

INDEX.

Hebrew tradition, reliable in essentials, 5; historical monuments, scarcity of, 6, 8, 9; inscription, the solitary, 7; legend fitted to Oriental history, 21.

Hebron, David's residence while tribal king, 71.

Helix, heads a rebellion in Jerusalem, 229.

Heliodorus, a Syrian official, tries to plunder the temple, 188; murders Seleucus IV., 188.

Hellas, see Greece.

Hellenism, 175; contrasted with the Oriental spirit, 176; influence of in Alexandria, 179; in Judea, 179–182, 187–192.

Hermon, Mount, 12.

Herod, son of Antipater, 228; avenges his father's murder, suppresses uprising in Galilee, 229; confirmed by Antony, flees before Antigonus, 230; made king of Judea, 231; takes Jerusalem by storm, 232; recalls Hyrcanus, appoints Ananel high priest, 232; displaces him for Aristobulus, murders the latter, resists the wiles of Cleopatra, 233; makes war on Malchus, wins the favor of Augustus, 234; estimate of his reign, 235–237; his last act to condemn two violators of the Roman dignity, 238.

Herod Antipas, son of Herod the Great, 240; sovereign of Jesus, founds Tiberias, 244; aided by Tiberius against Aretas, 252; quarrels with Agrippa, 254; removed and exiled by Caligula, 257.

Herod (III.), in charge of the temple, 259.

Herodeion, surrenders, 295.

Herodias, sister of Agrippa 254; goes into exile with her husband Herod Antipas. 257.

Hezekiah, 130; rebels against Sennacherib, visited by Merodach-baladan, also by Ethiopians, receives Padi of Ekron as prisoner, joins revolt, 132; submits to Sennacherib, gives up to him his own family, 133; refuses to surrender Jerusalem to Sennacherib, 134; expels the Philistines from Gaza, submits to Assyria, 136.

High priest, first notice of, 152.

High priesthood, limited to the sons of Zadok, 153; attitude of toward Hellenism, 182; furnishes the leaders in resistance to Rome, 276.

Hiram of Tyre, lends to Solomon, forecloses on borderlands, 91.

Historical records in Israel begin with the kings, 17.

Hittites, see Chatti.

Hophra, see Nahabra.

Horites, conquered by Edomites, 34.

Hosea the prophet the first to condemn the worship of Baal as heathenish, 128.

Hoshea, murders Pekah, tributary Assyrian ruler, 124.

Hushai, delays Absalom's pursuit of David, 80.

Hyksos in Egypt, 25.

Hyrcania, Jews deported to, 169.

Hyrcanus, escapes assassins. 208; beset by Antiochus VII., 209; treats with him, receives easy terms, takes aggressive, 210; conquers all Palestine, 211; deserts the Pharisees, allies himself with the Sadducees, 212; incongruity of his position, 213.

Hyrcanus (II.), high priest, 220; resigns in favor of Aristobulus, 221; defeats him, 222; appears before Pompey, 224; reappointed high priest, 225; confirmed by Cæsar, 227; mutilated by Antigonus, 230; recalled to Jerusalem by Herod, 232; murdered by Herod, 234.

IDUMEANS, called to Jerusalem by the Zealots, 280; massacre inhabitants, 281.
Immigration to Canaan, circumstances of, 33.
Isaiah, regarded the dependency of Judah on Assyria as a blessing, 146.
Ishmael, his relation to Israel, 32.
Ishmael, high priest, 265.
Ish-bosheth, son and successor of Saul, 71; quarrels with his general, Abner, 72; assassinated, 73.
Isopolity, 171.
Israel, its contribution to civilization compared with that of Greece and Rome, 3; immigration to Canaan established, 19; time of, 27; the people born of the Exodus, 42; learned agriculture from the Canaanites, 48; centrifugal tendency in, 48.
Israel, kingdom of, established, 96; combines with Damascus against Judah, 123; becomes an Assyrian dependency, 124; end of the kingdom, 124; much underrated, 126; its religion as pure as that of Judah, 127; not all taken captives by Shalmaneser IV., 126; the home of prophecy, 128; its peculiar mission, 146-147.
Israelites adopt the language of Canaan, 33.

JABESH-GILEAD, seeks help from all Israel, 55.
Jabin, king of Hazor, 49.
Jacob and Laban, stand for Israel and Aram, 31.
Jacob, meaning of name; represents a second emigration from Mesopotamia, 35.
Jacobitic emigrants unite with Abrahamitic, 37.
Jadduah, high priest, 170.
Jair and Machir, families of Manasseh, 49.
Jason, brother of Onias III., high priest, an ardent Hellenist, 189; deposed, 190; dies, 191.
Jebusites, held Jerusalem before David made it his capital, 75.
Jehoahaz, son of Jehu, his reign a wretched period, 112; beset by Hazael of Syria, 118; the unnamed king with Elisha, 119.
Jehoahaz of Judah, son of Josiah, made king, removed by Necho, 140.
Jehoash, see Joash.
Jehoiada, priest, saves Joash, 112; crowns him, 116.
Jehoiakim, son of Josiah, King of Judah as vassal of Egypt, 140; rebels against Nebuchadnezzar, dies, 141.
Jehoiachin, King of Judah, captured and taken to Babylon, 141.

INDEX.

Jehoram, of Judah, marries Athaliah, loses Edom and Libnah, 108.

Jehoram, of Israel, becomes king, 107; invades Moab, 107; retakes Ramoth, 108; murdered by Jehu, 109.

Jehoshaphat, of Judah, makes alliance with Israel, 103; fails in expedition to Ophir; supports Ahab against Damascus, 106; supports Jehoram against Moab, dies, 107.

Jehosheba, saves Joash, her nephew, from Athaliah, 112.

Jehu, selected to exterminate the house of Ahab, murders Jehoram of Israel and Ahaziah, 109; murders Jezebel, orders murder of Jehoram's sons, 110; murders princes of Judah, massacres the worshippers of Baal, 111; sends tribute to Shalmaneser II., 118; dies in peace, 117.

Jephthah, defeats the invading Ammonites, 51.

Jeremiah, contemporary of Josiah, 137.

Jericho, called the city of Palms, 12; taken by Joshua, 47; destroyed by King Ochus, 169.

Jeroboam, rebels against Solomon, is expelled, 93; King of Israel, 96; moves his capital to Penuel, 97; and again to Tirzah, 98.

Jeroboam II., restores Israel, subdues Moab, ruled from Edom to Damascus, 122.

Jerusalem, made the capital by David, 75; sacked by Joash, 121; besieged by Sennacherib, 134; destruction of, by Nebuchadnezzar, 142–143; walls rebuilt by Ezra, 159; torn down by order of Artaxerxes, 160; rebuilt by Nehemiah, 162–164; final siege and destruction, 286–297.

Jeshua, one of the Elders, 151; high priest, 152.

Jesus, his slight influence on Jewish history, 239.

Jesus, a conservative leader, 280; slain, 281.

Jesus Sirach, the Book, influenced by Hellenism, 181.

Jewish Canon, includes historical books among the prophetic, 4.

Jezebel, wife of Ahab, 101; responsible for murder of Naboth, 102; murdered, 110.

Jezreel, physical features of, 12.

Joab, David's nephew and general, defeats Abner, 72; murders Abner, compared with Hagen of Tronje, 73; defeats the Aramæans. punishes the Edomites, 77; intercedes for Absalom, 79; defeats and slays Absalom, 80; is dismissed, recalled, suppresses the revolt of Sheba the Benjaminite, 81; opposes Bath-sheba, 82; is executed, 83.

Joash, of Judah, saved from the phrenzy of Athaliah, 112; crowned, 116; checks the cupidity of the priests, 116; ransoms Jerusalem, 118; murdered, 120.

Joash of Israel, defeats Benhadad II., attacks Amaziah of Judah, 120; sacks Jerusalem, 121.

Joazar, high priest, 248.

Johanan, slain in the temple, 169.

John, a brother of Judas Maccabæus, treacherously slain, 200.

John the Baptist, executed under Herod Antipas, 244.

John of Gish-chala, leader against the Romans and Galilee, 277; flees to Jerusalem, 279; institutes reign of terror, 281; shut up in the temple by Simon, 283; driven out by Eleazar, 284; regains it by a ruse, 285; retires to the Upper City, 292; captured, dies in Rome, 294.

Jonathan, son of Saul, slays Philistine prefect, 60; makes an assault upon Philistine camp, 61; loves David, 66; suspected of a plot with David against his father, 67.

Jonathan, the Maccabean, succeeds his brother Judas Maccabæus, 200; makes a peace with Bacchides, sets up government at Michmas, courted by Demetrius, 201; high priest, 202; obtains concessions from Demetrius II., 203; supports Demetrius II., and then the rebel Trypho, 203; is betrayed by Trypho, and murdered, 204; his merits, 204, 205.

Jonathan, high priest, asks appointment of Felix, 263; murdered by Sicarii, 264.

Jordan, The River, 10, 11.

Joseph, compared with Æolus, 30; forced to migrate to Egypt, 37; invades Canaan, 47.

Joseph, son of Gorion, a leader of the war party, 276.

Josephus, the historian, one of the leaders chosen against the Romans, 276, 277; his defence of Jotapata, 278; becomes the adviser of Titus, 284.

Joshua, takes northern and middle Palestine, leads seven tribes into Canaan, 47.

Joshua, brother of Johanan, 169.

Josiah, a good king, 137.

Josiah, king of Judah, defeated by Necho, 140.

Jotapata, defended by Josephus, 278.

Judah, leads the Israelites into Canaan, 46; becomes Israel after the fall of Samaria, 128; finds the dependency on Assyria a blessing, 129.

Judaism, outward, imposed on Greeks by Alexander Jannæus, 219.

Judas Maccabæus, 193–200; frees Judea, 194; defeats two Syrian armies, restores the temple to the worship of Jahweh, 195; gathers the Jews into Judea, 196; defeated by Lysias, 197; defeats Nicanor, 198, 199; seeks a Roman alliance, 199; slain, 200.

Judas, a Pharisee, with Matthias, burned alive for cutting down the Roman eagle, 238.

Judas the Galilean, opponent of Roman dominion, 248.

Judea, becomes an Egyptian province, 170; made an immediate Roman province, 246; sequestered on the death of Agrippa, 259; finally conquered, 297, 298; the victory of the vanquished, 300, 301.

KADESH-BARNEA, the modern Ain Kudês, 43; temporary seat of the Hebrews, 43, 44.

INDEX.

Kar-Duniash, empire of, 24.
Kassites, see Cossæans, 24.
Kemosgad, King of Moab, subjected by Omri, 101.
Kir-haresheth, held by King Mesha of Moab, 107.
Kudur-Mabuk, King of the Elamites, 23.

Laish, conquered and name changed to Dan, 49.
Law, the priestly, proclaimed by Ezra, 164.
Lebanon and Anti-Libanus, 13.
Legends, Popular, their value as historical sources, 17.
Levi, punished for treachery in taking Shechem, 46.
Libnah, revolts from Judah, 108.
Lucilius Bassus, legate in Syria, completes the conquest of Judea, 295.
Lysias, regent of Syria, 194; defeated by Judas Maccabæus, 195; defeats Judas, 196-197; makes peace with the Jews, takes Antioch, 197; executed, 198.

Maccabees, see Mattathias, Judas, Jonathan, John, Simon, Hyrcanus, Aristobulus, Alexander Jannæus, Hyrcanus II., Aristobulus II., Alexander II., Antigonus.
Maccabees, Books of, 188.
Maccabean state, its inner inconsistency, 206.
Machærus, important fortress in last stand against Rome, 274; taken by the Romans, 295.
Malachi, his notes of conditions in Judea, 154.
Malichus, poisons Antipater, 229.

Manasseh, persecutes the prophets, 136.
Manasseh, son-in-law of Sanballat, expelled from Jerusalem, founds the congregation of Samaria, 167.
Mari, king of Damascus, subdued by the Assyrians, 122.
Mariannne, wife of Herod, 231.
Massada, important stronghold in the last contest with Rome, 273; its siege and notable defence, 296-297.
Marsus, legate in Syria, represses Agrippa, 258.
Mattathias, founder of the house of the Maccabees, revolts against Antiochus Epiphanes, 192-193.
Medes, threaten Assyria under Asurbanipal, 138.
Media, alliance with Babylonia, 148, conquest by Cyrus, 149.
Menahem, defeats and slays Shallum, 122; bribes the Assyrians, 123.
Menahem, grandson of Judas the Galilean, 273; engages in civil strife, 274.
Menelaus, high priest, murders Onias, 190; executed by Lysias, 197.
Merenptah, the Pharaoh of the Exodus, 41.
Merodach-baladan, visits Hezekiah. 132; assailed by Sennacherib, 132.
Mesha, King of Moab, his triumphal column, 7; retakes territory from Israel, resists invasion by Jehoram, 107.
Messiahs, suppressed by Felix, 264.
Metilius, a Roman tribune, 274.
Michal, Saul's daughter, loves David, 66.
Midianites, incursion of, 51.

Migration to Egypt, of all the Hebrew tribes, 38.

Mixed marriages, Ezra's zeal against, 156-159; Nehemiah's opposition to, 160-165.

Moab, with Ammon and Edom came out of Mesopotamia with Abraham, 32; relationship to Israel, 32; rebels from Solomon, 90.

Moabite language, 33.

Moabites, and Ammonites, driven out of their homes by Sihon, king of the Canaanites, 45; assail Israel, 51; attack David and are defeated, 74.

Modein, scene of beginning of Maccabean rebellion, 192.

Mohammedans, their debt to Israel. 4.

Moses, his name Egyptian, 41; leads the Exodus, 42; founder of Israelitish nationality, 48.

Mount Tabor, taken by the Romans, 279.

NABOPOLASSAR, 139.

Naboth, murder of, instigated by Jezebel, 102.

Nadab, son of Jeroboam, king of Israel, murdered by Baasha, 98.

Nahash, king of the Ammonites, besieges Jabesh-gilead, 55.

Naphtali, settled in the north, 49.

Naram-Sin, 21.

Neapolitanus, Roman tribune in Jerusalem, 270.

Nebuchadnezzar, defeats Necho, 140; takes Jerusalem and leads Jehoiachin and ten thousand Jews into captivity, 141; his connection with Media, his death, 148.

Nebuzaradan, Babylonian captain, destroys Jerusalem, 144.

Necho, Pharaoh, defeats King Josiah, defeated by Nebuchadnezzar, 140.

Nehemiah, governor of Jerusalem, his character, 160; his work in restoring Jerusalem, 161-164; increased zeal, 166-168.

Nicanor, Syrian general, defeated by Judas Maccabæus, 198-199.

Nineveh, destruction of, 139.

Nob, priests of, slain for favoring David, 68.

OBEDAS, an Arab sheik, defeats Alexander Jannæus, 217.

Ochus, King, destroys Jericho, deports Jews, 169.

Old Testament, does not claim to be history, 4.

Onias III., high priest, 183; hated by the Hellenists, 187; imprisoned in Antioch, 189; murdered, 190.

Onias, a conciliatory philosopher, 222.

Omri, overthrows Zimri, 99; overcomes Tibni and made king of Israel, founds Samaria, 100; invades Moab, acknowledges overlordship of Damascus, makes alliance with Tyre, pays tribute to Assyria, 101; peace with Judah, 101.

PADI, of Ekron, remains loyal to Assyria, and is imprisoned by his own people, 132.

Palestine, origin of name, 9; physical description of, 10-12; flora of, 13; isolation of, 14; products of, fauna of, 15; an Egyptian province under Ahmes, 26; defended by Ra-

INDEX.

meses III., against invading races, 44; naturally belongs to Syria, 172; taken by Syria, 173.

Pallas, favorite of Emperor Claudius, 263.

Parthians, invade Syria, aid Antigonus, 230.

Pashebchanen II., Solomon's father-in-law, subdues Gezer, and gives it to him, 92.

Patriarchs, stand for tribes, 30.

Pekah, slays Pekahiah, the last king of Samaria (North Israel), 123; slain by Hoshea, 124.

Pekahiah, son of Menahem, his brief reign, 123.

Penuel, chosen by Jeroboam as capital, 97.

Petronius, legate in Syria, ordered to set up altar to Caligula in the Holy of Holies, 253, 254.

Phannias, last high priest, 280.

Pharisees, origin of, 183; character, 184; origin of name, 185; oppose John Hyrcanus, 211–213; call in Demetrius III., 217; massacred by Alexander, 218; control Alexandra-Salome, 220.

Phasael, son of Antipater, 228; governor in Jerusalem, 229; confirmed by Antony, takes his own life, 230.

Philip, regent of Syria, overthrown by Lysias, 197.

Philip, son of Herod, 240; best of the family, 243; founds Cæsarea Philippi, 244.

Philistines, come in to Palestine under Rameses III., 45; subdue the Israelites, 54; attempt to suppress David, 74.

Philo of Alexandria, 255–256.

Philology, its aid in historical study, 17, 18.

Phœnicians, their contribution to civilization, 2; make naval expeditions with Solomon, 91.

Phraortes, 139.

Pithalaus, heads a rebellion against Rome, is executed, 226.

Pontius Pilate, Roman procurator in Palestine, 249; builds aqueducts, 250; massacres the Jews and the Samaritans, 251; removed from office, 252.

Pompey, conquering Asia, 223; invades Judea, 224; restores Hyrcanus II., 225, 227.

Popilius Lænas, Roman ambassador, in Egypt, 191.

Priests, their lukewarmness towards the reforms of Nehemiah, 165; leave Jerusalem for Samaria, 167.

Primogeniture in Hebrew law, 88.

Prophecy originated in Israel, not in Judah, 128.

Psammetichus I., frees Egypt from Assyria, 138.

Ptolemy V. married to daughter of Antiochus III., 186; dies, 190.

Ptolemy, son-in-law of Simon, murders him, 208.

Ptolemy Lathyros, wastes Judea, 216.

Ptolemies, their relation to the Jews, 170–174.

Pul, see Tiglath-Pileser II.

Pursta, Egyptian form of Philistines in inscriptions, 45.

RAMAH OF EPHRAIM, home of Samuel, 56.

Ramah, held by Baasha, 98; taken by Asa, 99.
Rameses II., his war with the Cheta, 39; impresses the Israelites for state labor, 40.
Rameses III., maintains Egyptian power in Palestine, 44.
Ramman-Nirari, of Assyria, son of Semiramis, 119.
Ramoth, retaken by Jehoram, 108.
Raphia, scene of the defeat of Shabaka, 130.
Red Sea, the passage of, 42.
Rehoboam, difficulties with Israel, 95; flees from Shechem, 96; loses the North Kingdom, 96, 97.
Reuben, claims the hegemony, 38; and Gad, remain east of the Jordan, 47.
Resin, King of Syria, loses land and life, 124.
Rizpah, Saul's concubine, taken by Abner, 72.
Romans, their contribution to civilization, 3.
Roman government of Judea, 246, 247.

SABINUS, Roman official, Herod's executor, besieged in Jerusalem, plunders the temple, 242.
Sadducees, origin of, 183; descendants of Zadok, 184; allied with John Hyrcanus, 212, 213; seek protection of Aristobulus II., 220.
Samaria, established as capital of Israel, 100; taken by the Assyrians, 125; colonized with foreigners, 126; destroyed by Hyrcanus, 211.
Samaritan, religious community, founded by Manasseh, 167.
Sammuramat, see Semiramis.

Samuel, feels the humiliation of Israel, 56; desires union, 57.
Sanballat, opposes the restoration of Jerusalem, 162.
Sargon of Agade, 21.
Sargon, conquers Samaria, 129; defeats Shabaka, 130; suppresses rebellion in Ashdod, 131; murdered, 131.
Saul, son of Kish, 57; seeks Samuel, anointed by him, 58; responds to the call from Jabesh-gilead, 59; crowned king in Gilgal, keeps a body-guard, calls to arms against the Philistines, 60; defeats them, organizes army, 61; mental weakness, not equal to the situation, 62; defects of his character, 63; attacks the Gibeonites, 64; defeats the Amalekites, but is too lenient toward them, 64; compared with Frederick William IV. of Prussia, 65; loves David, 66; gives him his daughter, suspicious of David, 67; assails him, punishes the priests of Nob, 68; at war with David, 69; defeated by the Philistines at Gilboa, kills himself, 70; summary, 70–71.
Scaurus, legate of Pompey, aids Aristobulus, 223.
Scopas, Egyptian general, 173.
Seleucus Nicator, favors Jews in Syria, 171.
Seleucus IV., 187.
Seleucidæ, 172; downfall of, 187; overthrown by a usurper, 202; 207; 208; 211; 217; 221.
Semiramis, invades Cœlesyria, 119, 120.
Semitic conquest of Babylonia, 22.
Sennacherib, 131; general re-

INDEX. 323

volt against him, 132; suppress it, 133; wastes Palestine, 134; fails to take Jerusalem, 136; murdered, 137.

Sepphoris, taken by the Romans, 277.

Septuagint, beginning of, 180.

Set-necht, grandson of Merenptah, 44.

Sextus Cæsar, legate in Syria, 228.

Shabaka, of Egypt, incites the Israelites against Assyria, 125; is defeated by Sargon, 130.

Shadduck, a Pharisee, opponent of Roman dominion, 248.

Shallum, murders King Zechariah, and is murdered, 122.

Shalmaneser II., of Assyria, invades Cœlesyria, 105; and again, 108; again, 117; receives tribute from Jehu, last incursion, 118.

Shalmaneser IV., destroys the kingdom of Israel, 125.

Shammai, a leader of the Sanhedrin, denounces Herod, 228.

Shamir, occupied by the family of Tolah, tribe of Issachar, 49.

Sheba, a Benjaminite, heads a revolt against David, is betrayed and slain by his own people, 81.

Shechem, taken by Simeon and Levi, 46; key to the mountain region of Ephraim.

Sheshbazzar, governor-general of Judea, 151.

Sheshenk, Pharaoh, harbors Jeroboam, 94; plunders Jerusalem, 97.

Shiloh, captured by the Philistines, 54

Shishak, see Sheshenk.

Sicarii, organized assassins hostile to Rome, 263, 273; pillage Southern Judea, 282.

Siege of Jerusalem by Titus, 286–293.

Sihon, of Canaan, founds Heshbon, 45; defeated at Jahaz, 46.

Simeon, absorbed by Judah, 47.

Simon II., high priest, 183.

Simon, a leader of the Hellenistic party, 187; causes riot, 188.

Simon, brother of Judas Maccabæus, aids Jonathan, 203; succeeds him, allies himself with Demetrius, takes the citadel of Jerusalem, hereditary prince and high priest, 205; his character, 207; murdered, 208.

Simon bar Giora, a leader of the Sicarii, 282; gathers an army, is admitted to Jerusalem, 283; holds the Upper City, 292; captured, 294; executed, 295.

Simon ben Shetach, head of the Pharisees, 220.

Sinai, a refuge for the fleeing Hebrews, 43.

Sisera, attempts to recover Canaan, 50.

Solomon, supplants Adonijah through the devices of Bathsheba, 82; varying views of his character, 86; endowment from his mother, 87; his task, 88–89; his defects, 90; loses Edom, re-subdues Moab, 90; financial measures, cedes territory to Tyre, impresses Canaanites, 91; impresses Israelites, builds temple, his Egyptian wife, 92; builds fortresses, expels the rebel Jeroboam, 93; cultivates art and literature, 84; a theme for poetic legends, death, 95.

Sosius, Antony's legate, 231, 232.

Stephanus, a Roman official, assaulted and robbed, 261.

Succoth and Penuel, chastised by Gideon, 52.

Sulla the younger, leads in the taking of Jerusalem, 224.

Sumerians, primitive inhabitants of Babylonia, 22.

Syria, contends with Egypt for Palestine, 172.

TACITUS, his description of the Jewish people, 16.

Tattenai, Persian satrap, 154.

Tell-el-Amarna, 26; great discovery of ancient Egyptian diplomatic correspondence there, 27.

Temple, originally a part of Solomon's palace, 92; reconstruction of, 153.

Ten Tribes, misrepresented by Judean historians, 126; the material and intellectual center of the race, 127.

Thamar, daughter of David, forced by her brother Amnon, 75.

Theudas, a prophet, slain by Fadus, 260.

Thotmes III., 25.

Tiberias, founded by Herod Antipas, 244.

Tiberius, 250, 252.

Tiberius Alexander, Roman procurator in Judea, 260.

Tibni, opposes Omri, and is defeated, 100.

Tiglath-Pileser, receives submission of Egypt, 45.

Tiglath-Pileser II. invades Cœlesyria, 123; called in by Ahaz, takes Damascus, subdues Israel, 124.

Tigranes, King of the Armenians, 221, 223.

Tirhakah, King of Egypt, conquered by Esarhaddon, 137.

Titus, takes Tarichæa, 278, 282; given command, 284; besets Jerusalem, 285; begins siege, 286; progress, 287-288; takes the Lower City, 290; takes the temple, 291-292; completes the capture, 293; celebrates his triumph, 294 295.

Tobiah, the Ammonite, opponent of Nehemiah, 162; cast out of the temple, 167.

Tribal kingdom, insufficiency of, 53.

Tribes, the Twelve, their relations, 35-36.

Tribe, average size of, 36.

Trypho, a general of Alexander Balas, rebels against Demetrius, II. 203; his treachery toward Jonathan, 294.

UAHABRA, Pharaoh, stirs Zedekiah to rebellion, 142.

Ummidius Quadratus, legate in Syria, 262.

Ur, the modern Mughier, 20.

Uzziah (Azariah), his prosperous reign, 121.

VALERIUS Gratus, Roman procurator in Palestine, 249.

Varus (Quintilius), legate in Syria, plunders Judea, 243.

Ventidius Cumanus, Roman procurator in Judea, 260; causes massacre in Jerusalem, persecutes the Jews, 261-262; removed, 262

Vespasian, directs the campaign against the Jews, 277; his policy, 282; made em-

INDEX.

peror, turns the command over to Titus, 284.

Vitellius, legate in Syria, 252.

YAMAN, in Ashdod, rebels against Sargon, defeated, flees to Egypt, and is delivered to Sargon, 131.

ZADOKIDÆ, 153.

Zealots, 263, try to rule Jerusalem, 280–282; divided into parties, 284.

Zebulon, settled in the north, 49.

Zechariah, son of Jeroboam II. murdered, 122.

Zedekiah, made king of Judah by Nebuchadnezzar, 141; rebels, 142; captured, blinded and taken to Babylon, 143.

Zerubbabel, leader of the Elders, 151; governor of Judea, 154.

Ziklag, David's residence while in exile, 69.

Zimri, murders Elah, overthrown by Omri, 99.

Zoilus, prince of Ptolemais, 215.